BEYOND
WORDS

Mark O. James
Norman W. Evans

Brigham Young University–Hawaii

BEYOND WORDS

An Advanced Reading Course

PRENTICE HALL REGENTS
Englewood Cliffs, New Jersey 07632

Library of Congress Cataloging-in-Publication Data

James, Mark O.
    Beyond words : an advanced reading course / Mark O. James, Norman
W. Evans.
        p.   cm.
    ISBN 0-13-074048-9
    1. English language--Textbooks for foreign speakers. 2. Readers
(Secondary)   I. Evans, Norman W. II. Title.
PE1128.J326 1989
428.6'4--dc19   89-30117
                                                               CIP

Cover design: Karen Stephens
Manufacturing buyer: Laura Crossland
Illustrations on pages 39, 157, and 159 by Jaime Mendame

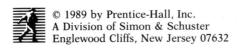 © 1989 by Prentice-Hall, Inc.
A Division of Simon & Schuster
Englewood Cliffs, New Jersey 07632

Photo Credits

Page 1: Pan American. *Page 43:* AP/Wide World Photos. *Page 48:* Library of Congress.
Page 59: Town & Country Photographers. *Page 103:* Laimute E. Druskis. *Page 114:* Ellen
Levine. *Page 121:* Eugene Gordon. *Page 123:* Eugene Gordon. *Page 136:* © Michal Heron
1982. *Page 205:* Ralph Westerhoff. *Page 216:* Marc Anderson. *Page 225:* Eugene Gordon.
Page 234: U.S. Department of Justice, Federal Bureau of Investigation. *Page 253:* A.T.&T.
Co. Photo Center. *Page 266:* Ken Karp. *Page 284:* A.T.&T. Co. Photo/Graphics Center. *Page
301:* N.Y. Convention and Visitors Bureau. *Page 304:* Library of Congress. *Page 309:*
Brown Brothers. *Page 312:* Library of Congress. *Page 318:* Courtesy of the Port
Authority of New York and New Jersey. *Page 319:* Courtesy of the National Park
Service. *Page 324:* Mak Takahashi.

Printed in the United States of America

10 9 8 7 6 5 4 3 2 1

ISBN 0-13-074048-9

Prentice-Hall International (UK) Limited, *London*
Prentice-Hall of Australia Pty. Limited, *Sydney*
Prentice-Hall Canada Inc., *Toronto*
Prentice-Hall Hispanoamericana, S.A., *Mexico*
Prentice-Hall of India Private Limited, *New Delhi*
Prentice-Hall of Japan, Inc., *Tokyo*
Simon & Schuster Asia Pte. Ltd., *Singapore*
Editora Prentice-Hall do Brasil, Ltda., *Rio de Janeiro*

CONTENTS

To the Instructor ix

Acknowledgments xiii

1 Hawaii—The Fiftieth State   *1*

Description: Purpose and Principle *3*

Reading One: *Hawaii—The Fiftieth State 7*

Vocabulary in Context *10*

Description: Figurative Language *12*

Reading Two: *Kilauea Volcano at Night 16*

Description: Appeal to the Senses *20*

Vocabulary: Contextual Paraphrasing *21*

Reading Three: *Impressions of Honolulu, 1873 24*

Vocabulary: Word Analysis *30*

Description: Technical Matters *33*

Reading Four: *Hawaiian Featherwork 36*

2 The Nuclear Age   *43*

Narration: An Introduction *45*

Reading One: *The Letter That Started the Nuclear Age 47*

Supplementary Reading: *The Father of the Atomic Bomb Was Not
Einstein 52*

Detecting Sequence: Narrated and Natural Order *53*

Reading Two: *The Day the Nuclear Age Was Born* 58

Narration: Chronological Expressions 65

Reading Three: *The Dawn of the Nuclear Age* 67

Narration: Reading Newspapers 74

Reading Four: *First Atomic Blast Gave Isolated Stretch of New Mexico Desert a Place in History* 77

Narration: Point of View 80

Reading Five: *Zero Hour: Forty-Three Seconds Over Hiroshima* 84

Narration: Verb Tense 91

Reading Six: *How I Designed an A-Bomb in My Junior Year at Princeton* 94

3 Marriage and Family 103

Comparison and Contrast—Pattern A: The "Point-by-Point" Approach 105

Reading One: *The American Family: Then and Now* 107

Understanding Tables 111

Comparison and Contrast—Pattern B: The "Whole" Approach 112

Reading Two: *Mom, How Did You Meet Dad?* 114

Understanding Bar Graphs 117

Comparison and Contrast—Pattern C: The "Same/Different" Approach 119

Reading Three: *The Amish and the Kibbutzim* 120

Comparison and Contrast: Equality 125

Understanding Line Graphs 126

Reading Four: *Marriage in Iran and America: A Study in Contrasts* 128

Understanding Pie Graphs 132

Reading Five: *Family Life in the People's Republic of China—Then and Now* 136

4   Ecology   *145*

Cause/Effect: Distinguishing Between Causes
and Effects *147*

Cause/Effect: Author's Emphasis *149*

Reading One: *A Delicate Balance 156*

Reading Two: *Historic Extinctions 166*

Understanding the Main Ideas: Sentences *171*

Reading Three: *Exploding Volcano: Full Impact Yet to Come 176*

Understanding the Main Idea: Paragraphs *182*

Supplementary Reading: *A Hard Look at Acid Rain 188*

Reading Four: *Storm Over a Deadly Downpour 189*

Supplementary Reading: *A Warmer Globe Just Around
Corner 196*

Reading Five: *The Silent Summer 197*

5   Crime   *205*

Reading One: *Crime: An Ever-Growing Problem 208*

Conclusions and Inferences: An Introduction *211*

Problem–Solution: The Everyday World *213*

Reading Two: *How to Keep Your Wallet Safe 215*

Conclusions and Inferences: From What? *220*

Problem–Solution: The Problem *222*

Reading Three: *Auto Theft Turns Pro 226*

Conclusions and Inferences: The Reader *231*

Problem–Solution: The Solution(s) *232*

Reading Four: *Commercial Piracy 235*

Problem–Solution: Purpose and Balance *243*

Reading Five: *There's a Burglary Every 10 Seconds—My Turn 245*

6   Language   *253*

Classification: The Everyday World   *255*

Reading One: *What Kind of Language Are You Using?   257*

Remembering What You Read: Association   *260*

Classification: The Principle   *262*

Reading Two: *The Variety of Conversations   265*

Remembering What You Read: Visualization   *270*

Classification: Organization and Purpose   *272*

Reading Three: *The International Language of Gestures   277*

Division: A Close Cousin   *282*

Reading Four: *Take Your Pick of Language Lessons   284*

Reading Five: *The Origin of Language   293*

7   Immigrants in America: A Land of Promise?   *301*
(Review Chapter)

Reading One: *America: A Nation of Nations   304*

Reading Two: *Why They Came   311*

Reading Three: *Angel and Ellis: Islands of Tears   320*

Reading Four: *Goree   329*

Reading Five: *Is America Closing the "Golden Door"?   338*

TO THE INSTRUCTOR

Beyond Words is designed primarily for advanced students of ESL (TOEFL score of 525+) though remedial students and those who speak English as a second dialect will also benefit from its use. The readings cover broad-based topics of interest, but are intended for students preparing for undergraduate coursework. Sources of readings include common newsstand magazines and newspapers, as well as more specialized sources such as textbooks and professional journals. The instructional approach of this text differs somewhat from the traditional "skills" approach. Although a number of skills have been integrated throughout, the book focuses on comprehensive text processing strategies that improve one's overall comprehension.

RATIONALE TO OUR APPROACH

Over the past few years much has been written about the interactive nature of reading. It is generally accepted that reading is not a passive activity and that the reader's responsibility and contribution to meaning and communication are as great as the writer's. To interact with what one reads, however, a person must have a foundation of knowledge on which to build. This text strengthens that foundation.

David Ausubel, a prominent educational psychologist, noted that the single most important factor influencing learning is what the student already knows. The question then is: What must a reader know to interact successfully with the text and to read efficiently with comprehension?

Specifically, a reader must know three things: (1) the language in which the passage is written, (2) something about the subject matter itself, and (3) the textual or discourse patterns used in that language to present or develop ideas. These, therefore, have become the three areas of focus in this text.

The first area of knowledge, known as *linguistic schema*, includes vocabulary and syntax. Although these are well covered in most reading texts, it is not enough for the reader to know the meanings of all the words and to be able to identify the grammatical structures of the prose.

It is also important that a reader approach the material to be read with as much prior knowledge about the topic as possible. This knowledge can come either through direct experience, prior reading, the media, or group discussion, and is used by fluent readers to form expectations about the reading task and material. In this text students build both vocabulary and background knowledge by progressing through thought-provoking pre-reading exercises, activities, and their accompanying readings, all of which are unified by a common chapter theme.

Much of the reading students encounter in their academic or work-related pursuits is expository in nature, and studies (with both native and nonnative learners) have shown that the reader's ability to detect the distinctive expository patterns or structures of the text is a crucial skill for effective comprehension and recall. More importantly, these studies reveal that these discourse patterns can be learned systematically in a reasonable amount of time, given the proper materials and instruction. To this end, each chapter in this text focuses on the instruction and analysis of one discourse pattern, which is modeled in its various forms by the readings in that chapter.

In addition, our experience tells us that the skills of reading and writing are closely intertwined and that practice in each is mutually beneficial. This has led to the inclusion of significant opportunities for students to write about what they know, what they've read, and how that knowledge can be applied to further reading.

ABOUT THIS BOOK

Beyond Words consists of seven chapters—six "instructional" chapters and one review chapter. Because a certain amount of skills reinforcement is recycled from chapter to chapter, it is recommended that the chapters be studied in sequence.

Each of the chapters has three basic objectives: (1) to introduce ESL readers to a common textual pattern used in English, (2) to reinforce a major related reading skill, and (3) to familiarize students with topics of current interest.

The subject area in each chapter is taught like most other subjects learned in school—through reading. Each passage builds knowledge of and familiarity with that particular theme. In contrast to classroom study of a subject, this book does not include introductory lectures for each theme. We therefore suggest that the instructor briefly discuss the topic of each chapter.

Preview activities allow for discussion and thought before each reading. When the subject matter is likely to be new to the student, we have included supplementary readings. These readings are general in nature and should be read as preview material for the main passage.

The textual patterns that are taught in each chapter are some of those most commonly used by English writers (e.g., comparison and contrast, cause and effect, problem–solution, narration, description).

Each pattern has distinct characteristics, vocabulary, and—in some cases—grammatical structures. To most effectively teach these patterns, each chapter has four or five lessons about the textual pattern and at least four reading passages written in that pattern.

The skills, much like the textual patterns, are also taught in short lessons, and these are followed by examples and exercises that serve as reinforcement. In addition, the skills in each chapter are usually related to the structure of the chapter. Chapter 2, for example, introduces a subject—the history of the nuclear age—that can be taught well in conjunction with narration. The skill introduced in this chapter, "detecting sequence," is a logical companion to the narrative discourse pattern.

HOW TO USE THIS BOOK

The first six chapters all have similar structures. Each chapter contains a number of readings related to a common theme. The first few readings in any chapter are more general and less complex than the later readings. These early readings provide the framework and background for the topic. In each chapter the readings are accompanied by lessons and exercises concerning aspects of the textual pattern or skill being taught.

Each reading is preceded by a preview section containing questions and activities. The objectives of these sections are (1) to arouse students' interest, (2) to activate and build on any prior knowledge students may have about the topic, and (3) to offer students the opportunity to make predictions about the reading through various skimming, scanning, and thought-provoking activities. This pre-reading phase can be completed either individually, in small groups, or as a class. Completing this phase as a class, however, gives the teacher the advantage of being able to evaluate how much the students know about the topic and how well prepared they are to read about it. In addition, through oral discussion students benefit from the experiences and viewpoints of others.

After completing the pre-reading activities, students should proceed to the reading itself. Most readings are intended as homework but can be done during class if the structure of the class period allows.

The readings are followed by three types of post-reading exercises:

1. **Review questions** that test general comprehension and suggest additional areas for discussion. Students should complete these immediately after reading the passage and should attempt them without referring back to the passage whenever possible.
2. **Textual pattern and skill review exercises** that test material covered in the lessons that precede the readings or lessons studied in earlier chapters. These exercises may require close analysis of the structure of the reading passage, so students may refer to the reading while completing the exercises.

3. **Questions for further discussion** that require students to take the information they have learned one step further by solving related problems or applying the information to their own lives (one of the main purposes of reading). These questions can be used in a number of ways: for individual short responses (either oral or written), as essay topics, for small group discussions, as debate topics, or for class discussions. We strongly suggest that these questions not be overlooked.

Chapter 7 is intended to reinforce what has been learned in the first six chapters. This chapter presents a new theme, but the readings represent a variety of textual patterns and review many of the skills learned in the previous six chapters.

A FINAL NOTE

It is our opinion that reading can be an enjoyable activity. In addition, we firmly believe that reading can be improved by practice—that is, people learn to read by reading. If one's reading is interesting and is accompanied by quality instruction, the practice becomes that much more effective. We hope that both students and teachers will find this text interesting and instructional.

ACKNOWLEDGMENTS

We would like to acknowledge a number of individuals and institutions without whose help this project would not have been possible. First, we have appreciated the opportunity to work with the editors and staff at Prentice Hall. We also owe a debt to the many anonymous reviewers for their insightful comments. Thanks also go to Karen Gibbons, Estelle Onaga, and Debbie Yang for their contributions in the creation of this final product. We express our gratitude to Brigham Young University–Hawaii and our colleagues for financial and professional support, as well as to the students and instructors of the English Language Institute who piloted the early drafts. But most especially, we wish to thank our families, whose patience and moral support made this text a reality.

M.O.J.
N.W.E.

CHAPTER 1

The loveliest fleet of islands that lies anchored in any ocean.

—Mark Twain

HAWAII—THE FIFTIETH STATE

Hawaii. One word—and yet it has the ability to call up strong, conflicting, emotional memories of romance, slave labor, war, sun, and fun. Hawaii is many things to many people. Some came as voyagers hundreds of years ago; some came as soldiers. Others came as daring business entrepreneurs, or simple immigrant laborers. And of course many come each year as tourists seeking paradise. In this chapter we will learn a little of Hawaii's people, geography, and culture as we learn about the patterns and devices used in descriptive writing.

DESCRIPTION

One of the most common types of writing is descriptive writing. The descriptive writer may be technical and objective, or perhaps impressionistic and subjective. This all depends on the purpose of the writer. Though all cultures share this mode of discourse, the tools and patterns differ slightly from one culture to another.

In this chapter we will discuss the purposes and styles of description, as well as the various devices used by writers to make their descriptions effective.

VOCABULARY IN CONTEXT

In addition to learning about patterns of descriptive writing, we will help you improve your word-attack skills and your ability to understand new words through context in order to improve your overall reading proficiency. To **understand** a word, however, does not necessarily mean you can correctly **use** the word in speaking or writing. This is the difference between your *passive* and *active* vocabulary. For the purposes of reading, we will concentrate on developing your *passive* vocabulary.

Description: Purpose and Principle

PURPOSE

Description is that form of writing which comes the closest to the fine arts because, like painting, sculpture, and film, it attempts to recreate a likeness or impression of a person, place, or situation for someone else. The writing may be technical and objective, in an effort to recreate every detail exactly as it is, or it may be imaginative and impressionistic, choosing to emphasize only one or two aspects of the whole. The purpose behind the description will determine the pattern and organization that are chosen and the selection of appropriate details. Read the following two descriptions.

> *Version 1:* "The man is approximately 6 ft., 1 in. tall. Weighs about 185 pounds. Dark, wavy hair; brown eyes. Caucasian. Muscular build with a small scar over the right eye. Speaks with a slight slur. He was last seen wearing a black jacket and blue-jeans. Thought to be unarmed but dangerous."

> *Version 2:* "He's a real hunk, Mom. He's tall, dark, and handsome with a really macho-looking face. Wow, and what a body! He looks like Rambo's kid brother. No kidding, Mom! He doesn't talk much, but I like men who are quiet. Anyway, I have to go now, Mom, he's picking me up soon. Bye!"

The two versions above describe the same person, although they are quite different in both detail and tone. Part of the responsibility of the reader is to determine the purpose of the writer in order to understand why the author selected certain details. Can you guess who the authors of these two descriptions might be?

1. _____police_____   2. _____a girl friend of_____

As mentioned above, descriptions can be either objective or subjective. In the first category, the author is interested in giving details *about* the subject in a systematic way. This type of description is used often in the fields of science and business, for example, where an engineer might describe a newly designed product, or a botanist might describe a rare species of flower.

As opposed to information *about* things, the second type of description, which is subjective, attempts to give us a recreation or feeling *of* things. The details may not be so systematic. This type of description, often used by artists, poets, and novelists, does not accurately portray each and every detail but uses language to bring out a certain impression, quality, or tone. In other words, the description of a river by a marine biologist would be quite different from a description of the same river by Mark Twain: They do not share the same purpose.

This does not mean, however, that we never find technical description in fiction or suggestive description in the world of science. Nor does this mean that the two forms cannot be found together in the same piece of writing.

EXERCISE   Mark each passage as either "obj" (objective) or "sub" (subjective). Underline words or phrases that help you decide.

sub 1.   By the time one has seen the villages, the afternoon is well along. White clouds sail lazily overhead.

obj 2.   Professionally produced and directed, the show consists of two acts that present the historical prologues and thirty-four scenes.

obj 3.   The *mamo* bird . . . was black in color, with small patches of orange-yellow feathers above the base of the tail, on the lower part of the back, and on the thighs.

sub 4.   The buses creep around back streets searching out their hotel stops, traveling close behind each other like multicolored caterpillars. They part together and travel together, picking up and disgorging loads of tourists together, as if afraid to be separated in the wilds of Waikiki.

PRINCIPLE

In the process of description, writers will choose an overall principle of organization. Whether describing a room, a group of objects, or a process, the writer chooses a principle (e.g., spatial, logical, chronological) that will organize the information for the reader. The purpose of the organization, of course, is to allow the reader a better chance of remembering the details. For example, a writer might describe a room from left to right, or from top to bottom. In describing his or her own family members, a writer might choose to start with the oldest and proceed to the youngest. Perceiving which principle the writer has chosen will greatly increase your ability to comprehend and recall the material you are reading.

PREVIEW | HAWAII—THE FIFTIETH STATE

Things to Think About

1.   When you see or hear the word *Hawaii*, what comes to mind?

Beaches, and bright colors, Hawaiian
girls dancing with bright floresh necklaces.

2. Have you ever been to Hawaii or read about it? If so, what can you remember about Hawaii?

_____Never._____

_____

_____

_____

3. If you haven't been to Hawaii, you may have thought about what tropical South Pacific islands look like. Write down your impressions.

It would look like a beautiful

place. Blond sand with palm

trees. Blue water, colorful fish.

Banjo music all around.

Beautiful girls with dark long hair.

_____

4. If you had the opportunity to stay in Hawaii for two weeks, would you go? If so, what would you do there?

Yes, Try to see everywere. And

take part in most of events possible.

_____

_____

_____

_____

Preview

1. Descriptive writing usually has an underlying organization to help the reader follow along. Look at the first sentence of each paragraph and write down how the author has organized this description of Hawaii.

_____

_____

_____

2. What are the names of the principal Hawaiian islands in the order in which they are presented in this reading?

a. _Big Island, Hawaii_ e. _MoloKai "The friendly Isle_
b. _Maui "The Valley Island"_ f. _Lanai "The Pineapple Isle"_
c. _Oahu "The Gathering Place"_ g. _Niihau "The Mistery Isle" or The Forbiden Isle_
d. _Kauai "The Garden Island"_ h. _Kahoolawe_

3. Before you begin reading, look at the maps below and determine exactly where Hawaii is and where the islands are in relation to each other.

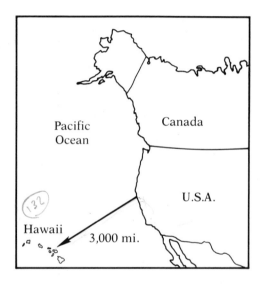

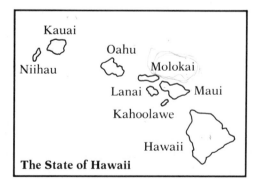

The State of Hawaii

READING ONE

HAWAII—THE FIFTIETH STATE

1   Hawaii, the "Aloha State," was the last territory to be admitted as a state in the United States. Alaska became the 49th state on January 3rd, 1959, and seven months later, Hawaii was given statehood on August 21st. In Hawaiian, "aloha" (pronounced Ah-LOW-ha) means "hello," "goodbye," "love," and "goodwill"—a very   5 useful word! And a very descriptive word for the people of Hawaii. Its people are friendly, relaxed, and congenial, and any visitor who stays more than a day or two soon catches the spirit. In addition to the balmy, sunny weather, the warm, crystal-clear water, or the scent of tropical flowers, this infectious "Spirit of Aloha" has made   10 Hawaii a paradise for millions of people for many years. As Mark Twain said, it is "one of the loveliest fleets of islands that lies anchored in any ocean."

2   There are 132 islands in the state of Hawaii, some no bigger than specks in the ocean. These islands are located about 2,500 miles   15 southwest of San Francisco and stretch over 1,000 miles from "The Big Island" of Hawaii, northwest to Midway Island. The eight primary islands that make up the Hawaiian Archipelago each have a character of their own.

3   First, there's "The Big Island," Hawaii, appropriately named   20 because it is the largest, having 4,038 square miles of land. Hawaii has the only remaining live volcanoes in the state, Kilauea and Mauna Loa. Mauna Loa is the world's largest active volcano. One inactive volcano, Mauna Kea is the site for the only snow skiing available in Hawaii. Skiers ride a helicopter to the summit of the   25 perfectly-shaped cone of the crater. Due to the volcanic rock, Hawaii has black sand beaches. It's also known occasionally as "The Orchid Isle" and is considered the Antherium capital of the world. The "Big Island" of Hawaii is the home of Kamehameha the First, the first king to rule all the Hawaiian islands, and founder of Hawaii's first   30 and only dynasty, which ruled until the turn of the 20th century.

4   Next in line according to size is Maui, "The Valley Island," with 720 square miles. East and west Maui have forested mountains, semi-arid plains, cow-country grasslands, and fertile valleys. From the winding road one can see some of the most dramatic beauty in   35 Hawaii including cascading waterfalls, white sandy beaches, dense forests of tropical ferns and rare indigenous birds. Maui's principal town, Lahaina, used to be a major whaling port. Maui is now dotted with condominiums and resort hotels and serves as a major tourist destination, yet much of Maui is still "country." First-time visitors   40 to Hawaii come to Honolulu and take tours every day until they're totally exhausted. Second-time visitors prefer the peaceful quiet of Maui, away from the hustle and bustle of tourist traps and souvenir shops. The entire island of Maui rises to a central geographical landmark: an extinct volcano called Haleakala (Hah-lay-ah-kah-   45

LAH) meaning "House of the Sun." Haleakala is the only place where the beautiful silversword plant grows.

5   Oahu, "The Gathering Place," is the most densely populated of all the islands. On this island is the capital of the state of Hawaii, Honolulu, and the vast bulk of the state's citizens. Honolulu is defined as the business, cultural and political center of Hawaii and the hub of Pacific commerce, yet despite its size, it still retains its small-town friendliness. Most of the more than 750,000 people packed into Oahu's 608 square miles live within the city of Honolulu or suburban areas around it. Protected from most heavy winds by the beautiful backdrop of the Koolau mountain range, Honolulu can boast an ideal climate that attracts people from all over the world to Waikiki, the tourist center of the state. There are many famous historical sites on Oahu that still remain: old sugar mills, the original missionary houses (the oldest standing wooden structures in the state), the Bishop Museum, the Royal Hawaiian Hotel and the Iolani Palace. Iolani is the only royal palace in the United States and former home of the ruling family begun by King Kamehameha the First in the 18th century. Some of the prominent geographical features include Pearl Harbor, one of the world's finest protected deepwater harbors (of World War II fame), and the Koolau Mountain range, which divides the northern and southern (also known as the windward and leeward) halves of the island. Other features include: Hanauma Bay, THE place for snorkeling and diving, Punchbowl, an extinct volcano that serves as a serene setting for the U.S. Pacific National Cemetery, and Diamond Head crater, another extinct volcano whose world-famous profile provides a dramatic backdrop for the beaches of Waikiki.

6   Kauai, "The Garden Island," is virtually undiscovered compared with its slightly larger sister islands. 40,000 permanent residents share its 553 square miles. It is considered the most beautiful island of the archipelago. Kauai is blessed with attractive beaches, fertile plains, serene valleys, majestic mountains, rain forests, lush green fern grottoes, and countless waterfalls. Kauai's most famous geographical feature is Waimea Canyon, often called "The Little Grand Canyon of the Pacific." It is similar in form and coloration to the Grand Canyon in Arizona. In contrast to Waimea Canyon, Kauai also sports the wettest spot on earth: Mount Waialeale, where over 400 inches of rain fall annually. It is known as the birthplace of rainbows to Hawaiians.

7   Then there's Molokai, "The Friendly Isle," with 261 square miles. It was not a very popular tourist site for many years because of its famed leper colony. This, however, is no longer the case. There are big name hotels and sightseeing packages. And you can visit the old leper colony, if that's the sort of thing that interests you. Molokai, an island that still retains its rural flavor, is rich in myth and legend, full of historic and religious sites. Near the east end of the island is a famous grove of kukui trees (named for the highly esteemed prophet Kalanikaula). The grove was considered sacred, and nuts from these trees were thought superior to all others. On the west end is Molokai Ranch Wildlife Park, a preserve of rare and

endangered African and Indian hoofed animals. Visitors can track and photograph these animals roaming freely in a habitat closely resembling their native environment. The only sizeable community, Kaunakakai, resembles the Hollywood set for a John Wayne West- 100 ern with its small business section made up of wooden buildings.

8   Lanai is known as "The Pineapple Isle," and for very good reason. The entire place is owned by the Dole Pineapple company and is planted with pineapple. Located just off the northwest end of Maui, it is relatively small and quiet, and is covered by gently slop- 105 ing plains and fields. Despite its close position to the Garden Isle, it is relatively barren, having no major mountains to hold on to the rain-bearing clouds. It looks more like the rolling hills of North Dakota than it does the tropical splendor of "The Garden Island," its closest neighbor. 110

9   Next there's Niihau which lies just off the west coast of Kauai. Known as "The Mystery Isle," or "The Forbidden Isle," this may be the most interesting of all the islands. One must be invited to Niihau because it is privately owned by the Robinson family, and they don't welcome visitors. To all appearances, it is the last stronghold 115 of tradition in Hawaii. Transportation, communication and entertainment are limited. There are no courts, nor is there a need for policing the 250 people that live on the island. This is the only place left where all the people still speak Hawaiian as their native language. The land is quite barren with little rainfall. The chief 120 industry of Niihau is ranching; sheep and cattle mostly.

10   Finally, the smallest island of the eight major islands is Kahoolawe, with only 45 square miles. I wouldn't plan to visit this once-sacred island though. Since 1941, it's been used strictly as a target range and bombing practice site by the U.S. Navy! 125

11   These together make up "home" for the Hawaiians, as well as thousands of immigrants from Japan, China, Portugal, the Philippines, and Mainland America—and "paradise" to the many artists, writers, sailors, and tourists who visit the islands each year.

REVIEW | HAWAII—THE FIFTIETH STATE

Comprehension

1. On which island is the capital city of Honolulu located? _____

2. Two islands are privately owned: Niihau and Lanai. Who owns them?

    Niihau: _____

    Lanai: _____

3. Which island is the Kamehameha family from? _____

4. Which of the eight major islands is the most popular with tourists?

   _____

5. When did Hawaii become the fiftieth state? _____

6. Can you define the "Spirit of Aloha"? _____

   _____

   _____

7. What makes Niihau's people unique among the major eight islands?

   _____

   _____

8. Two of the islands receive no tourists at all. Which ones are they,
   and why? _____   _____

   _____

   _____

Textual Pattern: Description

1. In what kind of publication do you think this type of description
   would be found?_____

2. What is the main purpose of this description of Hawaii?_____

   _____

   _____

3. In the preview section, you were asked about the principle of organization used by the author. Was it subjective or objective?

   _____

   _____

4. What other principle(s) might the author have chosen to organize a
   description of Hawaii?_____

   _____

Vocabulary in Context

As was pointed out in the introduction to this chapter, there is a difference between passive and active vocabulary. Passive vocabulary
includes words that you understand when you hear or read them but do
not necessarily know how to use when you are speaking or writing.

For the purposes of reading, most native language readers are satisfied with a general understanding of a word, without knowing its exact definition or various shades of meaning.

We see one good example in the first paragraph of the reading you just completed, beginning with line 7:

> Its people are friendly, relaxed, and **congenial**, and any visitor who stays more than a day or two soon catches the spirit.

When you understand the other two adjectives about the people of Hawaii, it is not hard to guess what might be the meaning of the word *congenial*. Though contexts many times do not offer enough for the reader to know the *exact* definition, there is usually enough to allow the reader to guess intelligently. If you had to pick one of the following words as being similar in meaning to *congenial*, which would you pick?

coldhearted
easygoing
mean
shy

If you picked *easygoing*, you did well. If you got this question right try explaining the process behind your choice to a classmate (or to the class).

This is not to say that *congenial* means easygoing. If you look *congenial* up in a dictionary, these are some of the definitions you will find: a person who is "sympathetic, agreeable, pleasant," or a person who is "liked because he or she has the same customs or behavior."

The entire context seems to be positive in its description of the land and people. To know that *congenial* is a positive personal adjective, not a negative one, is sufficient for the purpose of understanding the reading material.

We are not suggesting that this is the way to study for the vocabulary sections of the TOEFL or Michigan tests! Your purpose is not the same, and purpose determines method. Multiple exposures to the same word through a variety of contexts will, however, lead to greater comprehension and an ability to use the word successfully in your writing should you desire to do so.

EXERCISE A   It is not always possible to obtain the exact meaning of the word from its context. But knowing the exact meaning of a word is not necessary for comprehension of the passage. Let's look at a few more examples.

1. "The 'Big Island' of Hawaii is the home of Kamehameha the First, the first king to rule all the Hawaiian islands, and founder of Hawaii's first and only **dynasty**, which ruled until the turn of the 20th century."

What do you think a *dynasty* could be? It doesn't seem to be a person because of the word *which* following it. And yet it can rule.

family real line — *real family / line of Kings all of the same fam*

2. "From the winding road one can see some of the most dramatic beauty in Hawaii including **cascading** waterfalls, white sandy beaches, dense forests . . ."

   What do you think *cascading* means? What do waterfalls do?

   - water coming down steadily and rapidly.
   - water falling straight down over rocks sometimes from great

3. "Visitors can track and photograph these animals **roaming** freely in a habitat closely resembling their native environment."

   Now what is it that animals can do freely in this kind of place?

   moving across, through, over the fields in complete lazyness.

EXERCISE B   Try a few more from the past reading on your own.

1. "In addition to the **balmy**, sunny weather, the warm, crystal-clear water, or the scent of tropical flowers, this infectious "Spirit of Aloha" has made Hawaii a paradise for millions of people . . ."

   balmy *soft and warm. / that gives comfort to the spirit.*

2. "Honolulu is defined as the business, cultural and political center of Hawaii and the **hub** of Pacific commerce."

   hub *the center of active commerce.*

3. "Second-time visitors prefer the peaceful quiet of Maui, away from the **hustle and bustle** of tourist traps and souvenir shops."

   hustle and bustle *the uproar / the crowdness / hurried activity*

Description: Figurative Language

Choice of words is important to authors who create images. In addition to using words of exact measurement and chemical composition, authors have a variety of ways to create images.

One simple method is to string adjectives together. The tall teenage boy crawled into the deep, green, exotic, tropical forest. Since this kind of writing can get boring, authors use other techniques as well.

SIMILES

One of the most common devices is called a *simile*. A simile is a figure of speech in which a likeness between two objects is directly expressed with the words *as* or *like*.

Examples
He works like a bee.
Her face was red as a beet.
The train moved slowly up the curving tracks like a giant snake.

In these examples writers have described one object by comparing it to another. We understand that the man in example 1 is hard-working and dedicated to his task. We obtain a better view of the train in example 3 as it works its way along the winding track if we imagine how a snake moves.

METAPHORS

This is a similar device in which the words *as* and *like* are not used.

Examples
While the lone Indian looked on, the giant snake worked its way up the railroad tracks toward the tunnel.

Lifting his opponent off the ground, the modern-day Hercules threw him out of the ring for an easy victory.

In both sentences, one subject has been replaced by another, creating a comparison. We are to imagine the train in example 1 as if it were a giant snake. We understand the strength of the wrestler in example 2 by the comparison to Hercules, the muscular hero of Greek mythology.

This second example brings out another important point. In making comparisons, authors often refer to familiar people or places. On the phone you might tell your mother that your new roommate looks like Uncle George. You do this to help your mother envision this new roommate. In example 2 above, the modern wrestler is compared to Hercules. Do you know who Hercules was? Since most of the English material you will read is created for Western audiences, the comparisons naturally will be to people and places familiar to Western Civilization.

There are several common sources for references. The most common is *Western history*. Kamehameha the First (the first king of Hawaii) has often been referred to as the "Napoleon of the Pacific." To understand this comparison, the reader must know who Napoleon was; most native English speakers do.

Another source is *Western literature*. Certain works have become *classics*. The term can loosely be defined as works of literature that have come to be appreciated by a wide audience over quite a long period of time. Their characters and situations therefore often become labels for common events or behavior. Hawaii is often called a "paradise lost." This is in reference to Milton's famous book *Paradise Lost* about the war in heaven, an important event in Christian theology.

There are two sources in Western literature that deserve special attention. The first is Greek, Roman, Western European, and American *mythology*. Mythology refers to legends and stories of gods, goddesses, and heroes that have been handed down and told for centuries. The author assumes that readers are familiar with them. They are a favorite subject of children's storybooks. Greek and Roman mythology is a popular course of study for many English-speaking students. Hercules, a famous Greek hero, is a good example.

The second source is the *Bible*. Since much of the Western world is Christian, references are often made to biblical places and people. For example, we might hear, "This house is older than Methuselah. I'd never buy it!" According to the Bible, Methuselah lived to be 969 years old!

It is true that there is no quick solution to understanding these references, but then they make up only a small percentage of the vocabulary problems you are likely to encounter. Nevertheless, your understanding of these references will increase your reading comprehension and enjoyment.

Understanding the tools of the descriptive writer will help you better recreate the image and tone the author is trying to develop. Mark Twain is a master of description in this next selection on a visit to Kilauea Volcano. Be aware of his use of the tools discussed above.

PREVIEW | Kilauea Volcano at Night

Things to Think About

1. Who is Mark Twain, the author of this selection? When did he travel and write? _____

2. Can you think of any other writings of his? _____

   _____

   _____

3. What is a simile? _____

   _____

   Make up one example in a sentence about a favorite place you have visited. _____

   _____

4. What is a metaphor? _____

   _____

Make up one example in a sentence about a favorite place you have visited. _____

_____

Vocabulary in Context

Provide a synonym or definition for the following words according to their context. Remember, you are not expected to provide an accurate dictionary definition. Also be prepared to explain how you arrived at your definition.

1. "There was a heavy fog over the crater and it was splendidly illuminated by the **glare** from the fires below."

   glare _strong light_

2. ". . . the mists hung down their **gauzy** curtains and cast a deceptive gloom over all . . ."

   gauzy _thin curtains_

3. "You could imagine those lights the width of a continent away—and that hidden in the darkness were hills, and winding rivers, and weary stretches of plains and desert, and even then, the **vista** stretched on and on."

   vista _a view extended into the distance_

4. "Here and there were **gleaming** holes twenty feet in diameter, broken in the dark crust, and in them melted lava—their color a dazzling white with a bit of yellow—was boiling and surging furiously."

   gleaming _shining dimly_

5. "And from these holes branched numberless bright streams in many directions, like the **spokes** of a lady's fan or the wheel of a wagon." Draw an illustration below.

6. "Through the binoculars, the little fountains scattered about looked very beautiful. They boiled, and coughed, and **sputtered**, and let out sprays of stringy red fire—of about the texture of **mush** or oatmeal."

sputtered _____

mush _____

Preview

Read the italicized paragraph at the beginning of the article and answer the following questions:

a. Where are the Sandwich Islands? _____

_____

b. Why do you think Mark Twain wanted to go there? _____

_____

_____

c. What island is Kilauea on? _____

d. Explain why Twain wrote this description of his trip to Kilauea.

_____

_____

_____

READING TWO

KILAUEA VOLCANO AT NIGHT

In the early part of Mark Twain's literary career, he lived in California and worked for one of the largest and most popular newspapers in the West, the Sacramento Weekly Union. *In 1866, Twain wanted desperately to visit the romantic Sandwich Islands, as Hawaii was known then. The* Weekly Union *agreed to pay his way if he would write a series of articles on his travels. The following reading is taken from one of the articles he wrote while on the "Big Island" and is dated "Midnight, June 3rd, 1866."*

From Mark Twain, "Kilauea Volcano at Night," *Sacramento Weekly Union,* November 17, 1866.

abundant

1   By the path it is half a mile from the Volcano House to the lookout house. After a hearty supper we waited until it was thoroughly
dark and then started to the crater. The first glance in that direction
revealed a scene of wild beauty. There was a heavy fog over the
crater and it was splendidly illuminated by the glare from the fires   5
below. The illumination was two miles wide and a mile high.

2   Having arrived at the little thatched lookout-house, we rested
our elbows on the railing in front and looked abroad over the wide
crater and down over the sheer walls at the seething fires beneath us
. . . for a mile and a half in front of us and half a mile on either side,   10
the floor of the abyss was magnificently illuminated; beyond these
limits, the mists hung down their gauzy curtains and cast a deceptive gloom over all, which made the twinkling fires in the faraway
corners of the crater seem like the camp-fires of a great army miles
away. Here was room for the imagination to work! You could imag-   15
ine those lights the width of a continent away—and that hidden in
the darkness were hills, and winding rivers, and weary stretches of
plains and desert, and even then, the vista stretched on and on. You
could not comprehend it—it was the idea of eternity made tangible.

3   The greater part of the vast floor of the desert under us was as   20
black as ink, and apparently smooth and level; but over a mile
square of it was ringed and streaked and striped with a thousand
branching streams of liquid and gorgeously brilliant fire. It looked
like a huge railroad map of the state of Massachusetts created by
chain lightning on a midnight sky.   25

4   Here and there were gleaming holes twenty feet in diameter,
broken in the dark crust, and in them melted lava—their color a
dazzling white with a bit of yellow—was boiling and surging
furiously. And from these holes branched numberless bright
streams in many directions, like the spokes of a lady's fan or the   30

perpendicular

boiling

wheel of a wagon, staying straight for a while and then sweeping in huge rainbow curves, or broken at sharp angles looking like the fiercest lightning. These streams met other streams and they mingled and crossed and recrossed each other in every possible direction, like skate tracks on a popular skating ground. Through binoculars we could see these streams as they ran down small steep hills, first appearing pure white and then cooling to a rich red, colored from time to time with lines of black and gold. Every now and then, masses of the dark crust broke away and floated slowly down these streams like rafts down a river. Occasionally the molten lava flowing under the surface crust broke through, splitting an amazing streak, from 500 to a 1000 feet long. It seemed like a sudden flash of lightning, after which acre upon acre of the cold lava parted into pieces that turned up edgewise like cakes of ice when a great river breaks up, each plunging downward to be swallowed up in the fiery cauldron.

5   Through the binoculars, the little fountains scattered about looked very beautiful. They boiled, and coughed, and sputtered, and let out sprays of stringy red fire—of about the texture of mush or oatmeal, from ten to fifteen feet into the air, along with a shower of brilliant white sparks—producing what appeared to be a strange mixture of great quantities of blood and snowflakes!

6   The noise of the bubbling lava is not great, hearing it as we did from the height of the lookout house. It makes three distinct sounds—a rushing, a hissing, and a coughing or puffing sound. And if you stand on the edge and close your eyes, it is not difficult at all to imagine that you are sweeping down a river on a large steamship with the hissing of the steam around the boilers, the puffing of smoke from the escape pipes, and the churning rush of waters in the wake.

35

40

45

50

55

60

REVIEW | KILAUEA VOLCANO AT NIGHT

In the boxes provided below list the similes and metaphors used by Mark Twain in each paragraph. The first and second paragraphs have been done for you. (Review the introduction on figurative language if necessary before beginning.) This may be done in groups.

PARAGRAPH 1

Similes	Metaphors
none	*none*

PARAGRAPH 2

Similes	Metaphors
1. crater fires seem like campfires of a great army	1. the mists hung down their gauzy curtains

PARAGRAPH 3

Similes	Metaphors
floor was as black as ink / It looked like a huge railroad map of the state of Massachusetts	it was ringed and streaked and striped with thousand branching streams of liquid

PARAGRAPH 4

pag 18 (Top)

Similes	Metaphors
bright streams like the spokes of a lady's fan or the wheel of a wagon, looking like the fiercest lightning	and then sweeping in a huge rainbow curves,

like skate tracks ∘
masses floated slowly down like

PARAGRAPH 5

of about the texture of mush
or oatmeal

Similes	Metaphors
what appeared to be a strange mixture of great quantities of blood and snow flakes	the little fountains scattered They boiled, and coughed, and sputtered . . .

PARAGRAPH 6

Similes	Metaphors

In the second paragraph, Twain compares the crater fires to the campfires of a great army. What event in American history would make this a vivid comparison for Americans who would be reading this in 1866?

The civil war   North v South

Description: Appeal to the Senses

Success for the descriptive writer is measured by how vividly and accurately the object or feeling can be recreated in the reader's mind. As we have already discussed, authors use several methods for increasing the effectiveness of their descriptive writing.

In the first reading selection we saw how the author used the principle of size to organize his description of the Hawaiian Islands. We have also seen how authors, like Mark Twain, use similes and metaphors to create rich images.

Descriptive writing can be more realistic, with the use of words that appeal to the reader's sense of touch, smell, taste, and hearing. A description of a snowy day must include more than what the eye can see; otherwise, it is no more real than a black-and-white photograph. An author might mention the sound of the wind as it whistles lightly through empty branches, or the feeling of the snowflakes as they settle lightly on one's face, or the clean, penetrating, icy air as it stings the nostrils.

EXERCISE Skim through Mark Twain's description of his trip to the volcano and write down a few of the phrases that appeal to senses other than sight.

_____

_____

_____

_____

_____

_____

_____

_____

_____

Vocabulary: Contextual Paraphrasing

From time to time, the author will paraphrase (reword) an idea to make it clearer for the reader (as we have done in this sentence with the word *paraphrase*). These paraphrases are often set off by commas or parentheses, but not always. Good writers keep their audiences in mind when they write and offer help to the reader when they think it is necessary.

This is often done when using foreign words:

The *o'o*, or honeyeater, is now almost extinct on every island in Hawaii.

Here the native name for a tropical bird is used, but the English equivalent is also given.

There are two kinds of markers that writers often use to signal a coming paraphrase or example that will make the meaning clearer.

The first type includes punctuation. These include markers such as:

paired commas (, ... ,),
double dash (--),
set of parentheses (   ).

The second type consists of verbal clues. These include:

i.e. — in other words
e.g. — for example
that is — in other words
in other words — to say in a different way
for instance — for example
for example — for example
such as — for example

Consider these examples:

Nuclear war is likely to end in **mutual destruction**, that is, destruction in which both countries involved are destroyed.

The teacher said the coming exam would be a **bear**. In other words, we better study hard for this one.

People who eat too much spicy food are likely to suffer from **dyspepsia**—a condition commonly called indigestion.

The use of **hallucinogenics** such as LSD has declined over the past twenty years.

Of course, there is one other method for obtaining the meaning of a word— looking it up in the dictionary. From time to time, your purpose will require that you understand the word exactly. When other strategies fail, you will want to use a dictionary. If at all possible, use an English-English dictionary for reading purposes. With the proficiency of English that you possess, you should use a bilingual dictionary only sparingly when writing.

PREVIEW | IMPRESSIONS OF HONOLULU, 1873

Things to Think About

Have you ever gone back to a place that you have not visited for a long time? What sort of changes did you see? (Take a few minutes to think and write down what you can remember.)

_____

_____

_____

_____

_____

_____

_____

_____

_____

_____

_____

Vocabulary in Context

Write a definition or synonym in the blank.

1. "**Owing to** the clear atmosphere, we seemed only five miles off, but in reality we were twenty."

   Owing to __Due to/because of__   ⌐ deep cleft in the earth

2. "There were lofty peaks . . . but they were **cleft** by deep **chasms and ravines** of cool shadow."

   cleft __divided__ / __an opening made by splitting, a crack__ ⌐ a fissure .

   chasms and ravines __fissures, and long, deep, narrow hollows, usually made by a torrent deepening its bed,__

3. "The men displayed their **lithe**, graceful figures to the best advantage in white trousers and **gay** Garibaldi shirts.

   lithe _slim_

   gay _bright / brilliant_

4. "The conditions of life must surely be easier here, and people must have found rest from some of its burdensome **conventionalities**.

   conventionalities _customs_

5. "This place is quite unique. . . . It looks like a large village, or rather like an **aggregate** of villages."

   aggregate _add to / to come together / a collection_

Preview

1. Read the italicized paragraph at the beginning of the selection and answer the following questions.

   a. Who is Isabella Bird and why is she famous? _She travelled almost around the world and was the first woman accepted as a member of the Royal geographical society_

   b. When did she visit Hawaii? _1873_

      When did Mark Twain visit Hawaii? _1866_

   c. Do you think Twain's writing about the Sandwich Islands could possibly have influenced Isabella Bird's decision to come to Hawaii? As you read, look for a possible reference to Mark Twain.

   _____

   _____

   _____

2. What kind of description do you think this reading will be an example of: subjective or objective? (Circle one.) What makes you think so? _____

   _____

Note: As you read Isabella Bird's description of Honolulu as she remembers it in 1873, underline places where she appeals to your various senses other than sight: smell, touch, taste, and hearing.

READING THREE

IMPRESSIONS OF HONOLULU, 1873

*Isabella Bird (Mrs. J. F. Bishop, 1832–1904) was a
world-famous traveler. She spent half a year in the
"Sandwich Islands" in 1873. She married Dr. John F.
Bishop when he was forty and she was fifty, but she did
not let marriage interrupt her world travels. She
continued to travel, with her husband's blessing and
support, not only to Hawaii but also to the Rocky
Mountains (America), Japan, Malaya, Korea, the
Yangtze River, the vale of Kashmir, Tibet, and the
deserts of Morocco. She wrote accurate and interesting
books about all these places and was the first woman to
be accepted as a fellow (member) of the Royal
Geographical Society.*

—Hawaiian Hotel, Honolulu   —January 26, 1873

1   Yesterday morning at six-thirty I was aroused by the news that
"The Islands" were in sight. Oahu in the distance, a group of gray,
barren peaks rising verdureless out of the lonely sea, was not an
exception to the rule that the first sign of land is a disappointment.
Owing to the clear atmosphere, we seemed only five miles off, but in   5
reality we were twenty, and the land improved as we neared it. It
was the fiercest day we had had, the deck was almost too hot to

From Isabella L. Bird, *The Hawaiian Archipelago: Six Months in the
Sandwich Islands*, 1875, pp. 18–26.

stand upon, the sea and sky were both magnificently blue, and the unveiled sun turned every minute ripple into a diamond flash. As we approached, the island changed its character. There were lofty peaks, truly—gray and red, sun-scorched and wind-bleached, glowing here and there with traces of their fiery origin; but they were cleft by deep chasms and ravines of cool shadow and entrancing green, and falling water streaked their sides—a most welcome vision after eleven months of the desert sea and the dusty browns of Australia and New Zealand. Nearer yet, and the coastline came into sight, fringed by the feathery coconut tree of the tropics, and marked by the long line of surf. The grand promontory of Diamond Head, its fiery sides now softened by a haze of green, terminated the wavy line of palms; then the Punchbowl, a very perfect extinct crater, brilliant with every shade of red volcanic ash, blazed against the green skirts of the mountains. We were close to the coral reef before the cry, "There's Honolulu!" made us aware of the proximity of the capital of the island kingdom, and then, indeed, its existence had almost to be taken upon trust, for besides the lovely wooden and grass huts, with deep verandas, which nestled under palms and bananas, margined by the bright sea sand, only two church spires and a few gray roofs appeared above the trees.

2   We were just outside the reef, and near enough to hear that deep sound of the surf which, through the ever serene summer years, girdles the Hawaiian Islands with perpetual thunder, before the pilot glided alongside, bringing the news which Mark Twain had prepared us to receive with interest, that "Prince Bill" (Lunalilo) had been unanimously elected to the throne. The surf ran white and pure over the environing coral reef, and as we passed through the narrow channel, we almost saw the coral forests deep down under the Nevada's keel; the coral fishers plied their graceful trade; canoes with outriggers rode the combers and glided with inconceivable rapidity round our ship; amphibious brown beings sported in the transparent waves; and within the reef lay a calm surface of water of a wonderful blue, entered by a narrow, intricate passage of the deepest indigo. And beyond the reef and beyond the blue, nestling among coconut trees and bananas, umbrella trees and breadfruits, oranges, mangoes, and hibiscus, almost hidden in the deep, dense greenery, was Honolulu. Bright blossom of a summer sea! Fair Paradise of the Pacific!

3   We looked down from the towering deck on a crowd of two or three thousand people—whites, Kanakas, Chinamen—and hundreds of them at once made their way on board, and streamed over the ship, talking, laughing, and remarking upon us in a language which seemed without backbone. Such rich brown men and women they were, with wavy, shining black hair, large, brown, lustrous eyes, and rows of perfect teeth like ivory. Everyone was smiling. The forms of the women seem to be inclined toward obesity, but their drapery, which consists of a sleeved garment which falls in ample and unconfined folds from their shoulders to their feet, partly conceals this defect, which is here regarded as beauty. Some of these dresses were black, but many of those worn by the younger women

were of pure white, crimson, yellow, scarlet, blue, or light green. The men displayed their lithe, graceful figures to the best advantage   60 in white trousers and gay Garibaldi shirts. A few of the women wore colored handkerchiefs twined round their hair, but generally both men and women wore straw hats, which the men set jauntily on one side of their heads, and aggravated their appearance yet more by bandanna handkerchiefs of rich bright colors round their necks,   65 knotted loosely on the left side, with a grace to which, I think, no Anglo-Saxon dandy could attain. Without an exception the men and women wore wreaths and garlands of flowers, carmine, orange, or pure white, twined round their hats, and thrown carelessly round their necks, flowers unknown to me, but redolent of the tropics in   70 fragrance and color. Many of the young beauties wore the gorgeous blossom of the red hibiscus among their abundant, unconfined black hair, and many, besides the garlands, wore festoons of a sweet-scented vine, or of an exquisitely beautiful fern, knotted behind and hanging halfway down their dresses. These adornments   75 of natural flowers are most attractive. Chinamen, all alike, very long pigtails, spotlessly clean clothes, and an expression of mingled cunning and simplicity, "foreigners," half-whites, a few Negroes, and a very few dark-skinned Polynesians from the far-off South Seas, made up the rest of the rainbow-tinted crowd.   80

4   The "foreign" ladies, who were there in great numbers, generally wore simple light prints or muslins and white straw hats, and many of them so far conformed to native custom as to wear natural flowers round their hats and throats. But where were the hard, angular, careworn, sallow, passionate faces of men and women,   85 such as form the majority of every crowd at home, as well as in America and Australia? The conditions of life must surely be easier here, and people must have found rest from some of its burdensome conventionalities. The foreign ladies, in their simple, tasteful, fresh attire, innocent of the humpings and bunchings, the monstrosities   90 and deformities of ultrafashionable bad taste, beamed with cheerfulness, friendliness, and kindliness. Men and women looked as easy, contented, and happy as if care never came near them. I never saw such healthy, bright complexions as among the women, or such "sparkling smiles," or such a diffusion of feminine grace and gra-   95 ciousness anywhere. . .

5   In the crowd and outside of it, and everywhere, there were piles of fruit for sale—oranges, guavas, strawberries, papayas, bananas (green and golden), coconuts, and other rich, fantastic productions of a prolific climate, where nature gives of her wealth the whole year   100 round. Strange fishes, strange in shape and color—crimson, blue, orange, rose, gold—such fishes as flash like living light through the coral groves of these enchanted seas.

6   With two of my fellow passengers, we hired a buggy and left the ship. This place is quite unique. It is said that fifteen thousand   105 people are buried away in these low-browed, shadowy houses, under the glossy, dark-leaved trees, but except in one or two streets of miscellaneous, old-fashioned-looking stores, arranged with a dis-

tinct leaning toward native tastes, it looks like a large village, or
rather like an aggregate of villages. As we drove through the town 110
we could only see our immediate surroundings, but each had a new
fascination. We drove along roads with over-arching trees, through
whose dense leafage the noon sunshine only trickled in dancing,
broken lights; umbrella trees, bamboo, mango, orange, breadfruit,
candlenut, monkey pod, date and coco palms, huge-leaved, wide- 115
spreading trees, exotics from the South Seas, many of them rich in
parasitic ferns, and others blazing with bright, fantastic blossoms.
The air was heavy with odors of gardenia, tuberose, oleanders,
roses, lilies, and great white trumpet flowers, and myriads of others
whose names I do not know. 120

7   In the deep shade of this perennial greenery the people dwell.
The foreign houses show a very various individuality. The pecu-
liarity in which all seem to share is that everything is decorated and
festooned with flowering trailers. It is often difficult to tell what the
architecture is, or what is house and what is vegetation; for all 125
angles and verandas are hidden by jasmine or passion-flowers, or
the gorgeous flamelike bougainvillea. Many of the dwellings strag-
gle over the ground without an upper story, and have very deep
verandas, through which I caught glimpses of cool, shady rooms,
with matted floors. Besides the frame houses there are houses built 130
of blocks of a cream-colored coral conglomerate laid in cement; of
adobe, or large sun-baked bricks, plastered; houses of grass and
bamboo; houses on the ground and houses raised on posts; but
nothing looks prosaic, commonplace, or mean, for the glow and
luxuriance of the tropics rest on all. 135

REVIEW | IMPRESSIONS OF HONOLULU, 1873

Comprehension

1. What is Isabella Bird's first impression of Oahu?_____

_____

2. What are her impressions of the people of Hawaii?_____

_____

_____

3. What is her general impression of the architecture in Honolulu?

_____

_____

Textual Pattern: Description

1. How did Bird organize her description?_____

_____

2. In the preview exercises you were asked to think about the tone of the description. Now that you have completed the reading, do you think Isabella Bird was subjective or objective? Why is she so positive?

_____

_____

_____

_____

3. Can you think of any negative things that might have been said about Honolulu in 1873? Surely she could have mentioned a few!

    _____

    _____

    _____

    _____

4. As Isabella describes her impressions of her arrival and first day in Honolulu, what is her purpose? Who is her audience?

    _____

    _____

    _____

    _____

5. As we discussed, adding details that appeal to the reader's sense of taste, smell, or touch adds to the power of the writing to recreate in the reader's mind the writer's experience or emotions.

    Write down the passages you found in the reading that enriched the description by dealing with the senses of smell, taste, touch, and hearing.

    Smell:

    _____

    _____

    _____

    _____

    Taste:

    _____

    _____

    _____

    _____

    Touch:

    _____

    _____

    _____

    _____

Hearing:

_____

_____

_____

_____

_____

Vocabulary: Word Analysis

The preceding reading selection contains a number of unfamiliar words that are difficult to guess the meanings of. Let's look back at the first few lines of the reading. Define the two boldface words.

> Yesterday morning at six-thirty I was **aroused** by the news that "The Islands" were in sight. Oahu in the distance, a group of gray, barren peaks rising **verdureless** out of the lonely sea, . . .

aroused _____

verdureless _____

The first word, *aroused*, should be quite easy to understand by the context. Possible definitions might be *excited* or *surprised*. It is 6:30 A.M. when she hears the news, however, so it is also possible that she was *awakened* by the news.

The second word is not so easy. Oahu is described as "verdureless." It is probably a negative adjective, if it is to fit in with Bird's first impression of the island, but otherwise its meaning is difficult to guess at.

The context of this second word is a good example of the fact that context does not always make the meaning clear. As a reader, you must decide whether the word is worth pursuing or not. If you feel it's important to the meaning of the passage, there are other strategies available.

PREFIXES, SUFFIXES, AND ROOTS

Word analysis allows the reader to break down English words into their component parts. Roots or stems carry the basic meaning of a word. The meaning of these roots can be changed by adding prefixes (to the beginning of the words) and suffixes (at the end).

A good example is the word *conversation*, which can be broken down like this:

Prefix	**Root**	**Suffix**
con-	-verse-	-ation
(with)	(word, phrase, talk)	(changes a verb to a noun)

Converse means to talk with (someone).
Conversation means a talk with (someone).

This is another strategy, then, that makes it possible to understand a word. Here is a partial list of common prefixes, suffixes, and roots.

Prefix	**Meaning**	**Example**
anti-	against	antisocial
auto-	self	automatic, automobile
con-, com-, co-	with	cooperate
de-	away from, down	decrease
hyper-, hypo-	over, under	hyperactive, hypodermic
inter-, intra-	between, within	interpersonal
mini-, maxi-	small, large	minimum, maximum
mono-, bi-, poly-	one, two, many	monotone, polygon
pre-	before	preview
semi-	half, part	semiformal dress
sub-, super-	under, above	superman, subhuman
tele-	far	telephone
trans-	across	translate
ultra-	maximum, extreme	ultraconservative
un-, in-, im-, il-,	negative, not	impractical, illegal

Root	**Meaning**	**Example**
aud-	hear	auditorium
bio-	life	biology
carc-	cancer	carcinogen
dict-	speak, word	dictator
fest-	celebrate	festival
gen(e)-	to create, make	generate
graph-	write, writing	autograph
homo-, hetero-	same, different	homogeneous
hydro-	water	hydrotherapy
lat-	horizontal, side	latitude, lateral
man-, manu-	hand	manual
mar-, terr-	sea, land	marine, terrain
mov-, mot-, mob-	to move	motivate
palat-	taste	palatable

Root	*Meaning*	*Example*
ped-, pod-	foot	pedal
phon-	sound, hear	phonetic
photo-	light	photograph
port-	carry, move	portable
psych-	mental, brain	psychologist
spect-	to look at	spectator
vis-, vid-	to see, sight	visible, video

Suffix	*Meaning*	*Example*
-able, -ible	ability to	capable, responsible
-er, -or, -ist	a person who	actor, terrorist
-er, -est	more, most	taller, tallest
-ful	full of	beautiful
-hood	state of being	childhood
-ic, -ical	made of, about	political, fantastic
-ish	like, similar to	childish
-ite	a follower/member	Israelite
-ly	adverb of manner	quietly
-less	without	careless
-ness	state of being	calmness
-ship	state/office of	ambassadorship
-some	full of, causing	bothersome, awesome

EXERCISE A   Write a word of your own for each of the following:

1. pre- _____   **6.** inter- _____

2. mini- _____   **7.** anti- _____

3. ped- _____   **8.** -ly _____

4. phon- _____   **9.** -able _____

5. spect- _____   **10.** -er _____

EXERCISE B   Explain the following words by analyzing their parts.

1. photography _____

_____

2. international _____

_____

3. audiovisual _____

_____

4. superman _____

_____

5. submarine _____

_____

Description: Technical Matters

In descriptions that are technical in nature, writers tend to use many professional terms. Readers must decide, according to their purpose, which terms are important and which ones can simply be ignored.

A chemist reading an article on a chemical process would need to understand all the terms being used. A person reading a family medical encyclopedia for treatment of a common cold would not need to understand the scientific names of all the viruses that cause colds. Below we discuss briefly several categories of terms often encountered in technical reports and descriptions.

SCIENTIFIC NAMES AND LABELS

This category includes the Latin-based names for all organic and inorganic substances. These terms are often italicized and/or enclosed in parentheses. In most cases, the meaning is understood without discussion of scientific names for the objects. Here are two examples:

The monarch butterfly *(Danaus archippus)* is the most common butterfly found in the lowlands of Hawaii.

Of the five kinds of tuna, the bonito *(Euthynnus pelamis)* is the most common food source for South Pacific Islanders.

PROFESSIONAL TERMS AND JARGON

Each profession develops new words and phrases that are unique to that profession. This occurs usually out of the necessity to describe new products, services, and processes (e.g., laserprinting, drycleaning, software). Culture subgroups also introduce new words and change meanings of old ones. Users of CB radios call members of the police force "smokey bears." In the 1960s, "acid" referred to hallucinogenic drugs like LSD. Such words are used so commonly by those in a particular profession or culture group that they are often not defined for the outsider or general reader.

Sometimes words are used in a particular profession with a different meaning than they have in common usage. Many of these words arise so quickly that dictionaries cannot keep up. Since you won't be able to look many of them up, get professional advice about the vocabulary unique to your interests or profession.

EXERCISE   Translate the following terms into common English terms.

1.   "Yesterday's **learning module** was not well understood by the students, so they asked the teacher to review it again the following day."

   _____

2.   "The report indicates that **secretarial personnel** suffer from **temporary visual indications of fatigue** after **having interfaced** with computer terminals for extended periods of time."

   Who's suffering? _____(one word, please!)

   What's the problem? _____

   What were these people doing to cause the problem? _____

   _____

Certain professions and governmental agencies sometimes create new terms or use obscure language that does not aid in comprehension. Translate the following example into its common form:

   Members of an avian species of identical plumage congregate. (Hint: This is a proverb.)

   _____

FOREIGN NAMES

Often, when discussing a custom, plant, or material that is part of another culture or country, scholars will use terms in the native language of that area. These terms are not important for comprehension if the English equivalent is also found in the sentence. They are often set off by quotation marks or placed in italics. As with scientific names, these native terms are not important to understanding the text if one is reading for general comprehension.

Below are two examples:

The *ahu'ula*, or feathered cloaks, worn by the ruling chiefs of Hawaii, were made from thousands of little red and yellow feathers.

Light yellow feathers for the capes were gathered from the *o'o (Acrulocercus nobilis)*. This black-feathered bird, more commonly known as the honeyeater, has a few short yellow feathers beneath the tail and wings.

PREVIEW | HAWAIIAN FEATHERWORK

Things to Think About

1. What are feathers used for in your culture? Are different kinds of feathers used for different purposes? _____

    _____

    _____

    _____

2. What do you think Hawaiians use feathers for? _____

    _____

    _____

Vocabulary in Context

1. "Many people throughout the world have used feathers for decorating objects intended to be showy or attractive. These include . . . the helmets and **diadems** of the chiefs of New Guinea, trimmed with the beautiful **plumes** of the birds of paradise."

    diadems _____

    plumes _____

2. "This graceful black-feathered bird has a few short, yellow feathers beneath the tail, and a **tuft** of about 20 longer feathers below each wing."

    tuft _____

3. "The *ahu'ula* were made and worn only by men, being **taboo** to women."

    taboo _____

4. " . . . so was a Hawaiian king or chief symbolized by his *kahili*. This consisted of a **hulu** or clustered arrangement of feathers borne aloft on a long pole."

    hulu _____

Preview

1. Skim through the first paragraph to determine the time reference for this article on featherwork. Are the authors talking about how the feathers are used nowadays or in the past? How do you know? (What is the clue?)

   _____

   _____

2. Scan the boldface subtitles. What types of articles did the Hawaiians make with feathers?

   _____

   _____

3. What type of description do you expect here: subjective or objective? (Circle one.) As you read this selection, indicate with an asterisk (*) where you are fairly sure what kind of description this is.

4. In this reading you will encounter some words you are not familiar with. Circle them and decide whether or not they are important for comprehension.

READING FOUR

Hawaiian Featherwork

1   Featherwork in Hawaii was closely associated with royalty. Only the families of the kings and high chiefs in these islands were allowed to use feathers for adornment or decoration. In this way the gorgeous feather cloaks and helmets became the state robes of the kings and their close associates. The graceful *kahilis* became their   5
banners. The feather *leis* adorned only the heads of their queens and royal ladies. Feathers were used to decorate the images in their immediate charge.

2   Many people throughout the world have used feathers for decorating objects intended to be showy or attractive. These include the   10
images in temples of India, the feather scepters of rulers in Brazil and Venezuela, the headdresses of the Mayas and Aztecs, the helmets and diadems of the chiefs of New Guinea, trimmed with the beautiful plumes of the birds of paradise. In modern times we have the work of the milliner and costumer. But, although the birds in   15
Hawaii, whose feathers were used, were less brilliantly colored, none used feathers with more skill and artistic taste than did the Hawaiians.

Reprinted with permission from the *Honolulu Advertiser*, December 25, 1932.

LITTLE FOREST BIRDS

3   The feathers for most of the cloaks, helmets, *leis* and images were obtained from a very few species of native forest birds. The *kahili* makers also employed the feathers of the owl, crow, and several sea birds, such as terns, the *iwa* or frigate bird, and the *koa'e* or tropic bird. In more modern times, use was made of the feathers of such introduced birds as the peacock, the pheasant, and the domestic fowl, the feathers of the last being dyed.

4   The little forest birds whose feathers were most frequently used were the *mamo, o'o, i'iwi*, and less commonly the *apapane, ou* and *amakihi*. All of these except the *o'o* belong to a family of perching birds found nowhere else in the world. The *mamo (Drepanis pacifica)* was found only on the Island of Hawaii, never very commonly, and has not been seen at all since about 1870. It was black in color, with small patches of orange-yellow feathers above the base of the tail, on the lower part of the back, and on the thighs. It was these orange-yellow feathers which were used in featherwork, so one can easily imagine that cloaks and leis made of them are now quite valuable.

YELLOW, RED AND GREEN

5   Feathers of a lighter yellow, more commonly seen than those of the *mamo*, were from the *o'o (Acrulocercus nobilis)*. This graceful, black-feathered bird had a few short, yellow feathers beneath the tail, and a tuft of about 20 longer feathers below each wing. One frequently hears the statement that the *o'o* had only two yellow feathers, whereas, in reality, it has two tufts, with more nearly forty feathers.

6   The *o'o* was found only on the Island of Hawaii, but it had relatives, with much inferior yellow feathers, on Maui, Molokai and Kauai. The long, curved bill of this bird helped it to sip the nectar from the base of the long-tubed lobelia blossoms. It is now very scarce, perhaps extinct.

7   The *i'iwi (Vestiaria coccinea)*, which furnished the featherworker with scarlet feathers, is still fairly abundant in native forests throughout the larger islands. It is about the size of an English sparrow, bright scarlet except for the black wings and tail.

8   There are a few cloaks and capes which use the rich crimson feathers of the *apapane (Himatione sanguinea)*, and the greenish feathers of the *amakihi* (species of *Chlorodrepanis*) and female *ou (Psittirostra psittacea)*, but these are uncommon. . . .

CLOAKS AND CAPES

9   Hawaiian featherwork took its most gorgeous form in the cloaks and capes. The whereabouts, throughout the world, of about 120 of these beautiful garments is known. They are scattered far and wide in museums and private collections, because of the generosity of the Hawaiian chiefs in giving them to the early visitors to these islands. Only about 20 are preserved here in Hawaii, and most of these are in the Bishop Museum.

10   In making the *ahu'ula* (cloaks and capes) a strong network, called *nae*, was first made out of the fiber of the *olona* plant. The nets were knotted with various mesh, some very fine, and were usually made in strips about nine inches wide, which were tied together to form the groundwork of the cape or cloak. The feathers were tied   70 upon this in overlapping rows, like shingles on a roof, the quill of each feather being firmly held by a loop of *olona* fiber.

11   Contrasting patterns in the form of crescents, triangles, diamonds and other geometric figures were worked out in red and yellow, and some black. There are almost no two patterns alike. In   75 size, the *ahu'ula* varied from very short capes which scarcely covered the shoulders, to long cloaks which reached from the shoulders nearly to the ground on a tall man. The *ahu'ula* were made and worn only by men, being taboo to women. They were not only ceremonial robes of state, but also uniforms of the kings in battle, to   80 make them conspicuous points for their men. A victor in battle had the privilege of taking a fallen hero's cape for his own.

HELMETS AND KAHILIS

12   The feather-covered helmets or *mahiole* were worn by kings and chiefs rather as royal insignia than as protective coverings.   85 However, the heavy, tough foundation for the feathers, made of the aerial rootlets of the *ieie* vine and *olona* fibers, would have broken the force of a considerable blow. The helmet had a central raised crest which made it have a close resemblance to the ancient helmets of Greece and Spain. It is thought that the pattern more likely came   90 from the western Pacific, where in New Guinea and New Ireland there are found head coverings very similar in form. There are about forty *mahiole* preserved or known from illustrations, in the world.

13   As the feudal knights of old were recognized by their coats-of-arms and banners, so was a Hawaiian king or chief symbolized by   95 his *kahili*. This consisted of a *hulu* or clustered arrangement of feathers borne aloft on a long pole. The pole might be made of a hardwood spear, or might be more elaborately composed of alternate sections of ivory, human bone and tortoise shell. It was no dishonor to a person to have his bone in a kahili handle. Rather it did honor   100 to his memory.

14   The *hulu* was made up for the special occasion, ceremony or funeral procession, the feathers being put away with native tobacco leaves between uses. To aid in their effective display, the feathers were fastened to the ends of pieces of fiber. In addition to the feath-   105 ers of native forest birds, kahilis were also decorated with owl, crow and seabirds' feathers, and in recent times with dyed chicken feathers.

LEIS AND IMAGES

15   Royal women were permitted to wear feathers in the form of   110 leis, which were placed about their hair, and in more recent times about the neck. A feather lei was made by tying the feathers around

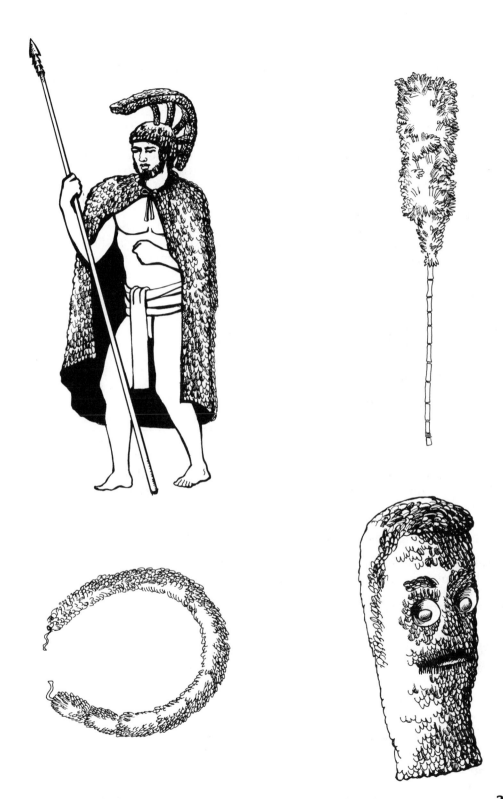

a central core of fiber. The old form was nearly cylindrical and of one color. Making them of variegated color is a more modern innovation. The *ilima* flower leis and paper leis are very good imitations of the yellow leis of *mamo* or *o'o* feathers.   115

16   Throughout the world there are known to be about ten or a dozen Hawaiian images made of fiberwork covered with feathers. Most of these are called "Ku-kaili-moku." The tradition is that the original feather god, Kaili, consisted of a couple of feathers kept in a   120 gourd. It, of course, could not be carried into battle, so these fearsome-looking images, with eyes of pearl shell, and mouths edged with dogs' teeth, were made to represent it, and at the same time to strike terror to the enemy.

17   All of these feather images, while different, are built after a   125 general pattern. One of the least hideous is on exhibition at Bishop Museum, where one may also see numerous representative examples of kahilis, cloaks, capes, and leis.

REVIEW | HAWAIIAN FEATHERWORK

Comprehension

1. What are the most popular colors for Hawaiian featherwork?

_____

_____

2. True or false? Most of the forest birds that once provided feathers for the traditional featherwork are now extinct or almost extinct.

_____

3. The best feathers seemed to be found on which island?_____

4. How does the featherwork of the Hawaiians compare to that of other cultures mentioned in the article?

_____

_____

5. From what you have read so far in this chapter on Hawaii, give two reasons why feathered cloaks, helmets, and leis are no longer made.

_____

_____

6. True or false? The Hawaiian featherworkers were very careful to copy the patterns of their teachers when making new cloaks or capes.

_____

7. True or false? Women were allowed to wear only the feather leis.

    _____

8. True or false? The only remaining examples of these cloaks, capes, leis, etc., are found only in the Bishop Museum.

    _____

9. What was the purpose of the Hawaiian feather "images"?

    _____

    _____

Textual Pattern: Description

1. In the preview activity section, you decided, after briefly skimming the selection, what type of description you thought this would be. Look back to that exercise to see what you had written. Of the following categories, which seems to accurately describe this reading? (Circle one.)

    objective   technical   emotional   subjective

2. What kind of publication do you think this selection was found in? Who was the intended audience?

    _____

    _____

3. At what point in the reading did you feel fairly confident about the answer to each of the two questions above? (Where did you put your asterisk?)

    _____

    _____

4. What has the writer done to help the audience follow the organization?

    _____

    _____

5. At first glance, there seem to be six major parts to this description of Hawaiian featherwork. In reality, however, there are only three. What are they?

    a. Introduction

    b. _____

    c. _____

Skill Review: Vocabulary

1. List several examples where the author helped the reader by para-
    phrasing or providing a synonym for a difficult term. (There's one in
    the first paragraph!)

    a. _____

    b. _____

    c. _____

    d. _____

    e. _____

2. List some of the professional terms the author used.

    a. _____

    b. _____

    c. _____

    d. _____

    e. _____

    What method did the author use to set these terms apart (to help the
    reader)?

    _____

3. Look over the words you circled. Are there any words we haven't
    discussed? (We are sure there are a few.) Since every reader's list
    will be different, the question is: Which ones do you think are worth
    taking time to look up in the dictionary? Write them down. *Not too
    many, please!* Look them up and note their meanings.

    a. _____ _____

    b. _____ _____

    c. _____ _____

    d. _____ _____

    e. _____ _____

CHAPTER 2

*Those who cannot remember
the past are condemned to
repeat it.*

—George Santayana,
"Reason in Common Sense"

THE NUCLEAR AGE

Many of the scientific achievements that we take for granted today have reached far beyond the dreams of scientists and science fiction writers of just seventy-five years ago. One of the most spectacular of these scientific accomplishments was the splitting of the atom. Life has never been the same since that event. From microwave ovens to electrical power and nuclear medicine, to ships that can sail the seas for as long as twelve years without refueling, the atom provides a better life for many of the inhabitants of the earth. Yet, this same power that is used today to detect genetic disorders in unborn children or to destroy a malignant cancer cell was the destructive force that killed over one hundred thousand people in Hiroshima and Nagasaki at the end of World War II. The splitting of the atom, the unleashing of its terrific power, poses the greatest single threat known to humanity. We now have the power to destroy in a matter of minutes a civilization that has taken centuries to develop. Never before has the power for such potential good or such total destruction existed.

In this chapter you will be reading about important events in the development of atomic energy.

NARRATION

These readings about the nuclear age are all told as narrations. Narration is one of the most common types of reading discourse you will encounter. Simply defined, narration tells a story. Authors using narration develop a story into events and arrange them in time. In short, narration answers the question, "What happened?"

In this chapter you will be reading narrative accounts of "what happened" at key events during the nuclear age.

DETECTING SEQUENCE

Because narration is a retelling of events, those events must be presented in some logical sequence or order. You will be learning in this chapter that a narration is developed in chronological or time order. Generally, when we narrate a story, the most understandable way to tell the story is to start at the beginning and continue to the end. In other words, we relate an event in exactly the same order as it actually occurred. However, you will discover, if you haven't already, that a beginning-to-end, first-to-last sequence is not always the way authors retell events. For various reasons which you will be reading about in this chapter, an author may rearrange the order of events. Being able to detect the actual sequence of events despite the way an author presents them is often necessary in order to understand what you are reading. Therefore, many of the exercises in this chapter will be helping you learn how to detect the sequence of events as they are told by authors.

Narration: An Introduction

If you were asked what a narration is, you might answer, "It's a story," or "It's a retelling of events." Both responses would be correct, but for our purposes it would be helpful to have a more detailed explanation of a narration.

A narration is a retelling of a story, and, in general, a story is a sequence of events (which may be historically true or false) presented in such a way that the reader's imagination can comprehend the action. The events used in a story must have some relationship to one another; writers generally do not add events to a narration that have nothing to do with the story.

Remember that a narration is more than a list of chronological events. There must be some purpose for the events' being put together. The following two paragraphs make this clearer.

> President Wilson presented his war message to Congress on April 6, 1917. War was declared. Thus the United States embarked on its first great adventure in world affairs. On April 8, 1917, just two days later, Albert Mayfield was born in Marysville, Illinois. He was a healthy baby and grew rapidly. By the time the peace treaty was signed he weighed 22 pounds. On December 12, 1918, the troopship Mason, returning to New York from Cherbourg, struck a floating mine off Ireland and sank. Two hundred and sixteen men were lost.

There is nothing to unify this paragraph. There is no purpose for listing these seemingly unrelated events together. Now read the same paragraph with a few more events added to unify the whole story.

> President Wilson presented his war message to Congress on April 6, 1917. War was declared. Thus the United States embarked on its first great adventure in world affairs. On April 8, 1917, just two days later, Albert Mayfield was born in Marysville, Illinois. Scarcely before the ink had dried on the headlines of the extra of the Marysville *Courier* announcing the declaration of war, Albert embarked on his own great adventure in world affairs. He was a healthy baby and grew rapidly. By the time the peace treaty was signed he weighed 22 pounds. On December 12, 1918, the troopship Mason, returning to New York from Cherbourg, struck a floating mine off Ireland and sank. Two hundred and sixteen men were lost. Among those men was Sidney Mayfield, a captain of artillery, a quiet, unobtrusive, middle-aged insurance salesman, who left a widow and an infant son. That son was Albert Mayfield. So Albert grew up into a world that the war—a war he could not remember—had defined. It had defined the little world of his home, the silent, bitter woman who was his mother, the poverty and the cheerless discipline and it had defined the big world outside.*

*Excerpts from *Modern Rhetoric*, Fourth Edition, by Cleanth Brooks and Robert Penn Warren, copyright © 1979 by Harcourt Brace Jovanovich, Inc., reprinted by permission of the publisher.

In the second paragraph, unlike the first, the events are purposefully related one to another and each adds to the bigger structure—the story of Albert's life.

As you begin reading narrative passages in this chapter and elsewhere, you should be aware that authors use each event purposefully to add to the whole structure—the story. In many ways, events are comparable to the pieces of a puzzle. Each piece by itself doesn't appear to be very significant, but when an entire puzzle is put together with one piece missing, you quickly see the value of one small piece. And so it is in reading: each event in a story serves a specific function; each adds to the whole structure.

PREVIEW | THE LETTER THAT STARTED THE NUCLEAR AGE

Things to Think About

1. When was Adolf Hitler in power in Germany?_____

2. Why would a political leader like Hitler be interested in nuclear research?

   _____

3. Who was Franklin D. Roosevelt?_____

4. When did World War II begin?_____

5. What effect did the beginning of World War II have on nuclear research?

   _____

6. Who was Albert Einstein, and what is he most famous for?

   _____

Preview

1. Quickly scan the reading for all dates. What is the general time frame of this reading?

   _____

2. What major world event was taking place at this time?

   _____

3. Now scan the reading for the names of countries. How many do you see?

   _____

4. Which countries did you see mentioned most often? _____

_____

5. What is the meaning of $E = mc^2$? (Scan the reading if you are not
   sure.)

_____

6. How could a letter start the nuclear age? _____

READING ONE

THE LETTER THAT STARTED THE NUCLEAR AGE

1   At Kaiser Wilhelm Institute in Germany, a rather shy, not very
tall, Jewish scientist had been working on experiments in radioactive elements. Her name was Dr. Lise Meitner, and she had begun
her brilliant career in 1908 as an assistant at the University of
Berlin. Little did Dr. Meitner realize that she was beginning work   5
which would eventually lead to one of the most historically important letters ever written.

2   By 1938, Dr. Meitner was conducting experiments with the element uranium in collaboration with Dr. Otto Hahn and Dr. F.
Strassmann. The three scientists were bombarding uranium atoms   10
with neutrons and producing what appeared to be a new radioactive element more powerful than uranium. At that point, they did
not know the answer to the puzzle. Drs. Hahn and Strassmann
could not quite accept the idea that the atom of uranium had been
split, but Dr. Meitner could, and she went ahead with the work on   15
that basis.

3   In 1938, Germany, under the rule of Hitler, was plunging back
into the barbarism of the Dark Ages. And just as Dr. Meitner was
reaching the most important and fascinating stage of her research,
she found herself being labeled as a member of a non-desired race in   20
Hitler's empire. As an Austrian national of Jewish descent, her life
was under a constant threat. As a result, she decided to stop her
work and flee for her life. Hitler put a great deal of pressure on her to
force her to remain in Germany and continue her work on the atom,
but with the help of friends and associates she managed to escape to   25
Stockholm, Sweden, taking in her notebook and in her brilliant
mind the information that could have won the war for Germany.

4   In 1939, shortly after her arrival in Stockholm, she solved the
mathematical mystery of the experiments in atomic fission (split-

_____

From *Albert Einstein* by Catherine Owens Peare. Copyright 1949 by
Holt, Rinehart and Winston, Inc. Adapted by permission of Henry Holt and
Company, Inc.

ting the atom) she and Drs. Hahn and Strassmann had been con-   30
ducting in Berlin. Dr. Meitner, along with her nephew, Dr. Otto R.
Frisch, published the results in a scientific magazine. Their results,
later known as the Berlin Fission, basically stated that Drs. Hahn
and Strassmann had in fact split the atom. And using Einstein's
famous formula $E = mc^2$, Dr. Meitner showed that one pound of   35
uranium would release as much energy as 8,000 tons (7,300 metric
tons) of TNT.

5   It was her nephew, Dr. Otto R. Frisch, who sent the results of Dr.
Meitner's experiments to Dr. Niels Bohr at Columbia University in
New York City. Dr. Bohr repeated Dr. Meitner's experiments, col-   40
laborating with Professor Enrico Fermi.

6   Dr. Leo Szilard at the University of Chicago was concurrently
working along similar lines, and he, Fermi, Bohr, and others understood well enough the military possibilities of Dr. Meitner's discov-
eries. These men communicated with Professor Albert Einstein.   45

7   Dr. Szilard prepared a long and careful scientific paper explaining the dangers of possible atomic warfare and emphasizing the fact
that American scientists were not at all sure they were keeping a
step ahead of German scientists in their research.

8   Dr. Einstein made a careful study of Dr. Szilard's paper and on   50
the second day of August, 1939, exactly one month before the
Second World War started, wrote a letter to President Franklin D.
Roosevelt:

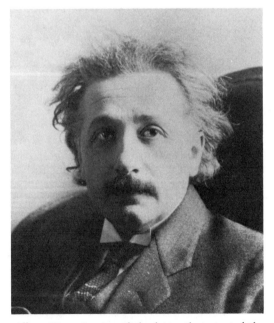

*Albert Einstein signed the letter that started the
nuclear age.*

August 2, 1939

Sir:

Some recent work by E. Fermi and L. Szilard, which has been communicated to me in manuscript, leads me to expect that the element uranium may be turned into a new and important source of energy in the immediate future. Certain aspects of the situation which has arisen seem to call for watchfulness and, if necessary, quick action on the part of the Administration . . . .

In the course of the last four months it has been made probable through the work of Joliot in France as well as Fermi and Szilard in America—that it may become possible to set up a nuclear chain reaction in a large mass of uranium, by which vast amounts of power and large quantities of new radium-like elements would be generated. Now it appears almost certain that this could be achieved in the immediate future.

This new phenomenon would also lead to the construction of bombs, and it is conceivable—though much less certain—that extremely powerful bombs of a new type may thus be constructed. A single bomb of this type, carried by boat and exploded in a port, might very well destroy the whole port together with some of the surrounding territory. . . .

I understand that Germany has actually stopped the sale of uranium from the Czechoslovakian mines which she has taken over. That she should have taken such early action might perhaps be understood on the ground that the son of German Under-Secretary of State, Von Weizsacker, is attached to the Kaiser-Wilhelm-Institut in Berlin, where some of the American work on uranium is now being repeated.

Yours very truly,
A. Einstein

9   On October 11, 1939, two weeks after the Nazi war machine had invaded and crushed Poland, Dr. Szilard's paper and Dr. Einstein's 55 accompanying letter reached President Roosevelt.

10   When Albert Einstein published his first papers on relativity in 1905, he included a mathematical formula stating the relationship between mass and energy ($E = mc^2$). The formula stated that mass could be converted to energy and that some day a way might be 60 found to smash the atom and make it give up its energy.

11   In 1939, thirty-four years later, when Einstein read Dr. Szilard's paper stating that the atom of the element uranium had been successfully split, and that it had proved to be a source of terrific energy, he knew exactly what it meant. He sat down and wrote his 65 history-making letter to President Roosevelt immediately. Fortunately for the world, President Roosevelt took Dr. Einstein's warning seriously.

REVIEW | THE LETTER THAT STARTED THE NUCLEAR AGE

Comprehension

1. When did Dr. Meitner begin conducting experiments on radioactive elements?

   _____

   _____

2. Why did Dr. Meitner leave Germany?

   _____

   _____

3. Why did Hitler put pressure on Dr. Meitner to stay in Germany?

   _____

   _____

   _____

4. What was the Berlin Fission?

   _____

   _____

   _____

5. What math mystery did Dr. Meitner solve while she was in Stockholm?

   _____

   _____

   _____

6. How much energy would one-half pound of uranium release?

   _____

   _____

7. According to this reading, who wrote the letter that started the nuclear age? Who received it?

   _____

   _____

   _____

8. What part did Albert Einstein have in the whole process that led to the writing of the letter that started the nuclear age?

_____

_____

9. The reading never directly states how the letter started the nuclear age. It does give us enough information to make some educated guesses. In what ways do you think the letter started the nuclear age?

_____

_____

_____

10. Read the supplementary reading "The Father of the Atomic Bomb Was Not Einstein" on page 52. What differences are there between that account and the one you just read?

_____

_____

_____

Textual Pattern: Narration

1. List below all the events narrated in the story that you think led to the writing of the letter that started the nuclear age. You may not need to use all the lines provided.

Event: *1908, Dr. Meitner begins her career at Berlin University*

Event: _____

Event: _____

Event: _____

Event: _____

Event: _____

Event: _____

Event: _____

Event: _____

Event: *October 11, 1939 Roosevelt receives the letter.*

2. The third paragraph discusses Hitler's hatred for Jews and Dr. Meitner's escape from Germany. How does this information add to the overall structure of the story? (How does it help complete the puzzle?)

_____

_____

_____

_____

Questions for Further Discussion/Composition

1. It is unfortunate that atomic theory and research were being developed at the same time the world was heading into a world war. Do you think atomic research would be where it is today if circumstances had been different when Dr. Meitner and others were first beginning their research?

2. What people do you think were responsible, either directly or indirectly, for the letter that started the nuclear age? List as many as you can think of and briefly discuss how you think they were responsible. For example, how were Hitler and the German corps of scientists responsible for the letter? You may want to reread the supplementary reading "The Father of the Atomic Bomb Was Not Einstein" below.

SUPPLEMENTARY READING

THE FATHER OF THE ATOMIC BOMB WAS NOT EINSTEIN

1   Albert Einstein's 1939 letter to President Franklin Roosevelt urging development of an atomic bomb—the famous document that started the Nuclear Age—was not written by Einstein at all. It was ghost-written for him by a relatively little-known Columbia University physicist named Leo Szilard.   5

2   In 1939, Szilard and Princeton scientist Eugene Wigner approached Einstein to ask a vital favor. Given his great stature, would he lend his name to the promotion of a serious study of

_____

From Irving Wallace, "The Father of the Atomic Bomb Was Not Einstein," *Parade Magazine*, September 27, 1981.

nuclear energy's wartime applications and the design and construction of an atomic bomb?   10

3   Einstein agreed, although he confessed relative ignorance about
nuclear chain reactions. Szilard wrote a draft and presented it to
him for his signature on Aug. 2. It spoke of the "vast amounts of
power and large quantities of new radium-like elements [that]
would be generated" by a nuclear chain reaction set off in a large 15
chunk of uranium.

4   The message finally went to Roosevelt. Later, Einstein did write
and sign two follow-up messages which, together with the first, led
to the 1942 formation of the Manhattan Project, which developed
the bombs dropped on Japan in 1945. Szilard was one of the proj- 20
ect's guiding forces; Einstein had nothing whatsoever to do with it.
"I . . . only acted as a mailbox," Einstein later wrote. "They brought
me a finished letter, and I simply mailed it."

Detecting Sequence: Narrated and Natural Order

Since a narration is a retelling of events, it is necessary for a reader to be
able to detect the order or sequence of those events. A good reader
should be able to tell the relationship of one event to another. A recipe,
for example, is a narrative that presents the events, or steps, in precisely
the order in which they should be done by the cook. Being able to detect
the correct sequence of events in a recipe is usually quite easy because
the order of steps is made very clear by the writer.

Another reason the sequence of a recipe or a process is usually quite
easy to follow is that the author uses a very logical sequence of events—
first to last. This first-to-last sequence is sometimes called the natural
order of events, in other words, the order in which the events actually
happened. However, not all narrations are told in a natural order. An
author may present events in an order different from the order in which
they actually happened. For example, the first event you read in a passage may have happened last in real time. An author may begin telling
you about a scientist who has just discovered an important step in a
chemical process. The story may then cut back and tell you how and
why the scientist first started working on that experiment. Authors rearrange the natural order of events for a variety of reasons—for example,
to get the reader's attention, to place more emphasis on a particular
event, or to build suspense. In order to be an effective reader it is necessary to be able to distinguish the narrated order of events from the
natural order of events. The time lines in the figure below graphically
point out the difference between the natural and narrated order of
events. Each letter represents one event in a story.

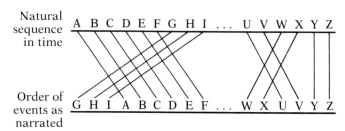

Natural order of action in time
A B C D E F G H I ... U V W X Y Z

Natural sequence in time
A B C D E F G H I ... U V W X Y Z

Order of events as narrated
G H I A B C D E F ... W X U V Y Z

Source: Modern Rhetoric, Fourth Edition, by Cleanth Brooks and Robert Penn Warren, copyright © 1979 by Harcourt Brace Jovanovich, Inc. Reprinted by permission of the publisher.

EXERCISE

1. Review the first reading, "The Letter That Started the Nuclear Age." Which order is most closely followed: a narrated or a natural order? Explain your answer.

    _____

    _____

    _____

    _____

2. The following paragraphs have been taken from passages in this chapter. Listed below the paragraphs are a few of the events that have been narrated. In the blank beside each event place a number indicating the events' *natural order*. If two or more events occur at the same time, give them the same number.

    > On January 25, Dr. Fermi, Herbert Anderson, who was then a graduate student, and John Dunning, who had made Columbia a center of neutron research, began conducting fission experiments in their laboratory. By Jan. 29, Dr. Fermi had outlined an entire program of forthcoming experiments. He and Dr. Anderson set to work with natural uranium. Dr. Dunning was working with U-235, an isotope of uranium, having similar properties but different atomic weight. And on a different floor of the same laboratory, Dr. Szilard and Walter Zinn conducted photoneutron experiments.

    J. 29 Dunning and Dr. Anderson start work with natural uranium.

    J.29 Dr. Fermi has entire program outlined.

7.25 ___ Dr. Fermi, Herbert Anderson, and John Dunning begin experiments.

7.29 ___ Dr. Szilard and Walter Zinn conduct photoneutron experiments.

Dr. Szilard prepared a long and careful scientific paper explaining the dangers of possible atomic warfare and emphasizing the fact that American scientists were not at all sure they were keeping a step ahead of German scientists in their research.

Dr. Einstein made a careful study of Dr. Szilard's paper and on the second day of August, 1939, exactly one month before the Second World War started, wrote a letter to President Franklin D. Roosevelt.

On October 11, 1939, two weeks after the Nazi war machine had invaded and crushed Poland, Dr. Szilard's paper and Dr. Einstein's accompanying letter reached President Roosevelt.

When Albert Einstein published his first papers on relativity in 1905, he included a mathematical formula stating the relationship between mass and energy ($E = mc^2$). The formula stated that mass could be converted to energy and that some day a way might be found to smash the atom and make it give up its energy.

_____ Einstein publishes his famous formula $E = mc^2$.

_____ Einstein studies Dr. Szilard's paper.

_____ Einstein writes a letter to President Roosevelt.

_____ Nazis invade Poland.

_____ Einstein's letter reaches President Roosevelt.

_____ Dr. Szilard prepares a long scientific paper.

. . . in 1933, Sir Ernest Rutherford, who had discovered the nucleus of the atom in 1912, gave a speech in which he ridiculed the whole notion of harnessing atomic energy. Szilard evidently took the remarks as a challenge, and by 1934 he proclaimed, and his colleagues agreed, that he had figured out how, in theory, to do it. That same year, Dr. Fermi, in his laboratory in Rome, moved science a stage closer to the goal when he succeeded in actually altering basic nuclear matter. Dr. Fermi bombarded 60 different elements with neutrons and produced artificial radiation in 40 of them. Finally, when he bombarded uranium with neutrons, he produced a new element (No. 93) in the atomic table.

Dr. Fermi was awarded the Nobel Prize for his work in 1938 and he used his trip to Stockholm for the ceremonies as an opportunity to get himself and his family permanently out of Mussolini's Italy. They came to New York on January 9, 1939 and he was given a post at Columbia University.

Now, the pace of events, particularly at Columbia, began to quicken. Exactly one week later Niels Bohr, the physicist, arrived in New York from Copenhagen, bubbling over with news of the fission experiment in Berlin. Dr. Bohr had learned of it from Lise Meitner, a German mathematician who had fled to Copenhagen to escape the Nazis and who had first analyzed the Berlin fission.

_____ Fermi goes to New York.

_____ Fermi alters basic nuclear matter.

_____ Szilard takes Rutherford's remarks as a challenge.

_____ Fermi is given the Nobel Prize.

_____ Rutherford ridicules the idea of harnessing atomic energy.

_____ Niels Bohr arrives in New York.

_____ Rutherford discovers the nucleus of the atom.

PREVIEW | THE DAY THE NUCLEAR AGE WAS BORN

Things to Think About

1. What would cause a scientist to flee from Italy and Germany to the United States in the early 1940s?

   fascist regimes. Shortly before World War II

2. Who were Fermi, Bohr, Szilard? What countries did they come from?

   Scientist from Italy, Copenhagen and Hungary respectivelessly.

3. Who were Mussolini and Hitler? *were dictators. The first Italian the theorist in Germany*

4. What contribution did Dr. Lise Meitner make to the development of atomic energy?

   She was the first to analyze the Berlin fission.

5. What is a chain reaction? What would a sustained chain reaction *does not stop* be? What would a controlled sustained chain reaction be? *a sequence of reactions*

   It is a reaction follows another and another. When this reaction is sustained by itself, A self sustain

6. What does a sponge do to water? What would a neutron sponge do?

    Absorbs it. absorb energy

    _____

    _____

7. The story takes place in 1942. Why would there be a race between the United States and Germany to be the first to succeed at controlling atomic energy?

    _____

    _____

Preview

1. Where was this reading first printed? _____

    _____

2. Scan the reading for definitions of the following words:

    Manhattan Project (paragraph 3) _____

    _____

    fission (paragraphs 9 and 10) _____

    _____

    pile (paragraphs 12 and 14) _____

    _____

    Geiger counter (paragraph 21) _____

    _____

    cadmium (paragraph 20) _____

    _____

3. The title suggests that there was a day on which the nuclear age was born. Scan the reading to find out which day it was.

    _____

    _____

4. Scan the reading for any dates. List each date you see. When do most of the events seem to take place? What year is mentioned most often?

    _____

    _____

READING TWO

THE DAY THE NUCLEAR AGE WAS BORN

1   Forty years ago this week, on the afternoon of Dec. 2, 1942, a group of 42 scientists, working under the direction of Enrico Fermi, gathered in an indoor squash court under the west grandstands of Stagg Field, the football stadium of the University of Chicago.

2   What they achieved that afternoon was the first sustained   5
nuclear chain reaction to be made by man. On a larger scale, what they launched was the nuclear age.

3   Dr. Fermi's colleagues, several of whom had fled, as he did, from fascist regimes in Europe shortly before World War II, had all been working in separate, smaller groups—in Princeton, Chicago, New   10
York, California—to control atomic energy. Now, brought together by the Government as part of what was called the Manhattan Project, they were embarked upon an all-out effort to create a controlled nuclear reaction. Until they knew they could do that, they would have no idea whether they could make an atomic bomb.   15

4   In 1938, German scientists in Berlin, taking the first step in that direction, had succeeded in splitting a single atom of uranium. Wartime planners and scientists in the United States were thus convinced that a fatal race was on. Indeed, Eugene Wigner, the eminent Princeton physicist who worked with the Fermi group, recalls that   20
within two weeks after they produced their chain reaction, they received a telegram from a German scientist working in Switzerland which read: "Hurry up. People here are working on it, too."

5   But the American scientists were not absolutely sure before that   25
Dec. 2 afternoon that they would succeed. "There was no real certainty that we could do it," Herbert Anderson, Dr. Fermi's longtime collaborator, said in a recent interview. And his remark reflects the improbabilities that run through the whole story of the development of controlled nuclear chain reaction, as reconstructed now   30
from a series of interviews, memoirs and other accounts.

6   The basic idea for the chain reaction was first patented by Leo Szilard, a Hungarian scientist who was said to have been inspired by reading "The World Set Free," the 1914 novel by H. G. Wells. Wells had read that uranium naturally disintegrates by emitting   35
alpha particles containing neutrons and protons, a process that yields a million times more energy per atom than ordinary fire but over a period of thousands of years. The novel dramatized what might be done with such energy if the process could be speeded up and controlled, something Wells envisioned as occurring in 1933.   40

Enrico Fermi

7   Yet, in 1933, Sir Ernest Rutherford, who had discovered the nucleus of the atom in 1912, gave a speech in which he ridiculed the whole notion of harnessing atomic energy. Szilard evidently took the remarks as a challenge, and by 1934 he proclaimed, and his colleagues agreed, that he had figured out how, in theory, to do it.   45
That same year, Dr. Fermi, in his laboratory in Rome, moved science a stage closer to the goal when he succeeded in actually altering basic nuclear matter. Dr. Fermi bombarded 60 different elements with neutrons and produced artificial radiation in 40 of them. Finally, when he bombarded uranium with neutrons, he pro-   50
duced a new element (No. 93) in the atomic table.

8   Dr. Fermi was awarded the Nobel Prize for his work in 1938 and he used his trip to Stockholm for the ceremonies as an opportunity to get himself and his family permanently out of Mussolini's Italy. They came to New York on Jan. 9, 1939 and he was given a post at   55
Columbia University.

9   Now, the pace of events, particularly at Columbia, began to quicken. Exactly one week later Niels Bohr, the physicist, arrived in New York from Copenhagen, bubbling over with news of the fission experiment in Berlin. Dr. Bohr had learned of it from Lise Meitner, a   60
German mathematician who had fled to Copenhagen to escape the Nazis and who had first analyzed the Berlin fission.

10   On Jan. 25, Dr. Fermi, Herbert Anderson, who was then a gradu-

ate student, and John Dunning, who had made Columbia a center of neutron research, began conducting fission experiments in their lab- 65
oratory. By Jan. 29, Dr. Fermi had outlined an entire program of forthcoming experiments. He and Dr. Anderson set to work with natural uranium. Dr. Dunning was working with U-235, an isotope of uranium, having similar properties but different atomic weight. And on a different floor of the same laboratory, Dr. Szilard and 70
Walter Zinn conducted photoneutron experiments.

11   It is clear that there was great excitement and an astonishing amount of communication among American scientists in those days. To be sure, there was some secrecy, though not as much as the Army, and Maj. Gen. Leslie Groves, head of the Manhattan Project, 75
would have liked. . . .

12   The key to the development of the Chicago pile was Dr. Fermi's work on "exponential piles" of uranium. For several years at Columbia he had experimented arranging uranium and graphite in lat-
ticed structures, attempting to increase atomic fission in the piles. If 80
enough uranium of the proper kind were packed into the proper shape and area, an energetic neutron escaping from an atomic nucleus might strike another atom, splitting it into two lighter atoms, in the process releasing more neutrons to strike more atoms. Since each fission, or splitting, would release several neutrons, the 85
chances for increased fission would rise exponentially.

13   Behind the notion of the eventual atomic bomb, or indeed of nuclear reactors, is the release of tremendous energy in each fission. As the atom splits it loses part of its mass. Since early 1938 scientists had known that the fission of a uranium atom would yield 200 90
million electron volts of energy (the formula is a practical applica-
tion of Einstein's theory that energy equals mass—or, in this case, loss of mass—times the speed of light squared—$E = mc^2$) and Lise Meitner's analysis of the Berlin fission late that year confirmed the figures. Obviously, if a self-sustaining reaction were allowed to get 95
out of control, there would be a tremendous explosion.

14   The scientists were ready to put their theories to the test in the stadium squash court by the summer of 1942. Mr. Anderson spent weeks searching Chicago lumberyards for 4-by-6-inch timbers for the piles framework. It then took two shifts of workers 16 days to 100
construct Chicago pile No. 1 (cp 1). Uranium and graphite blocks piled up 57 layers measured roughly eight feet by eight feet at the bottom, and the structure rose to a height of about 16 feet.

15   The mere physical labor was enormous, and dirty. Graphite, which was intended to reflect the flying neutrons and thus increase 105
the chain reaction, is a dry lubricant. Its dust was deep-seeping and slippery. One scientist recalled that the men working with the graphite would wash off dust, only to watch more of it ooze out of their pores, and it made the squash court as glassy as the floor of a dance hall. 110

16   As the scientists built up the layers, they regularly measured the rising levels of neutron production. By Dec. 1, it was clear they should try their experiment within 24 hours.

17   The day of Dec. 2 was bitter cold. And the stadium was not heated. Dr. Zinn recalled that while excitement and hard work kept 115 the scientists warm, there was some concern about the security guards who had to stand at the entrances. Someone found a trunk of old raccoon coats, left over from the days when Chicago was one of college football's Big Ten. So the guards were persuaded to stand outside draped in raccoon while Dr. Fermi and his team prepared to 120 turn on the ultimate fire machine.

18   There was concern, too, about more than just the guards. Ten years later, at a seminar, Dr. Fermi said of the reaction, "If we had let it continue it would have become very hot." (In fact, Mr. Anderson says there was a great deal of concern from the beginning about 125 the temperatures a reactor might reach. The pile under the football stands taught them a lot about that, in the weeks they kept it operating after Dec. 2. They could cool it off by opening a window and letting some Chicago winter air in.

19   Originally, the pile was to have been built in Argonne Forest, 130 about 25 miles west of the city, in a facility under construction that would be shielded from radiation, but a laborers' strike prevented its completion. Arthur Holly Compton, dean of physical sciences at the university and general scientific chief of the project, decided to let Dr. Fermi use the stadium. Dr. Compton later wrote that he 135 should have obtained approval from the university's president, Robert Maynard Hutchins. However, he said, Dr. Hutchins would have had to consider the safety of the university and the whole city of Chicago, and would have had said no. "But that would have been the wrong answer," Dr. Compton concluded. He did not tell Dr. 140 Hutchins until much later.

20   With everything set, Dr. Zinn and Mr. Anderson manned instruments on the north end of a balcony 10 feet above the floor of the squash court. The others stood at the other end of the balcony. The safety measures were interesting: On the floor, one man held onto 145 the main control rod—made of cadmium, which acts as a neutron sponge—designed to halt the reaction. There were two other such rods: One was automatic, set to drop into the pile when a certain level of fission was recorded. Another was held by a rope tied onto the balcony rail. One of the project leaders stood next to it holding 150 an ax, ready to chop the rope and drop the rod into the pile, if need be. In addition, three men stood on a wooden platform above the pile as a "liquid control squad." They were to flood the pile with cadmium-salt solution in case the control rods did not work.

21   Dr. Fermi ordered the first control rod and the emergency rod 155 withdrawn and tied, leaving only the hand-operated rod in the pile. Then he told the man on the floor to begin withdrawing the final rod by specific distances, making calculations at each level. Geiger counters and a paper graph chart on a cylinder resembling those that measure earthquakes recorded the rise in levels of fission. 160

22   As the manual control rod was pulled out foot by foot, Dr. Fermi would calculate the rate of fission in the pile on his own tiny slide rule and predict exactly the level at which the reaction would stop.

Repeatedly they had to adjust the counting ratios of their counters and the graph scale upward, as the reaction reached higher levels. 165 At 3:25 P.M. Dr. Fermi ordered the control rod pulled one last foot out of the pile.

23 "Now," he said to Dr. Compton, "it will become self-sustaining." He added, with reference to a graph depicting the rise in radiation: "The trace will climb and continue to climb. It will not level 170 off." For several minutes he continued checking the rise in the neutron count and finally said to the group:

24 "The reaction is self-sustaining. The curve is exponential." The pen on the graph drew a line rising steadily on the paper. At 3:53 Dr. Fermi ordered the control rod put back into the pile and the reac- 175 tion subsided immediately.

25 Dr. Wigner says now that, though others were less certain, he was so sure that they would succeed that he bought a bottle of Chianti months before, while he was still at Princeton, and had yet to join the Chicago effort. At this point, he brought out the Chianti 180 and everyone drank a toast.

26 Dr. Compton called James B. Conant, the president of Harvard University, who was coordinating the atomic energy project for the Government, and said: "The Italian navigator has landed in the New World." Mr. Conant asked: "How were the natives?" "Very 185 friendly," Dr. Compton said. It was their notion of a code.

REVIEW | THE DAY THE NUCLEAR AGE WAS BORN

Comprehension

1. Who was in charge of the project aimed at developing a sustained chain reaction?

_____

2. Why was a sustained nuclear reaction necessary before any further research could be conducted?

_____

_____

3. Why were United States' wartime planners so sure there was an atomic energy race?

_____

_____

4. According to the reading, where did Dr. Szilard first get the idea that a controlled atomic chain reaction was possible?

5. What was Sir Ernest Rutherford's reaction to the idea of controlling atomic energy?

6. Why did they need timber and graphite for the project? _____

7. Where was the project originally going to be built? Why was the location changed?

8. What measures were taken to make sure the reaction didn't get out of control? Describe each one.

9. What role did the president of Harvard University have in the project?

10. What did Dr. Fermi mean when he said, "The reaction will become self-sustaining"?

11. How was the reaction controlled so it could be scientifically measured?

12. If the reaction had not subsided, what most likely would have happened? How do we know this?

13. What did Dr. Compton mean when he called James Conant and said, "The Italian navigator has landed in the New World"?

_____

Skill Review: Detecting Sequence

The events listed below are described in the reading "The Day the Nuclear Age Was Born." The numbers on the left indicate the natural order in which the events occurred. In the blanks on the right indicate the order in which the same events were narrated by the author. Several have been done for you.

1. In 1933 Sir Ernest Rutherford said the idea of controlling atomic energy was ridiculous.   *3*

2. H. G. Wells's novel of 1914, *War of the Worlds*, inspired Dr. Szilard to pursue the possibility of controlling atomic energy.   *2*

3. By 1934, Dr. Szilard had, in theory, devised a way to control atomic energy. He had taken Sir Rutherford's speech as a personal challenge to control atomic energy.   *4*

4. In 1938, German scientists successfully split a single atom creating the first observed chain reaction.   **1**

5. Dr. Fermi was awarded the 1938 Nobel prize for his work in altering basic nuclear matter.   *5*

6. Dr. Fermi used his trip to Stockholm for the Nobel prize ceremonies as an excuse to escape from Italy.   *6*

7. In January of the following year, Dr. Fermi came to New York to work on the Manhattan Project.   *8*

8. Exactly one week after Dr. Fermi's arrival, Niels Bohr arrived in New York to begin work on the project.   *7*

9. By January 29, Dr. Fermi had a complete outline of all the preliminary experiments necessary to start the project.   *9*

10. By the summer of 1942 the scientists were ready to make the final experiment—a sustained atomic chain reaction.   *10*

11. On December 2, the final experiment was conducted in Chicago.   **11**

Questions for Further Discussion/Composition

1. There was a great deal of uncertainty that December morning back in 1942 about whether or not the experiment would work. In fact, if it had not worked, "there would have been a tremendous explosion." Should the group of scientists have gone ahead with the experiment at Stagg Field?

2. Who do you think was most responsible for the success of the first sustained nuclear chain reaction? Why? *Dr. Fermi*

Narration: Chronological Expressions

Like the textual patterns discussed in other chapters, narrations also have certain vocabulary and signal words unique to that particular style of writing. Authors of narrations will use these words to signal to the reader the relationship of one or more events to other events. These signals are given to help the reader understand their sequence. Being familiar with their meaning and knowing how these signal words are used can be helpful to a reader.

The words and expressions of time listed below are some of the most common terms used to tie sentences together chronologically, thus clarifying the sequence of events in a passage.

> at
> in
> on
> by
> during
> in the course of
> until
> between _____ and _____
> first, second, third, etc.
> previous(ly), prior to, before, ago
> simultaneous(ly) (with), at the same time, concurrent (to, with), by
>   the time, at that time, just as, now, then, as, meanwhile
> afterward, after, later, next, subsequently, next, then, in the next
>   place
> finally, eventually, at last
> dates, days, and time

Here are some examples of the use of these expressions:

We arrived *at* six o'clock.

In the winter the weather cooled the nuclear reactor.

On October 11, 1939, Dr. Einstein's letter was sent.

By 1939, Dr. Meitner was conducting experiments with uranium.

During the experiment Dr. Fermi would calculate the reaction.

In the course of the following centuries chemistry grew more and more.

Not *until* the turn of the century did nuclear studies really begin.

Between 1939 *and* 1942 research on nuclear reaction was at a peak.

EXERCISE   Go back to the reading "The Letter That Started the Nuclear Age" and underline all of the time signal words and phrases you can find. How many did you find? ___*13*___

PREVIEW | THE DAWN OF THE NUCLEAR AGE

Things to Think About

1. What is the meaning of *dawn*? _____

2. Who really wrote the letter that started the nuclear age? (See the supplementary reading "The Father of the Atomic Bomb Was Not Einstein" on page 52.)

   ___*Leo Szilard*___

3. Why was Einstein's letter sent to President Roosevelt?

   ___*Because he was an eminent scientist*___

4. What is a code used for? ___*To avoid people know what it's been talking about.*___

5. Why would atomic research need to be kept a secret in 1942?

   ___*Because of the world war II*___

6. Where, besides Europe, were U.S. military forces involved during World War II?

   ___*Japan*___

7. What was the Manhattan Project?

   ___*A project to control atomic energic*___

8. What is the meaning of *era*? _____

Preview

1. Scan the reading looking for all dates. Write down each date in the order in which it is presented in the reading. What is the general time frame of this story?

    _____

    _____

2. What kind of sequence does the author seem to be using—a natural or a narrated sequence?

    _____

3. The author of this reading uses headings to inform the reader about the topic of each section. What are the topics presented in this reading?

    _____

    _____

4. Where is New Mexico located? _____

5. Is New Mexico heavily populated? _____

READING THREE

THE DAWN OF THE NUCLEAR AGE

1   On Oct. 11, 1939, as German invaders subdued the last remnants of the Polish Army, a New York banker named Alexander Sachs went to the White House to visit his personal friend President Franklin Roosevelt. Sachs carried a letter signed by the eminent physicist Albert Einstein and partly written by another physicist, 5
Leo Szilard, who had enlisted Sachs as a messenger. The letter explained that scientists might soon be able to transform the element uranium into a new source of energy which could be used to make "extremely powerful bombs" and that the Germans were already hard at work on the same research. Sachs read the letter to 10
Roosevelt, and the following morning, as the two had breakfast, the President finally understood the magnitude of the message. "Alex," he said to Sachs, "what you are after is to see that the Nazis don't blow us up?" Sachs nodded, and Roosevelt summoned his aide, Gen. Edwin ("Pa") Wilson. "Pa," the President declared, pointing to 15
the letter, "this requires action."

Adapted with permission from Bob Levin, "The Dawn of the Nuclear Age," *Maclean's*, July 22, 1984.

2   With that, the bomb-building effort began, one that would evolve into the Manhattan Project, among the most massive, literally earth-shaking scientific undertakings ever. By the time of its dramatic climax in a mushroom cloud in the New Mexican desert in July, 1945, the project would cost about $2 billion, spawn new factories and even new towns and employ roughly 200,000 Americans, Britons and Canadians—including a conspicuous core of European refugees—all working under the strictest secrecy. Forty years later many of those scientists are still arguing over whether the atomic bomb should have been dropped on Japan at all and how to control the awesome force they unleashed.

3   **Explosive**: But in 1939 they saw only the most distressing of circumstances: the world was hurtling inexorably toward full-scale war just as physicists were confirming the basic principle behind atomic power—that neutron bombardment of uranium can break apart its atomic structure and release enormous quantities of energy—and it seemed vital to beat the Germans to the bomb. The scientists called the breakdown "fission," and they determined that a self-sustaining, potentially explosive "chain reaction" of fission could be triggered by neutron bombardment. "Once the chain was discovered," recalls Hans Bethe, a German emigré to the United States who became a prominent member of the bomb project, "every scientist foresaw what was possible—the Europeans, the Soviets, everyone."

4   Roosevelt's call for action resulted in the formation of a Uranium Committee, which was immediately plagued by excessive secrecy and a tight budget. At the same time, British scientists were making significant atomic progress, but, with their country consumed by the spreading war in Europe, they appealed to their U.S. counterparts to make an all-out effort.

5   Finally, in June, 1942, after a six-month trial program and the U.S. entry into the war following the bombing of Pearl Harbor, Roosevelt ordered a crash effort to build the bomb. The project was assigned to the U.S. Army, which code-named the cross-country network of laboratories the Manhattan Engineering District because their new commander, Gen. George Marshall, was headquartered in New York. Soon, however, the Manhattan Project was turned over to career officer Brig.-Gen. Leslie Groves. Beefy and brusque, a dogged organizer, "Greasy" Groves quickly set out to survey his new domain, visiting several labs before arriving at the University of California at Berkeley. There, he met a gaunt and dynamic 39-year-old physicist named J. Robert Oppenheimer, who was to become the central figure of the Manhattan Project. . . .

6   **New weapon:** By the time Groves showed up in California, Oppenheimer was working on an actual bomb mechanism under a title even he found comic—the co-ordinator of rapid rupture—and he had become convinced of the need for a superlab where scientists could pool their knowledge to produce the new weapon.

7   Groves liked the idea and settled on Oppenheimer to direct the new facility. . . .

8   **Ramshackle:** Oppenheimer, who had ridden his horse over the rugged terrain around his summer home in northwest New Mexico, even knew just the place for an isolated superlab: the Los Alamos Ranch School for boys, set on a mesa 7,300 feet up in the Jemez 70 Mountains. The army acquired it and began pounding together makeshift laboratories and apartments, creating a ramshackle town of unpaved streets, soot-producing coal furnaces and chronic water shortages. Meanwhile, Oppenheimer toured the country recruiting his team of scientists, including such prominent emigrés as Bethe, 75 Edward Teller from Hungary and Enrico Fermi from Italy, until he had assembled what Groves called "the greatest collection of egg-heads ever."

9   Los Alamos was not the only new Manhattan Project com-munity. Immediately after assuming his job, Groves had approved 80 construction on a site at Tennessee's Clinch River called Oak Ridge, home to four new factories by war's end. Three of the plants extract-ed uranium-235 from uranium ore. The fourth was a pilot plant for making a new fissionable element, plutonium. (That process was based on a major breakthrough at Chicago's Metallurgical Labora- 85 tory, where, in December, 1942, Fermi had finally achieved the long-theorized fission chain reaction.) Later, a larger plutonium fac-tory—and a third new town—went up at Hanford, Wash. . . .

breakthrough = first controlled chain reaction

10   **Code:** The new Manhattan Project towns remained officially nonexistent. At barbed wire-enclosed Site Y—code name for Los 90 Alamos—all incoming mail went to Box 1663, Santa Fe, down in the valley; all outgoing mail was censored. Robert Porton, now 69, who was a technical sergeant in the army's Special Engineering Detach-ment in Los Alamos, remembers that in letters to his mother in Florida he wrote only that "I'm out here in the West, the scenery is 95 beautiful, and the weather is very nice." Still, as a steady stream of strangers disappeared into the mountains, Santa Fe residents knew something was going on. "But in those days people just didn't ask questions," recalls Betty Brousseau, who was 15 years old when her family moved to Los Alamos in 1943. . . . 100

11   By late 1944 the original reason for the project—the threat of the German bomb—had all but disappeared. The Allied invasion of Europe, begun at Normandy in June, reached Strasbourg in November. There, U.S. investigators expected to find a centre of advanced A-bomb research, but instead they discovered documents 105 showing that the Nazis were at least two years behind the Allies. In April the man who initiated the Manhattan Project, Franklin Roos-evelt, died at Warm Springs, Ga., at the age of 63, and his successor, Harry Truman, had to be told about the new weapon. A month later the Germans surrendered, but by then the bomb work had a 110 momentum of its own. The brutal island-hopping battles in the Pacific had taken thousands of lives, and some U.S. leaders believed the only thing that would force the Japanese to surrender would be an even bloodier invasion of their mainland—or a couple of well-placed A-bombs. 115

12   **Target:** In the end, after a series of hearings in Washington, an

Interim Committee of politicians and scientists, appointed by Truman, arrived at a clear-cut conclusion: to use the bomb as soon as possible, without prior warning, against a Japanese target that had military significance but was also surrounded by the kind of 120 densely packed civilian buildings most susceptible to its fiery blast—in other words, a city. Another committee was already considering likely candidates, including Hiroshima and Nagasaki.

13   / The Interim Committee recommendations filtered out to project sites around the country—and ignited a brushfire of protest. The 125 strongest reaction came from Chicago's Metallurgical Laboratory, where scientists, removed from the frontline frenzy of Los Alamos and Oak Ridge, had time to consider the consequences of the bomb and had already called for international controls. The university appointed a committee chaired by Nobel Prize winner James 130 Franck. In June the Franck report warned that if the United States were the first to use a nuclear weapon in warfare, "she would sacrifice public support throughout the world, precipitate the race of armaments and prejudice the possibility of reaching an international agreement on the future control of such weapons." The report 135 also recommended giving a warning demonstration of the bomb in some isolated spot, in part to try to stun the Japanese into surrender. But Oppenheimer advised the Interim Committee that he did not think that "exploding one of these things as a firecracker over a desert was likely to be very impressive," and the committee 140 rejected the Franck report.

14   But even then, Oppenheimer and his crew were preparing to explode an A-bomb in the desert, not as a public warning but as a private test of the plutonium implosion device—know as "Fat Man." The site selected for the first-ever atom blast lay about 325 145 km south of Los Alamos, in a blistering-hot New Mexican desert that formed part of the U.S. Air Force's Alamogordo Bombing Range. Oppenheimer, taking the name from a John Donne sonnet, nicknamed the site Trinity, and on July 13 a team of physicists gathered in a ranch house to assemble the core. Prominent among 150 them was 31-year-old Louis Slotin of Winnipeg, who would die in a radiation accident the following year, but at the time he and the others handled their delicate task flawlessly. "There was a lot of tension," recalls Raemer Schreiber, a physicist who later became deputy director of the lab. "Nobody wanted to drop the thing." 155 Then, the core was transported 1½ miles to Ground Zero, where it was inserted into the explosive assembly and hoisted to the top of a 100-foot steel tower. Finally, at 5:10 A.M. on July 16, heavy rains subsided and the countdown began.

15   **Death:** Twenty minutes later came the flash. "It was just 160 unbelievable," remembers physicist John Manley, now 78, who was in charge of measuring the predawn blast from a bunker 10,000 m from Ground Zero. "The familiar features, like mountain peaks and passes, just stood clearly out of pitch dark." Other observers, looking through plates of dark glass, described intense heat, then a ball 165 of fire, a dust-filled mushroom cloud and an enormous explosion. Later, Oppenheimer, who reportedly bet $10 that Fat Man would

not work, recalled thinking of words from the Hindu book the *Bhagavad Gita*: "I am become death, the shatterer of worlds." But other scientists said they had no such deep thoughts. "No Armaged- 170 don," says Bradbury, "no visions of hell. Just 'By hell, the damn thing worked.'" It worked so well, in fact, that the light frightened a blind girl riding in a car 80 km away, and the army, besieged by inquiries, issued a false press release about an ammunition dump exploding.   175

16   Thus began the nuclear age, with an odd whimper but mostly with a bang. . . .

17   **Ultimatum:** The date was July 24. The cruiser Indianapolis, carrying a lead container of enriched uranium, was already nearing the Pacific island of Tinian, the planned launching pad for the atomic 180 attacks. Two days later the Americans, British and Chinese issued an ultimatum demanding that the Japanese surrender immediately but making no mention of the nuclear weapon, and two days after that the Japanese refused. There would be no second chance. At 8:15 A.M. on Aug. 6, 1945, the U.S. Air Force Superfortress Enola Gay 185 dropped a uranium-charged "Little Boy" A-bomb on Hiroshima, and three days later another B-29 released a plutonium "Fat Man" bomb over Nagasaki. For the first and only time, human beings experienced the unimaginable wrath of the new era.

REVIEW | THE DAWN OF THE NUCLEAR AGE

Comprehension

1. What did President Roosevelt mean when he said, "This requires action"?

_____

_____

2. What action did President Roosevelt take?

_____

_____

3. What event caused Roosevelt to make the bomb project an "all-out effort"?

_____

4. How did the project get the name "Manhattan"?

_____

_____

5. What was the "co-ordinator of rapid rupture"?

_____

_____

6. Whose idea was it to create a superlab in which the scientists could work together on the new weapon?

_____

7. Where was the superlab finally built?_____

8. The Manhattan Project had communities in various locations across the United States. Where were they, and what were they used for?

_____

_____

9. Why were the Manhattan communities called "nonexistent towns"?

_____

10. Why did work continue on the bomb even though Germany had surrendered?

_____

11. What was the Franck Report?

_____

12. What was the difference between the "Fat Man" bomb and the "Little Boy" bomb?

_____

13. What was the Enola Gay? _____

14. Did Oppenheimer think the first test bomb would work? How do we know?

_____

Skill Review: Detecting Sequence

1. The events listed below are some of the major events in the story "The Dawn of the Nuclear Age." They are not listed in a natural or narrated order. In each blank, write a number listing the events in either a natural or a narrated order. You will have to go back to the reading to complete this assignment.

____2____ The U.S. begins an all-out effort to build the bomb.

____3____ President Roosevelt dies.

_____4_____ The Germans surrender.

_____13_____ The cruiser Indianapolis carries bomb supplies to the Pacific Ocean.

_____1_____ The Germans invade Poland.

_____11_____ The first experimental bomb is assembled.

_____7_____ Oppenheimer becomes the central figure in the Manhattan Project.

_____5_____ The U.S. bomb building effort begins.

_____9_____ Work begins at Los Alamos, New Mexico.

_____15_____ A bomb is dropped on Hiroshima.

_____14_____ An ultimatum is issued to the Japanese.

_____6_____ Brig.-Gen. Leslie Groves becomes the head of the Manhattan Project.

_____8_____ Construction begins at the Tennessee Oak Ridge site.

_____10_____ Franck report warns of bomb effects.

_____12_____ First trial bomb is exploded.

_____16_____ A bomb is dropped on Nagasaki.

2. The following passage has ten chronological signals. As you read it, underline as many signals as you can identify.

By late 1944 the original impetus for the project—the threat of the German bomb—had all but disappeared. The Allied invasion of Europe, begun at Normandy in June, reached Strasbourg in November. There, U.S. investigators expected to find a centre of advanced A-bomb research, but instead they discovered documents showing that the Nazis were at least two years behind the Allies. In April the man who initiated the Manhattan Project, Franklin Roosevelt, died at Warm Springs, Ga., at the age of 63, and his successor, Harry Truman, had to be told about the new weapon. A month later the Germans surrendered, but by then the bomb work had a momentum of its own. . . .

The date was July 24. The cruiser Indianapolis, carrying a lead container of enriched uranium, was already nearing the Pacific island of Tinian, the planned launching pad for the atomic attacks. Two days later the Americans, British and Chinese issued an ultimatum demanding that the Japanese surrender immediately but making no mention of the nuclear weapon, and two days after that the Japanese refused. There would be no second chance. At 8:15 A.M. on Aug. 6, 1945, the

U.S. Air Force Superfortress Enola Gay dropped a uranium-charged "Little Boy" A-bomb on Hiroshima, and three days later another B-29 released a plutonium "Fat Man" bomb over Nagasaki.

Questions for Further Discussion/Composition

1. By now you should understand that the first atomic bomb was the result of thousands and thousands of hours of work and research. Would the first atomic bomb have been possible without Oppenheimer's "superlab"?

2. The Franck Report, issued in June 1945, warned that if the United States were the first to use a nuclear weapon in warfare, "she would sacrifice public support throughout the world, precipitate the race of armaments, and prejudice the possibility of reaching an international agreement on the future control of such weapons." Were those warnings accurate? Give specific examples in your answer.

Narration: Reading Newspapers

Nearly every article found in newspapers and news magazines is a narration of one kind or another. However, because these sources of news have a specific audience and purpose they are usually not written like other narratives.

Most people who read news stories will give the passage four or five sentences to get their interest. If they are not interested by then, they will quickly move to a new story. Therefore, the first two paragraphs of a news story will provide immediate answers to the journalistic questions: What happened? Who did it? When, how, and where did it happen? And perhaps, Why did it happen? Why is it important? Sometimes even the headline of a story will answer these questions. By skimming the headline and the first few paragraphs of the story, a hurried reader can get the most important information in a story and decide whether he or she has the time and interest to read on for further details.

Because a news writer must get a reader's attention quickly, it is not uncommon for exciting final events to be reported in the first paragraphs of the story. As a result, the natural order of events is frequently disrupted in a news narration.

Another characteristic common in news narrative is the lack of descriptive details. Because space in a newspaper or magazine is extremely valuable, news writers must present their stories as concisely as possible. This demand for conciseness sometimes results in readings that seem like a listing of facts without much descriptive detail. This is especially true in newspapers. The next reading in this chapter, "First Atomic Blast Gave an Isolated Stretch of New Mexico Desert a Place in History," is a good example of a story that lists many important facts without much descriptive detail. In news reporting only the most essential facts are included. Another example of this conciseness in newspapers is the way headlines are presented. You may have noticed that many grammatical elements such as articles and adjectives are left out of headlines. The news stories are much the same as their headlines—only essential facts are included.

EXERCISE Four of the readings in this chapter have been taken from either a newspaper or a news magazine. List the titles of those stories in the space provided below.

1. _____

2. _____

3. _____

4. _____

Now read the first two paragraphs of each story. As you read, pay particular attention to see whether the journalistic questions *who*, *what*, *where*, *when*, *how*, and *why* are answered.

PREVIEW | FIRST ATOMIC BLAST GAVE ISOLATED STRETCH OF NEW MEXICO DESERT A PLACE IN HISTORY

Things to Think About

1. What is the meaning of *isolated*? *place apart*

2. Why would the United States government want to test an atomic blast in an isolated desert?
   because they wanted to keep the test in secret.

3. Would it be possible to keep an atomic blast completely secret? Explain your answer.
   No. Because it created a ball of fire, and a dust-filled mushroom cloud and an enormous explosion which would not be kept in completly secret.

4. How far away would an atomic blast be visible?

80 Km away .

Preview

1. Where and when was this article first printed?_____

2. Scan the reading for dates. What date appears most often? When did the first atomic blast occur?

_____

3. Where was the first bomb exploded?_____

4. In the paragraphs below use the context to determine the meanings of the boldface words. In the space provided write a definition of, synonym for, or description of each of the vocabulary items.

a. All the scientists waited in the darkness to see if atomic elements could be split at once, releasing vast quantities of energy and creating an immense explosion. **Zero hour** told them they were right. The explosion lit the desert sky as never before.

zero hour _____

_____

b. The explosion around **ground zero** was so intense that the steel tower that held the test bomb in place was **vaporized**. Only a crater in the ground showed where it had stood.

ground zero _____

vaporized _____

c. Today all that can be seen at ground zero is an **obelisk** declaring, "Trinity Site, where the world's first nuclear device was exploded on July 16, 1945."

obelisk _____

READING FOUR

FIRST ATOMIC BLAST GAVE ISOLATED STRETCH OF NEW MEXICO DESERT A PLACE IN HISTORY

1   TRINITY SITE, N.M.—Radiation warning signs posted on a mesh fence are about the only evidence today of the violence unleashed here 40 years ago.

2   This isolated stretch of desert on the northern fringes of what is now the White Sands Missile Range has a place in history because of a brief moment in the pre-dawn hours of July 16, 1945—the explosion of the first atomic device. It was the beginning of the nuclear age, which changed the world forever.

3   As the countdown to change began, the bomb sat in a steel cab atop a 100-foot tower, awaiting an electrical signal that would set off its combination of plutonium, explosive and detonators.

4   Only a few scientists and politicians had knowledge of the bomb's development or the hopes it might provide a way to end World War II.

5   Scattered about the secret site about 210 miles south of Albuquerque were the men and women who had worked on the bomb in the "Manhattan Project."

6   Some of the scientists sat protected in three concrete bunkers 10,000 yards from ground zero. Others were perched atop nearby hills.

7   All waited in the darkness to see if their theory that atoms of certain heavy elements could be split at once, releasing vast quantities of energy and creating an immense explosion, would hold true.

8   Zero hour told them they were right.

9   The blast lit the desert sky of south-central New Mexico as never before. A mass of flame hurled rocks and debris into the air. A deafening roar filled the valley as a mushroom cloud slowly rose overhead.

10   The steel tower was vaporized. Only a crater in the ground showed where it had stood.

11   Three weeks later, similar devices were dropped on the Japanese cities of Hiroshima and Nagasaki, forcing the Japanese surrender.

12   "It probably saved 1 million to 2 million lives. An invasion of Japan would have probably resulted in the loss of many more lives," said Norris Bradbury, who supervised the assembly of "Fat Man," as the bomb was nicknamed.

13   Bradbury watched the July 1945 detonation from a hill about 10 miles from ground zero.

From Judy Giannettino, "First Atomic Blast Gave Isolated Stretch of New Mexico Desert a Place in History," *The Salt Lake Tribune,* August 4, 1985. Reprinted with permission from The Associated Press.

14   "The most impressive thing, of course, was the light," Bradbury recalled in an interview at his Los Alamos home. "It was a very, very bright light. Just as bright as daylight."

15   Bradbury, who served as director of Los Alamos National Laboratory from 1945–70, was "dog-tired" and asleep just hours before the explosion, which was delayed by rain.

16   "Someone woke me up and I saw it. We weren't to look directly at it, but, of course, a little peeking went on," he said.

17   Bradbury had left Stanford University in 1941 for a Naval Reserve commission. In 1944, he was ordered to Los Alamos, the secret community in the Jemez Mountains west of Santa Fe, where the Manhattan Project scientists worked on the bomb under the direction of physicist J. Robert Oppenheimer.

18   Bradbury, 76, said he did not learn of the bomb project, which was begun at Los Alamos in 1943, until his arrival. His job was to "make sure the thing was put together correctly," he said.

19   "I had no deep thoughts right before it went off," Bradbury said, "I was worried just about making sure I was doing what I was supposed to do. Most of my thinking was trivial and pedestrian."

20   The director of the Manhattan Engineer District, Maj. Gen. Leslie R. Groves, once wrote: "As we approached the final minute, the quiet grew more intense. I was on the ground. . . . As I lay there in the final seconds, I thought only of what I would do if the countdown got to zero and nothing happened."

21   Though the Manhattan Project was kept successfully from the public, secreted away in the mountains of northern New Mexico and on this sparsely populated desert, the explosion did not go unnoticed outside the bombing range.

22   The brilliant light was seen nearly 300 miles away—as far north as Santa Fe and as far south as El Paso, Texas. Windows rattled in Silver City, more than 100 miles away, and in Gallup, nearly 200 miles to the northwest.

23   A woman driving near El Paso saw the sky turn from deep black to bright white in a matter of seconds.

24   The government explained the strange occurrence by saying a munitions dump had been blown up—a story that held until Aug. 6, 1945, when the world learned an atomic bomb had been used on Hiroshima.

25   Since the detonation, Trinity Site has become a tourist attraction, though it has returned to its original state—dusty, windswept land dotted with desert flora.

26   The crater caused by the blast has been filled in.

27   About two miles from ground zero, the ranch house where the bomb was assembled stands freshly renovated.

28   At ground zero is an obelisk declaring, "Trinity Site, where the world's first nuclear device was exploded on July 16, 1945."

29   A careful search of the site can turn up bits of trinitite, the green glassy substance formed when the blast melted the desert sand.

30   Otherwise, only the fence with its radiation warning signs hints that this piece of land is different from any other on the missile range.

31   White Sands spokesmen say the levels of radiation at the site are extremely low, but still monitored biannually.

32   Visitors are usually allowed at the site only one day a year, but this year the area was open on the anniversary date and will also be open on the usual tour day in October.   95

REVIEW | FIRST ATOMIC BLAST GAVE ISOLATED STRETCH OF NEW MEXICO DESERT A PLACE IN HISTORY

Comprehension

1. Who witnessed the first atomic blast?

   _____

2. Where is Trinity site? _____

3. What is Trinity site used for today? _____

   _____

   _____

4. What evidence is there today of the first atomic blast? List as many things as you can.

   _____

   _____

   _____

5. True or false? The first atomic blast did not work as the scientists had expected.

   _____

   _____

6. Most of the quotations are firsthand experiences of whom? What were his responsibilities at the project?

   _____

   _____

7. How far away from the site was the blast seen? _____

8. How did the government explain the big explosion and bright light to people outside the project who had seen it?

_____

_____

9. If you wanted to visit the historical site of the first atomic blast, when would you be able to do so?

_____

Textual Pattern: Newspaper Narrations

Which of the following journalistic questions are answered in the first two paragraphs of this article? If the answer to the question is given, write it in the space provided.

Who _____

What _____

Where _____

When _____

How _____

Why _____

Questions for Further Discussion/Composition

1. The author states that the explosion at Trinity Site, New Mexico, was the beginning of the nuclear age and the explosion changed the world forever. Do you agree with the two parts of this statement?
   a. The first atomic blast was the beginning of the nuclear age.
   b. The first atomic blast changed the world forever.

2. If you had to select a site on which to build and test the first atomic bomb, what requirements would the site location need to meet?

Narration: Point of View

A very important part of comprehending a narrative passage is knowing who is telling the story and what relationship that person has to the events being related. In narration that relationship is called the author's point of view. By understanding the point of view, we understand how the author is involved in the action. Generally speaking, that involvement can be either as an observer or as a participant. In short, point of view concerns (1) who the narrator is and (2) what the narrator's relationship is to the action.

There are two possible points of view in narration: first person and third person. A narration is said to be in the first person when the author tells his or her own story. When you read:

> The first semester of my junior year at Princeton University was a disaster, and my grades showed it. A note from the dean had put me on academic probation.

you know you are reading first person point of view. The author is telling his own story. A story is in the third person when someone tells another person's story. The same passage about the Princeton student told in the third person would read something like this:

> The first semester of John's junior year at Princeton University was a disaster, and his grades showed it. A note from the dean had put him on academic probation.

Notice the pronouns used in this next example of third person narration. How do the pronouns differ from those in the first person example?

> At Kaiser Wilhelm Institute in Germany, a rather shy, not very tall, Jewish scientist had been working on experiments in radioactive elements. Her name was Dr. Lise Meitner, and she had begun her brilliant career in 1908.

In both examples of third person narration the author is telling someone else's story.

Even though there are only two points of view, there are several different ways in which each can be used. First person, for example, can be told by (1) the main character (as in an autobiography) or (2) a minor character who narrates the events going on around him or her. Third person narrative, on the other hand, can be told by a narrator who (1) sees into any or all the characters (this is sometimes called "all-seeing"), (2) sees into only one character (major or minor), or (3) sees the entire action objectively (not seeing any character in particular but objectively reporting everything that happens). Not all these methods are used in this chapter, but it is important to keep in mind just how a writer can report events in a narration. The following diagram illustrates the different ways a story can be told from the two points of view.

Point of view of:	Told by:
First person (a participant)	a main character
	a minor character
Third person (a nonparticipant)	someone who sees into the mind of any or all characters
	someone who sees into the mind of only one character
	someone who sees everything, like a camera on the wall

EXERCISE   Scan each of the readings listed below for the answers to the questions: (1) What point of view is used in the reading? (2) Who is telling the story? Use the diagram above to help answer the questions.

A.   "How I Designed an A-Bomb in My Junior Year at Princeton" (page 94)

1. _____

2. _____

B.   "The Letter That Started the Nuclear Age" (page 47)

1. _____

2. _____

C.   "The Dawn of the Nuclear Age " (page 67)

1. _____

2. _____

PREVIEW | ZERO HOUR: FORTY-THREE SECONDS OVER HIROSHIMA

Things to Think About

1.   What do *zero hour* and *ground zero* mean?

_____

_____

2.   Why is Hiroshima important in nuclear history?

_____

3. What do you think took forty-three seconds to happen?

    _____   _____

4. Have you ever read a first-hand account of a person who experi-
    enced the first atomic bomb? What kinds of things would a person
    tell about such an event?

    _____

    _____

Preview

1. Quickly scan the first paragraph. What point of view is being used,
    and who is telling the story?

    _____

    _____

2. Who does the main character appear to be? _____

3. Carefully read the first sentence. What could be meant by "the
    beginning of the end"?

    _____

    _____

4. Scan the reading for all dates. What dates do you see?

    _____

    _____

5. When and where was this story first published?

    _____

    _____

6. Read the first paragraph again. Does the author answer all the jour-
    nalistic questions: *who, what, when, where, how, why?*

    _____

    _____

7. How does this news narrative appear to be different from the one
    you just finished reading, "First Atomic Blast Gave Isolated Stretch
    of New Mexico Desert a Place in History"?

    _____

    _____

    _____

8. In the sentences below use the context to determine the meanings of the boldface words. In the space provided write a definition of, synonym for, or description of each of the vocabulary items.

a. Kaz and her friend were gossiping happily in the warmth of the morning when they heard the **drone** of a B-29 bomber plane six miles up.

    drone _____

b. The plane did not frighten Kaz. She had been born in California, and she liked to tell people she was the American in the family. She even felt a kind of **kinship** with the B-29s that flew regularly overhead.

    kinship _____

c. What remained of the life he had made was blown to **kindling** on the day the bomb exploded, though his home was more than a mile from the **hypocenter**.

    kindling _____

    hypocenter _____

d. "Look at this house," she said, **gesturing** toward what was left of it, a pile of boards on the ground

    gesturing: _____

e. She found a bottle of wine, left behind by a man fleeing the city. "We don't have any perfume, so this will be the perfume," she said. She **doused** her brother with it, trying to drown the **stench** of death.

    doused _____

    stench _____

READING FIVE

ZERO HOUR: FORTY-THREE SECONDS OVER HIROSHIMA

1   On a brilliant summer's morning in 1945, Kaz Tanaka looked up into the sky over Hiroshima and saw the beginning of the end of her world. She was 18 then, slender and pert, and her mind was filled with teen-age things. She had wakened with a slight fever, just

_____

From Peter Goldman, "Zero Hour: Forty-Three Seconds Over Hiroshima," *Newsweek*, July 29, 1985. © 1985 Newsweek, Inc. All rights reserved. Reprinted by permission.

bothersome enough to keep her home from her job as a messenger in   5
a war plant. But she felt well enough to be up and about; the August
sun was already oppressively hot, and her father had asked her to
water a tree in front of their property. She ran across the courtyard
and let herself out the great front gate. A girlfriend was standing
across the street. Kaz waved, and the two were gossiping happily in   10
the warmth of the morning when they heard the drone of a B-29
bomber six miles up. It was a minute or so before 8:15.

2   The plane did not frighten Kaz. For one thing, Hiroshima had
gone almost untouched by the air war, though it was Japan's eighth
largest city and was home to a major Army garrison. For another,   15
Kaz had been born in California, and although her father had
repatriated while she was still in diapers, she liked to tell people she
was the American in the family. The word itself had a kind of magic
to her. The first time they made pictures at her nursery school, she
had filled her sheet with scribblings in the brightest colors of   20
crayon. "What is it you're drawing, Kaz?" her teacher had asked,
and she had replied, "America."

3   She even felt a kind of distant kinship with the B-29s that flew
regularly overhead, bound north for Tokyo and other targets. People
in Hiroshima called them *B-san* (Mister B), but Kaz thought of them   25
as her American silver angels. "It's just the angel," she thought,
squinting up into the brightness of that August morning; just
another American angel come to see them.

4   She waved at the plane. "Hi, angel!" she called.

5   A white spot appeared in the sky, as small and innocent-looking   30
as a scrap of paper. It was falling away from the plane, drifting
down toward them. The journey took 43 seconds.

6   "Oh, my gosh," she said, "don't tell me that's a *parachute!*" No
man could be *that* brave, she was thinking, and then the air
exploded in blinding light and color, the rays shooting outward as   35
in a child's drawing of the sun, and Kaz was flung to the ground so
violently that her two front teeth broke off, except she didn't know it
then; she had sunk into unconsciousness.

7   Words failed the Japanese, trying later to describe that split-
second glimpse of the apocalypse; they had to create a new one,   40
pika-doun, or flash-boom, as if the nearly childlike simplicity of the
term could make what had happened somehow comprehensible.
When Kaz wakened from it, the world around her was as still as
death. Her girlfriend lay beside her. Her mother lay pinned under
the wreckage of the gate; she had come out to scold Kaz for having   45
left it open. Her father had been out back tending the vegetables,
working in his undershorts so as not to dirty his clothes. When he
came staggering out of the garden, blood was running from his nose
and mouth; by the next day the exposed parts of his body would
turn a dark, chocolate brown. What had been the finest house in the   50
neighborhood teetered crazily for a few moments at a 45-degree
angle to the ground. Then it came crashing down in splinters, so
loudly that the neighbors thought a second bomb had fallen.

8   Kaz had herself been hit in the back by a flying timber and cut
by shards of wood. She felt nothing. People were only shapes in a   55

dense, gray fog of dust and ash. A mushroom cloud towered seven miles over the remains of the city, the signature of a terrifying new age. Kaz never saw it. She was inside it.

9   Kaz Tanaka had wakened in a frightening new world—a world whose fixed points of reference lay reduced to kindling and whose   60 dominant sound was a silence broken only by the cries of the dying. The very air seemed hostile, so thick with dust and ash that she could barely see. She fought free of the daze cobwebbing her mind and found her girlfriend next to her.

10   "What happened?" they both blurted at once. There were no   65 answers; no one knew.

11   "Are you hurt?" Kaz asked.

12   "No, I can get up," her girlfriend answered.

13   "Thank heaven!" Kaz said. She struggled to her own feet then, bleeding from her cuts, and took her first steps onto the ravaged new   70 terrain of her life.

14   That life had been a comfortable one, wanting in nothing—not, at least, until the war. Kaz's father had been born to a family of some wealth and social position in Hiroshima, and had migrated to America in the early 1920s in the spirit of adventure, not of need or   75 flight; he never intended to stay. He had opened a produce market in Pasadena and had run it until he tired of it, doubling its business every year for four years. He moved back to Hiroshima then, at 40, *for the ancestors;* it was expected of him as the sole male heir to their name. But he brought his American baby girl with him, and a life-   80 style flavored with American ways.

15   The house he built, on a hill commanding a view of the Inland Sea, was a spacious one, two stories high; a row of rental properties stood like satellites across the street, testimony to his and his family's well-being. There was a courtyard in front of his place, guarded   85 by a large, ornamented gate, and two gardens in back, one to provide vegetables, one to delight the eye in the formal Japanese fashion. A tall *butsudan,* a family altar, dominated the interior, but one of the two living rooms was American, with easy chairs instead of *tatami,* and so were the kitchen and bathroom fittings. Dinner   90 was Japanese, the family sitting on the floor in the traditional way. Breakfast was American, pancakes or bacon and eggs, taken at the kitchen table.

16   The split vision never changed, even when war commanded the undivided allegiance to their homeland. When the news came that   95 the Japanese had bombed Pearl Harbor, Kaz's father retired, brood-ing, to his garden and stayed all day, shaking his head and refusing to speak to anyone. "Pitiful! *Pitiful!*" But he could not shut the war out of the sheltered world he had built for himself and his family. His children went to the factories part time. His servants were con-   100 scripted for war work. Food was short; his vegetable garden became less a hobby than a necessity, helping feed not only his own house-hold but his neighbors as well.

17   What remained of the life he had made was blown to bits kind-ling the day of pika-doun, though his home was more than a mile   105 from the hypocenter. He was working on the side facing zero, and

white heat of the flash, even at so great a distance, seared the front of his body; only his loins were protected by the thin covering of his underwear. "I'm hurt," he cried, stumbling out of the garden. His face was red with blood, and his flesh, when Kaz touched him, had 110 the soft feel of a boiled tomato.

18   Even time seemed broken in fragments, its pieces tumbling in Kaz's mind and memory like spilled bits of a mosaic. She was walking toward her aunt's house across the city, seeking shelter, with some dried rice and some first-aid supplies. She came upon a person 115 with a broken arm. The bone was sticking out through the flesh. Kaz improvised a splint out of two sticks and a length of rope and went on. She found a girl she knew, the sister of a classmate. There was a hole in her chest. Kaz wasn't sure she was still alive. She found a piece of cotton in her bag, laid it gently over the wound and kept 120 going. She passed a baby barely old enough to walk, standing unsteadily between its mother and father. The baby, naked but unhurt, was waiting for them to wake up. They were dead. Kaz kept walking.

19   She was at home again when a tall figure appeared, a silhouette 125 standing where the gate had been. "He's back, he's back!" she shouted; her brother, at six feet, towered over most Japanese men, and she knew at a glimpse that it was he. But when she drew closer she could barely recognize him through his wounds. His school had fallen down around him. His neck had been laid open, spilling blood 130 everywhere. He had struggled to a makeshift first-aid station. They had splashed some Mercurochrome on the open gash, tied it with a bandage and sent him on his way; he had willed himself home from there.

20   For a moment, he stood swaying at the ruins of the gate, smiling 135 at Kaz. She stared at him. His blood had congealed on his face and turned his white shirt brown. He looked like he came from another race, another country.

21   "Do you have any perfume?" he asked.

22   "Look at this house," she said, gesturing toward what was left of 140 it, a pile of boards on the ground. "How could I have any perfume?"

23   It was then that the smell of his blood engulfed her, as violent as the odor of a charnel house. She thought she might retch. She found a bottle of wine, left behind by a man fleeing the city. "We don't have any perfume, so *this* will be the perfume," she said. She doused 145 her brother with it, trying to drown the stench of death.

24   Later, when night had fallen, Kaz and her brother made for the mountains; a friend from Kaz's factory lived in a village on a hill behind the city and had offered to take them in. It was midnight by the time they found her place. Kaz looked back. The city was ablaze. 150 She felt a spasm of fear, not for herself but for her parents. She left her brother behind, and then she was running again, down the hillside toward the flames. The streets were clotted with the dead and the barely living, shadows backlit by a thousand fires, and a hidden sickness was sprouting like a black flower in Kaz's own body; still, 155 she kept on running, knowing only that she had to be home.

25   Kaz's family had been luckier than most. Her father was in

agony for weeks, lying outdoors on a *tatami* with his burns, and her brother's wounds refused to close. But they had at least survived, and they began, painfully, to rebuild their lives. They had two wells 160 for water and an uncle who lived on an island off the coast brought them a great sack of food every week. Kaz's father found a carpenter willing to raise a new house out of the wreckage of the old in exchange for whatever wood was left over. The house more nearly resembled a hovel, two slap-sided rooms with *tatami* for furniture; 165 Kaz could see the first snowflakes of winter through cracks between the boards on the roof. By the standards of Hiroshima after the bomb, it was a mansion.

26   In time the visible wounds healed. The burns on Kaz's father's chest left a tracery of ropy keloid scarring; he liked to say they made 170 maps of Japan and America, side by side the way they ought to be, and when the subject of the bomb came up, he resisted blaming anyone. "The war," he would say, "is finished."

27   But as the others were recovering, Kaz had fallen ill with all the symptoms of radiation sickness. The malady was one of the fright- 175 ening aftershocks of the bomb; the scientists in Los Alamos were surprised by its extent—they thought the blast would do most of the killing—and the doctors in Japan were unschooled in its treatment. All Kaz knew was that she felt like she was dying. She was aflame with fever. She felt nauseated and dizzy, almost drunk. Her gums 180 and her bowels were bleeding. She looked like a ghost. A friend saw her one day while she was still mobile and did not recognize her; Kaz had to tell her, "Hi, it's me, it's me!"

28   By October she had taken to her bed, her body ice cold. She could barely breathe or eat; tangerines were the only food that 185 tasted good to her, and as she grew weaker she could not peel one without help or even lift a single section to her lips. A doctor came to see her; he had heard of such cases, but had no idea what to do. "I can't save her," Kaz heard him saying through the haze of her illness. She found herself oddly unafraid. "Well, I'm next," she 190 thought matter-of-factly; she was an 18-year-old girl waiting her turn to die.

29   In memory she would mark the first day of 1946 as the start of her second life, though she remained ill for many months thereafter. It was an old superstition among the Japanese that a person would 195 spend the entire year as he or she spent New Year's Day, and Kaz's mother was determined that Kaz would spend at least a bit of it on her feet. A neighbor helped; they wrapped Kaz in a kimono, got her outside and propped her upright for few wobbly minutes. The medicine worked better than anything in the doctor's bag, since the only 200 known treatment for radiation sickness was rest. Death no longer seemed quite so inevitable, and as winter gave way to spring and spring to summer, Kaz began to mend.

30   The illness had not really left her; it had gone into hiding instead, and the physical and mental aftereffects of August 6, 1945 205 would trouble Kaz all the rest of her life.

REVIEW | ZERO HOUR: FORTY-THREE SECONDS OVER HIROSHIMA

Comprehension

1. Why does the title contain the phrase "forty-three seconds over Hiroshima"? What is significant about the forty-three seconds?

   _____

2. Where was Kaz Tanaka when the bomb exploded? How far was she from ground zero?

   _____

3. What did Kaz think of Americans before the bomb was dropped?

   _____

4. Why was she so close to Americans?_____

   _____

5. What was Kaz's life like before the bomb fell? Give as much detail as you can.

   _____

   _____

   _____

6. Why was Kaz's father so badly burned?_____

   _____

7. What were the most serious physical effects the bomb had on

   a. Kaz's brother:_____

   _____

   b. Kaz's father:_____

   c. Kaz: _____

   _____

8. What did Kaz's father think about the war between Japan and the United States before and after the bomb? Give details from the reading to support your answer.

   Before _____

   _____

   After_____

   _____

9. Why did Kaz's brother want perfume?

_____

10. The reading tells us that after the bomb fell, Kaz and her family were luckier than most. In what ways were they lucky?

_____

_____

11. What did most of the killing after the bomb had been dropped? Why couldn't doctors cure it?

_____

_____

Textual Pattern: Point of View

A. Use the diagram on page 82 to answer the following questions.

1. What point of view is used to tell this story?

_____

2. Who is telling the story?

_____

3. Underline some example sentences in the reading that indicate which third person is telling the story (someone who sees into the mind of only one character, someone who objectively sees everything, etc.).

4. Where are you first aware of the point of view being used?

_____

5. List some of the grammatical parts of speech that tell you what point of view is being used.

_____

B. Read the first paragraph of "Zero Hour: Forty-Three Seconds Over Hiroshima." If any of the following journalistic questions are answered, put the answer in the space provided.

Who _____

What _____

When _____

Where _____

Why _____

How _____

Skill Review: Detecting Sequence

The events listed below are in the order in which they actually happened (natural order). Place a number next to each event to indicate the order in which the events are described by the author (narrated order).

_5_ Kaz's father is born in Hiroshima.

_6_ Kaz's father migrates to America.

_2_ Kaz is born while the family is in America.

_7_ Family moves back to Japan.

_8_ Family builds a spacious home in Hiroshima.

_9_ The war starts between Japan and the U.S.

_1_ Kaz stays home from work on August 6, 1945.

_3_ The first atomic bomb is dropped on Hiroshima.

_4_ Kaz falls unconscious.

_10_ Kaz seeks shelter and supplies from her aunt.

_11_ When she returns home, Kaz sees her brother for the first time since the bomb was dropped.

Narration: Verb Tense

If someone asked you what tense is most frequently used to narrate an event, you would very likely respond, "past tense." Such an answer would be accurate; however, narrations do not have to be in the past tense. A sports announcer, for example, giving a play-by-play account of a soccer game, is narrating in the present tense. Other examples of present-tense narration include recipes and accounts of how an annual event such as a parade or ceremony is observed or how a typical businessman in Hong Kong spends his working day. A story does not have to be told in the past tense to be a narration.

The next reading in this chapter is a good example of a narration in the present tense. John Aristotle Phillips tells how he developed an A-bomb for his junior-year project at Princeton University. Rather than tell how he *did* it, Phillips tells the entire story in the present tense. By doing this he allows the reader to sense just what it was like to go through the rigors of sleepless nights, hours and hours of research, and the innumerable pages of calculations required to finish his project. Notice the verb tenses used in the following paragraph from "How I Designed an A-Bomb in My Junior Year at Princeton."

Over spring vacation, I *go* to Washington, D.C., to search for records of the Los Alamos Project that were declassified between 1954 and 1964. I *discover* a copy of the literature given to scientists who joined the project in the spring of 1943. This text, *The Los Alamos Primer*, carefully *outlines* all the details of atomic fissioning known to the world's most advanced scientists in the early '40s. A whole batch of copies *costs* me about $25. I *gather* them together and *go* over to the bureaucrat at the front desk. She *looks* at the titles, and then *looks* up at me.

"Oh, you want to build a bomb, too?" she *asks* matter-of-factly.

PREVIEW | HOW I DESIGNED AN A-BOMB IN MY JUNIOR YEAR AT PRINCETON

Things to Think About

1. Do you think a college student could design a working model of an atomic bomb? Why or why not?

   _____

2. In reference to government documents, what is the meaning of the word *classified*? Look it up in a dictionary if you are not sure.

   _____

3. What do you think would be the most difficult part about building an atomic bomb?

   _____

4. What materials would a person need to build an atomic bomb?

   _____

   _____

5. Where would a person get the necessary information to build a bomb?

   _____

   _____

6. If you decided to build a bomb how would you begin? What would your first step be?

   _____

   _____

7. Why is Los Alamos important in the history of nuclear research?

   _____

   _____

Preview

1. When was this story written?_____

2. Who wrote it?_____

3. Quickly read the introductory material. Why is David Michaelis listed as one of the authors?

    _____

    _____

4. The boldfaced words in the following passages are important to your understanding of the story "How I Designed an A-Bomb in My Junior Year at Princeton." Use the context provided to determine the meaning of each boldfaced word.

    a. "It takes only 15 pounds of plutonium to fabricate a crude atomic bomb," adds the teacher. The class discusses a possible **scenario**. A 200-pound shipment of plutonium disappears en route to a nuclear reactor. State and local police discover only an empty truck and a dead driver. Two weeks later, a crude fission bomb is detonated in downtown New York City.

        scenario _____

    b. Silence falls over the room as the students realize the **titanic** proportions of the destruction caused by a bomb.

        titanic _____

    c. Ted Taylor **postulates** that a terrorist group could easily steal plutonium from a nuclear reactor and then design a workable atomic bomb.

        postulates _____

    d. At subsequent meetings Dyson explains only the basic principles of nuclear physics, and his responses to my calculations grow **opaque**. If I ask about a particular design, he will glance over what I have done and change the subject.

        opaque _____

    e. During the next week I read that a high-**explosive** blanket around the beryllium shield might work. But after spending an entire night calculating, I conclude that it is not enough to guarantee a successful **implosion** wave. Seven days before the design is due, I'm still **deadlocked**.

        explosive _____

        implosion _____

        deadlocked _____

    f. "Aren't you the boy who designed the atomic bomb?" "Yes, and my paper wasn't handed back." She takes a deep breath. "The question has been raised by the department whether your paper should be **classified** by the U.S. government."

classified _____

READING SIX

HOW I DESIGNED AN A-BOMB IN MY JUNIOR YEAR AT PRINCETON

Most of us would assume that building a nuclear weapon would at the outset require genius, special expertise, and highly classified information. Unfortunately, however, that may not be the case. The following is an account of how a junior on academic probation at Princeton designed a workable atomic bomb as a term project in physics. John Aristotle Phillips had two goals in writing his term paper: showing how easily a nuclear device could be assembled by terrorists and getting an A in the course. He accomplished both, and his term paper was immediately classified. In collaboration with his former classmate, David Michaelis, Phillips wrote the following account, which comes from their book, Mushroom: The Story of the A-Bomb Kid *(1978).*

1   The first semester of my junior year at Princeton University is a disaster, and my grades show it. D's and F's predominate, and a note from the dean puts me on academic probation. Flunk one more course, and I'm out.

2   Fortunately, as the new semester gets under way, my courses   5 begin to interest me. Three hours a week, I attend one called Nuclear Weapons Strategy and Arms Control in which three professors lead 12 students through intense discussions of counterforce capabilities and doomsday scenarios. The leader is Hal Feiveson, renowned for his strong command of the subject matter. Assisting   10 him is Marty Sherwin, an authority on cold-war diplomacy, and Freeman Dyson, an eminent physicist.

3   One morning, Dyson opens a discussion of the atomic bomb: "Let me describe what occurs when a 20-kiloton bomb is exploded, similar to the two dropped on Hiroshima and Nagasaki. First, the   15 sky becomes illuminated by a brilliant white light. Temperatures

Adapted with permission from John A. Phillips and David Michaelis, *Mushroom: The Story of the A-Bomb Kid* (New York: William Morrow and Co., Inc., 1978). © 1978 by J. A. Phillips.

are so high around the point of explosion that the atmosphere is actually made incandescent. To an observer standing six miles away the ball of fire appears brighter than a hundred suns.

4   "As the fireball begins to spread up and out into a mushroom-shaped cloud, temperatures spontaneously ignite all flammable materials for miles around. Wood-frame houses catch fire. Clothing bursts into flame, and people suffer intense third-degree flash burns over their exposed flesh. The very high temperatures also produce a shock wave and a variety of nuclear radiations capable of penetrating 20 inches of concrete. The shock wave levels everything in the vicinity of ground zero; hurricane-force winds then rush into the vacuum left by the expanding shock wave and sweep up the rubble of masonry, glass and steel, hurling it outward as lethal projectiles."

5   Silence falls over the room as the titanic proportions of the destruction begin to sink in.

6   "It takes only 15 pounds of plutonium to fabricate a crude atomic bomb," adds Hal Feiveson. "If breeder reactors come into widespread use, there will be sufficient plutonium shipped around the country each year to fashion thousands of bombs. Much of it could be vulnerable to theft or hijacking."

7   The class discusses a possible scenario. A 200-pound shipment disappears en route between a reprocessing facility and a nuclear reactor. State and local police discover only an empty truck and a dead driver. Two weeks later, a crude fission bomb is detonated in Wall Street. Of the half-million people who crowd the area during the regular business day, 100,000 are killed outright. A terrorist group claims responsibility and warns the President that if its extravagant political demands are not met, there will be another explosion within a week.

8   "That's impossible," a student objects. "Terrorists don't have the know-how to build a bomb."

9   "You have to be brilliant to design an A-bomb," says another. "Besides, terrorists don't have access to the knowledge."

10   Impossible? Or is it? The specter of terrorists incinerating an entire city with a homemade atomic bomb begins to haunt me. I turn to John McPhee's book *The Curve of Binding Energy*, in which former Los Alamos nuclear physicist Ted Taylor postulates that a terrorist group could easily steal plutonium or uranium from a nuclear reactor and then design a workable atomic bomb with information available to the general public. According to Taylor, all the ingredients—except plutonium—are legally available at hardware stores and chemical-supply houses.

11   Suddenly, an idea comes to mind. Suppose an average—or below-average in my case—physics student could design a workable atomic bomb on paper? That would prove Taylor's point dramatically and show the federal government that stronger safeguards have to be placed on the storage of plutonium. If I could design a bomb, almost any intelligent person could. But I would have to do it in less than three months to turn it in as my junior independent project. I decide to ask Freeman Dyson to be my adviser.

12   "You understand," says Dyson, "my government security clearance will prevent me from giving you any more information than
that which can be found in physics libraries? And that the law of 'no
comment' governing scientists who have clearance to atomic   70
research requires that, if asked a question about the design of a
bomb, I can answer neither yes nor no?"

13   "Yes, sir," I reply. "I understand."

14   "Okay, then. I'll give you a list of textbooks outlining the general
principles—and I wish you luck."   75

15   I'm tremendously excited as I charge over to the physics office to
record my project, and can barely write down:

John Aristotle Phillips
Dr. Freeman Dyson, Adviser
"How to Build Your Own   80
Atomic Bomb"

16   A few days later, Dyson hands me a short list of books on
nuclear-reactor technology, general nuclear physics and current
atomic theory. "That's all?" I ask incredulously, having expected a
bit more direction.   85

17   At subsequent meetings Dyson explains only the basic principles of nuclear physics, and his responses to my calculations grow
opaque. If I ask about a particular design or figure, he will glance
over what I've done and change the subject. At first, I think this is
his way of telling me I am correct. To make sure, I hand him an   90
incorrect figure. He reads it and changes the subject.

18   Over spring vacation, I go to Washington, D.C., to search for
records of the Los Alamos Project that were declassified between
1954 and 1964. I discover a copy of the literature given to scientists
who joined the project in the spring of 1943. This text, *The Los*   95
Alamos Primer, carefully outlines all the details of atomic fissioning
known to the world's most advanced scientists in the early '40s. A
whole batch of copies costs me about $25. I gather them together
and go over to the bureaucrat at the front desk. She looks at the
titles, and then looks up at me.   100

19   "Oh, you want to build a bomb, too?" she asks matter-of-factly.

20   I can't believe it. Do people go in there for bomb-building information every day? When I show the documents to Dyson, he is
visibly shaken. His reaction indicates to me that I actually stand a
chance of coming up with a workable design.   105

21   The material necessary to explode my bomb is plutonium-239, a
man-made, heavy isotope. Visualize an atomic bomb as a marble
inside a grapefruit inside a basketball inside a beach ball. At the
center of the bomb is the initiator, a marble-size piece of metal.
Around the initiator is a grapefruit-size ball of plutonium-239.   110
Wrapped around the plutonium is a three-inch reflector shield made
of beryllium. High explosives are placed symmetrically around the
beryllium shield. When these detonate, an imploding shock wave is
set off, compressing the grapefruit-size ball of plutonium to the size

of a plum. At this moment, the process of atoms fissioning—or split- 115
ting apart—begins.

22   There are many subtleties involved in the explosion of an atomic
bomb. Most of them center on the actual detonation of the
explosives surrounding the beryllium shield. The grouping of these
explosives is one of the most highly classified aspects of the atomic 120
bomb, and it poses the biggest problems for me as I begin to design
my bomb.

23   My base of operations is a small room on the second floor of Ivy,
my eating club. The conference table in the center of the room is
covered with books, calculators, design paper, notes. My sleeping 125
bag is rolled out on the floor. As the next three weeks go by, I stop
going to classes altogether and work day and night. The other members at Ivy begin referring to me as The Hobo because of my
unshaven face and disheveled appearance. I develop a terrible case
of bloodshot eyes. Sleep comes rarely. 130

24   I approach every problem from a terrorist's point of view. The
bomb must be inexpensive to construct, simple in design, and small
enough to sit unnoticed in the trunk of a car or an abandoned U-
Haul trailer.

25   As the days and nights flow by, linked together by cups of coffee 135
and bologna sandwiches, I scan government documents for gaps
indicating an area of knowledge that is still classified. Essentially, I
am putting together a huge jigsaw puzzle. The edge pieces are in
place and various areas are getting filled in, but pieces are missing.
Whenever the outline of one shows up, I grab my coffee Thermos 140
and sit down to devise the solution that will fill the gap.

26   With only two weeks left, the puzzle is nearly complete, but two
pieces are still missing: which explosives to use, and how to arrange
them around the plutonium.

27   During the next week I read that a high-explosive blanket 145
around the beryllium shield might work. But after spending an
entire night calculating, I conclude that it is not enough to guarantee a successful implosion wave. Seven days before the design is
due, I'm still deadlocked.

28   The alarm clock falls off the table and breaks. I take this as a 150
sign to do something drastic, and I start all over at the beginning.
Occasionally I find errors in my old calculations, and I correct them.
I lose sense of time.

29   With less than 24 hours to go, I run through a series of new
calculations, mathematically figuring the arrangement of the 155
explosives around the plutonium. If my equations are correct, my
bomb might be just as effective as the Hiroshima and Nagasaki
bombs. But I can't be sure until I know the exact nature of the
explosives I will use.

30   Next morning, with my paper due at 5 p.m., I call the Du Pont 160
Company from a pay phone and ask for the head of the chemical-
explosives division, a man I'll call Mr. Graves. If he gives me even
the smallest lead, I'll be able to figure the rest out by myself. Otherwise, I'm finished.

31   "Hello, Mr. Graves. My name is John Phillips. I'm a student at   165
Princeton, doing work on a physics project. I'd like to get some
advice, if that's possible."

32   "What can I do for you?"

33   "Well," I stammer, "I'm doing research on the shaping of
explosive products that create a very high density in a spherically   170
shaped metal. Can you suggest a Du Pont product that would fit in
this category?"

34   "Of course," he says, in a helpful manner.

35   I don't think he suspects, but I decide to try a bluff: "One of my
professors told me that a simple explosive blanket would work in   175
the high-density situation."

36   "No, no. Explosive blankets went out with the Stone Age. We
sell [he names the product] to do the job in similar density-problem
situations to the one you're talking about."

37   When I hang up the phone, I let out a whoop. Mr. Graves has   180
given me just the information I need. Now, if my calculations are
correct with respect to the new information, all I have to do is
complete my paper by five.

38   Five minutes to five, I race over to the physics building and
bound up the stairs. Inside the office, everybody stops talking and   185
stares at me. I haven't shaved in over a week.

39   "Is your razor broken, young man?" asks one of the department
secretaries.

40   "I came to hand in my project," I explain. "I didn't have time to
shave. Sorry."   190

41   A week later, I return to the physics department to pick up my
project. One thought has persisted: If I didn't guess correctly about
the implosion wave, or if I made a mistake somewhere in the
graphs, I'll be finished at Princeton.

42   A secretary points to the papers. I flip through them, but don't   195
find mine. I look carefully; my paper is not there.

43   Trying to remain calm, I ask her if all the papers have been
graded.

44   "Yes, of course," she says.

45   Slowly I return to my room. The absence of my paper can only   200
mean that I blew it.

46   In the middle of the week, I go back to the physics-department
office, hoping to catch the chairman for a few minutes. The secretary looks up, then freezes.

47   "Aren't you John Phillips?" she asks.   205

48   "Yes," I reply.

49   "Aren't you the boy who designed the atomic bomb?"

50   "Yes, and my paper wasn't . . ."

51   She takes a deep breath. "The question has been raised by the
department whether your paper should be classified by the U.S.   210
government."

52   "What? Classified?"

53   She takes my limp hand, shaking it vigorously. "Congratula-
tions," she says, all smiles. "You got one of the only A's in the

department. Dr. Wigner wants to see you right away. He says it's a ₂₁₅
fine piece of work. And Dr. Dyson has been looking for you everywhere."

54   For a second I don't say anything. Then the madness of the
situation hits me. A small air bubble of giddiness rises in my throat.
Here I have put on paper the plan for a device capable of killing ₂₂₀
thousands of people, and all I was worrying about was flunking out.

REVIEW | HOW I DESIGNED AN A-BOMB IN MY JUNIOR YEAR AT PRINCETON

Comprehension

1. True or false? Phillips actually built an atomic bomb. _____

2. Where did Phillips first get the idea to build an atomic bomb?

_____

3. What was Phillips' academic standing as the semester started?

_____

4. Why does Phillips finally decide to design an A-bomb? What were
his reasons?

_____

5. Where would a person get most of the supplies necessary to build an
atomic bomb?

_____

6. What would be the most difficult supply to obtain? Why?_____

_____

7. Why was Phillips' adviser so limited in the amount of help he could
give on the project?

_____

8. What was Phillips' purpose in going to Washington, D.C.? _____

_____

9. What was his adviser's reaction to the documents Phillips had
photocopied, and why did he react the way he did?

_____

_____

10. What were Phillips' biggest problems in actually designing the bomb? How did he finally solve these problems?

_____

_____

11. What was Phillips' reaction when he first discovered that his paper was not in the stack of corrected papers?

_____

12. What was his reaction when he found out that his paper had been classified?

_____

_____

Skill Review: Detecting Sequence

A. Some of the steps taken by Phillips to design an atomic bomb are listed below. Write in any others you think are major events in the story. You do not need to list every single event—only the most important.

1. *Phillips attends his Nuclear Weapons Strategy and Arms Control class.*
2. *Following a class discussion he decides to build a bomb.*
3. *He records his project in the division office.*
4. _____
5. _____
6. *Phillips shows his advisor what he has photocopied.*
7. *He begins his work on the second floor of Ivy.*
8. _____
9. _____
10. *With less than 24 hours to go he calls the DuPont company in hopes of getting his missing information.*
11. _____
12. _____
13. *Phillips returns again only to find that his paper has been classified by the U.S. government.*

Does Phillips tell this story in the natural sequence in which the events happened, or does he mix up the natural sequence? How do you know this?

_____

_____

B. The following paragraph is the account given by Phillips' instructor of what might happen if a 20-kiloton bomb exploded. The sentences have been taken out of their correct order. Without turning back to the reading, write a number in each blank indicating the order in which the events were narrated by the instructor.

_____ Wood-frame houses catch fire.

_____ Temperatures are so high around the point of explosion that the atmosphere is actually made incandescent.

_____ The shock wave levels everything in the vicinity of ground zero.

_____ To an observer standing six miles away the ball of fire appears brighter than a hundred suns.

_____ First, the sky becomes illuminated by a brilliant white light.

_____ Hurricane-force winds then rush into the vacuum left by the expanding shock wave and sweep up the rubble of masonry, glass, and steel, hurling it outward as lethal projectiles.

_____ Clothing bursts into flame, and people suffer intense third-degree flash burns over their exposed flesh.

_____ As the fireball begins to spread up and out into a mushroom-shaped cloud, temperatures spontaneously ignite all flammable materials for miles around.

_____ The very high temperatures also produce a shock wave and a variety of nuclear radiations capable of penetrating 20 inches of concrete.

Questions for Further Discussion/Composition

1. What kind of security measures need to be taken in order to ensure that an atomic bomb is not made by anyone who wants to make one?

2. Who should have the information necessary to build an atomic bomb? Would it be possible to keep the information on building a bomb completely classified?

3. In your opinion, who gave Phillips the most useful information? Why?

4. What does Phillips mean when he says, "For a second I don't say anything. Then the madness of the situation hits me. A small air bubble of giddiness rises in my throat. Here I have put on paper the plan for a device capable of killing thousands of people, and all I was worrying about was flunking out"?

5. Imagine that you are a newspaper reporter relating to your readers some of the most important events in the history of the nuclear age. Tell *how* you are going to present those events. (Hint: Review the Narration and Skill Review lessons that discuss natural and narrated sequences, reading newspapers, point of view, and verb tenses.)

CHAPTER 3

Through all the drama,
whether damned or not—
Love gilds the scene,
and women guide the plot.

—Richard Sheridan

MARRIAGE AND FAMILY

Marriage and families have been around a long time, but they have not always meant the same things to various groups of people through different periods of time. In this chapter you will be reading about some of the contrasting customs, roles, and responsibilities of family members in different cultures. In addition, several of the reading selections will discuss the changes that are taking place in the institutions of marriage and the family.

COMPARISON AND CONTRAST

Every day as you choose from a menu, shop, or decide which class is easier, you are comparing. You weigh the advantages and disadvantages, pros and cons, similarities and differences, and choose the item or person that you find most appealing.

Comparing and contrasting are not particularly difficult; these are things that the mind is accustomed to doing all the time. From the reader's point of view, following a writer's comparison should not be very difficult as long as the reader is familiar with the organizational pattern the writer has chosen. In this chapter you will be introduced to the three most common patterns of comparison and contrast.

UNDERSTANDING TABLES AND GRAPHS

With modern computers, the creation of tables and graphs is as easy as the push of a button. This has made graphic representations more popular and useful than ever before, and the ability to read and comprehend them has become a valuable reading skill. After each reading in this chapter, you will have the opportunity to learn about the various kinds of tables and graphs that are popular today and how to interpret them.

Comparison and Contrast—Pattern A:
The "Point-by-Point" Approach

The first reading in this chapter is an example of what we shall call the "point-by-point" method of comparison and contrast. With this method, the author chooses several aspects of two objects to compare and measure and uses these points as a basis for the paragraphing. That is, each paragraph is about one aspect.

For example, if an author wanted to compare two families that he knew, he could talk about many things: diet, family responsibilities, activities, religion, sleeping habits, favorite TV programs, roles of the spouses, the accomplishments of their children, and so forth. To remain organized, the author would narrow the focus of his writing. An outline of this comparison might look like this (each Roman numeral represents a paragraph):

Religion in the Lives of Two Families
  I. Introduction to the two families
 II. Eating
       The Abdullah family
       The Singh family
III. Clothing
       The Abdullah family
       The Singh family

 IV. Holidays
       The Abdullah family
       The Singh family
  V. Conclusion

Notice that in each paragraph the order in which the families are talked about is kept the same: first the Abdullah family and then the Singh family. If the author has been careful, your job as a reader is easier since the points of comparison can be clearly remembered. As you begin the following reading on the American family, which is an example of the "point-by-point" method, keep in mind the principles we have discussed about this method of organization.

PREVIEW | THE AMERICAN FAMILY: THEN AND NOW

Things to Think About

1. Have you ever seen photographs of your parents or grandparents when they were young? How did their appearance differ from that of people today?

_____

_____

_____

2. Have your parents or grandparents ever talked to you about their youth, their experiences, and their families? Did they experience the same things you experienced? Explain.

    _____

    _____

    _____

3. How have families changed since the time your parents were young?

    _____

    _____

    _____

4. What caused these changes to take place? Inventions? Technology? Change of location or citizenship? Education?

    _____

    _____

    _____

Preview

1. What two objects or persons are being compared in this essay?

    _____   _____

2. How many points of comparison does the author use? _____
    List them below:

3. Now read the conclusion. What is the author's main point?

    _____

    _____

    _____

READING ONE

THE AMERICAN FAMILY: THEN AND NOW

point-by-point
size ∫ then
       ∫ now

1   Whenever I talk to my grandfather, I always leave with a greater awareness of the differences between his family and mine. Thinking back to our many conversations and shared memories, there are several ideas about families that seem to have changed considerably between the days of his youth and mine.   5

2   The first thing that comes to mind is the difference in size of his family and mine. Size refers to two different things here. First, he was one of ten children. I am one of three. Anybody with ten children today would be viewed as strange, antique, or, even worse, unpatriotic—"You are contributing to the depletion of resources   10
cargas
and overpopulation of our country!" A large number of children are no longer needed to carry on the work of the family and are no longer a source of security or pride. Today, in our urban lifestyles, they are simply economic burdens, costing tens of thousands of dollars to house, feed and clothe. Second, the size of the word "fam- 15
ily" itself has diminished. In my grandfather's time, the meaning of "family" included uncles, aunts, cousins, and grandparents, who almost all lived near enough to be a regular part of one's life. Today, the word "family" means the nuclear family (parents and children), not the extended family of the old days. In addition, due to a   20
number of unfortunate causes, the family increasingly consists of only one parent.

3   The second area of change that has occurred between my grandfather's time and mine is the role and status of the husband and wife. In the old days, according to my grandfather, the respon-   25

sibilities assigned to the man and woman were quite separate. The man's place was outside the home, earning a living to support the physical needs of his family. The woman's place was in the home, giving birth to and raising children, caring for and feeding the family, nursing the sick and the aged. On the other hand, the great majority of mothers today are employed at least on a part-time basis outside the home, and are expected to supplement the husband's income. Women are much more active in the affairs of politics, business, and government than they ever were in the days of my grandfather's youth. Today, more than ever, women are becoming equal partners in marriage.

4   The third area of difference which I have noticed is in the very practice of marriage itself. In the days of my grandfather, the word "marriage" meant only one thing: the union of one man and one woman, for good or for bad, until "death do they part." Marriage was traditionally looked upon as something permanent, a sacred bond between man and woman for the purpose of raising a family. In comparison, marriage today can mean different things to different people. And to some people it doesn't mean much at all. There are a number of alternatives to the traditional marriage, none of which was acceptable fifty years ago. There are homosexual marriages, group marriages, communal living arrangements, and swingers' groups, each of these being different from the others in the number and type of relationships desired. The word "relationship" is often used today when talking about marriage. The word reveals an underlying understanding that marriage today, in its many forms, is no longer a permanent or lifelong situation. It is a transient, temporary development that two or more people agree to until it is no longer mutually beneficial.

5   As a result of all these changes, the statistics of the typical marriage have also changed. My grandfather told me that he hardly knew any divorced people, yet half my classmates have divorced parents! In my grandfather's time it seems that everyone was eager to get married. These days, however, more and more people are choosing to marry at a later age, and a growing number have decided to remain single. Today, being single does not mean a life without sex, however. It simply means that some do not feel that the legal act of marriage is necessary to have successful intimate relationships with other people—something unheard of in my grandfather's day.

6   It seems that the very word "marriage" has changed in meaning. I suppose our emphasis on change and consumerism has led to all these new varieties that characterize today's marriages and families. I told my grandfather that I was sure I would get married someday and have a family as he had. The question is, what those words will mean when I come to that day.

REVIEW | THE AMERICAN FAMILY: THEN AND NOW

Comprehension

1. What is being compared in this passage?

   The family in the past and now

2. What specific points of comparison were discussed by the author?

   5

3. You were asked before to identify the author's main idea by reading the conclusion. Now that you have read the entire essay, what do you think is the real reason the author wrote this comparison?

4. In the conclusion, the author says that the meaning of the word *marriage* has changed. Explain.

5. Does the author express a personal opinion about the changes being described? (Is he for or against the changes taking place nowadays?)

Textual Pattern: Comparison and Contrast

Below is a partial outline of the reading you just completed. Fill in the missing portions.

The American Family: Then and Now
   I. Introduction
  II. Family size
       Then
       Now
 III. _Men and women roles_
       Then
       Now

IV. Marriage practices

    _____They_____

    _____Now_____

V. _____statistics_____

    _____they_____

    _____now_____

VI. Conclusion

Phrases of Comparison

When writers compare or contrast things, they often use certain words and phrases that help us to key in on the main points and relationships that they want us to remember. Following are lists of the most common terms. Look for these words in the reading you have just finished and <u>underline</u> all the words that you see from the following two lists.

Comparison	Contrast
also (too)	on the other hand
like	in contrast (with)
likewise	by contrast
similar(ly)	but
compared to	however
as well as	unlike
same	despite
as _____ as	differ, different, difference
in common	as opposed to
by the same token	contrary to
	whereas, while, although

Questions for Further Discussion/Composition

1. In all countries customs change—some faster than others. How have the traditions of marriage and family changed in your country?

2. How do these changes occur? Who or what changes them?

3. Why do countries have traditions? What purposes do they serve in the culture? Are they really necessary?

4. What does current society in your country perceive as the ideal family size? Does your government have any policies on this subject? If so, how are they enforced?

5. If you could change one thing about the customs of your culture concerning marriage or the family, what would you change?

Understanding Tables

In the first reading we are introduced to some of the changes that the American family is currently undergoing. Through the exercises we will take a closer look at some of these changes.

Read the following paragraph, which compares the percentages of married men and women in the United States between the years 1974 and 1980.

> It is interesting to look at the percentages of married men and women in the United States during the last few years. In the year 1974, 73.7 percent of the men were married as compared with 67.6 percent of the women. In 1975, married men represented 72.8 percent of the male population, whereas married women represented only 66.7 percent of their population. In the following year . . .

If you are like most readers, you would probably have a difficult time remembering any of the above percentages, or, more importantly, perceiving any significant trends revealed by the percentages.

Let's see what the discussion looks like in the form of a table:

PERCENTAGE MARRIED

	1974	1975	1976	1977	1978	1979	1980
Men	73.7	72.8	72.2	70.9	70.1	69.2	68.6
Women	67.6	66.7	66.2	65.3	64.2	63.5	63.1

It becomes clear immediately that in every year from 1974 through 1980, a larger percentage of men were married than women. In addition, it is evident that for both men and women, the percentage of those who were married dropped every year. Often tables can present relationships between percentages, amounts, etc., more clearly than text can. Tables also save time and space by providing the same information without all the words that are required in grammatical sentences.

EXERCISE   Fill in the answers to the following questions from the table on page 112.

1. What percentage of men were divorced in 1976? _____4.5_____

2. What percentage of nonwhite males had never been married by 1976? _____48.0_____

3. Did the percentage of white males who were divorced increase or decrease between the years 1978 and 1979? ___*NO*___ By how much? ___*0*___

4. Which sex had the higher percentage of divorced persons in 1979? ___*F.*___

5. Overall, which sex has the higher percentage of divorced persons? ___*F.*___

6. What pattern or trend do you notice in the divorce percentages during the years 1975–1980? ___*increase*___

MARRIAGE AND DIVORCE TRENDS

Sex and Race	1975	1976	1977	1978	1979	1980
Percentage Married						
Male	72.8	72.2	70.9	70.1	69.2	68.6
White	73.9	73.4	72.3	71.7	70.7	70.1
Nonwhite	63.5	62.0	60.6	58.4	57.5	57.1
Female	66.7	66.2	65.3	64.2	63.5	63.1
White	68.0	67.6	66.7	65.7	64.2	64.8
Nonwhite	57.3	56.2	55.4	52.6	51.8	51.5
Percentage Divorced						
Male	3.7	4.0	4.5	4.7	4.8	5.2
White	3.6	3.8	4.4	4.5	4.5	5.0
Nonwhite	4.6	5.5	5.0	6.3	6.6	6.6
Female	5.3	5.7	6.2	6.6	6.6	7.1
White	5.0	5.5	6.0	6.3	6.4	6.8
Nonwhite	7.1	7.4	8.2	8.8	8.3	8.9

Comparison and Contrast—Pattern B: The "Whole" Approach

The essay you are about to read is an example of another method writers use to compare two or more items. The comparison is basically divided into two parts; the first half is all about the first of the two items or persons being compared, and the second half is about the other. It may not be as easy for the reader to remember specific points of comparison or contrast with this method since the paragraphs are not based on the individual aspects of comparison as they are in the "point-by-point" approach. This pattern may appear simply to be two descriptions; one after the other. This is not entirely true, however. A careful reading of the second half of this type of writing will reveal a purposeful *comparative* description. Ideas and phrases will constantly remind or refer the reader to ideas stated about the first item or person.

The following outline summarizes the basic structure of this pattern. Compare this pattern with the point-by-point outline of the same comparison on page 105.

Religion in the Lives of Two Families
  I. Introduction
 II. Religious lifestyle of the Abdullah family
     Food
     Clothing
     Holidays
III. Religious lifestyle of the Singh family
     Food
     Clothing
     Holidays
 IV. Conclusion

Writers will often keep the points of comparison in the same order. This is not always the case, however. In fact, writers may not even keep to the same points of comparison between the two items.

PREVIEW | MOM, HOW DID YOU MEET DAD?

Things to Think About

1. Have you ever thought about why people get married? Is love always the reason? What are some other possible reasons?

   Money, promise, compassion, business, moral obligation, parent, tradition.

2. Did your parents ever tell you about how they met or got married?

3. What is a "blind date"? Have you ever had one? *To have a date with some one unknown.*

4. Can you guess what a "blind" marriage might mean?
   To get married with an unknown people.

Preview

1. What country are we reading about? _____China_____

2. What exactly is being compared in this passage? _The last generation and the recent one_

3. What time periods is the author referring to? _from 1975 to 1980_

4. In this reading, the main idea is given most clearly in the concluding paragraph. Write it down here.

_____

_____

READING TWO

Mom, How Did You Meet Dad?

1   As children begin to grow up, one of the questions they ask their parents most is how they met or how they decided to get married. In many countries the answers to these questions haven't always been as romantic as the movies we often watched. This is particularly true in China, the land of my ancestors. Things are not the same   5 today as they were before my parents left the country in 1949.

2   In the old days, the youth were not at all involved in the actual
mate selection process. The youth did not spend a lot of time, therefore, looking for a potential marriage partner. It would have just
been a waste of time. As in many countries, the men and women   10
were well separated throughout most of the day. The men had their
work to do, and the women had theirs. For thousands of years,
marriage was primarily an instrument for the continuation of the
family line through its male members. It was a social arrangement
between two families; not two individuals. Romance, therefore, was   15
not a factor in the selection process. In fact, it was regarded as a
potential threat to the proper conduct and calm considered essential in such important matters. In those times, 100 percent of the
marriages were arranged either by the two respective heads of families, or by professional matchmakers. The importance of the   20
matchmakers is clearly revealed in this well-known Chinese
proverb: "You can't sew without a needle." Matchmakers, who were
popular for a long time, would help the family of the daughter find a
suitable mate by doing some investigating. The matchmaker would
then place the name and date of birth of the man and woman on two   25
papers. These papers were then taken to a fortune teller. The fortune
teller determined if the two were right for each other according to
their horoscopes. If all was right, the marriage contract was signed;
not by the couple, but by the two patriarchal heads of the couple's
families. The couple didn't actually meet each other until the day of 30
the marriage!

3   These practices have changed considerably during this century
though. The changes have been brought about by two major influ-
ences in the lives of the Chinese people. The first was the people's
revolution, which succeeded in 1949. With the communist govern-   35
ment's emphasis on collective work organizations, many youth
were brought together to work, either on farms, or on other work
projects. As a result, youth today have a much greater opportunity
to meet a variety of other young men and women while working and
going to public school. In the 1950s, the percentage of couples who   40
married as a result of an arrangement by their families or
matchmaker dropped to 72 percent (29% family, and 43%
matchmaker). The remaining percentage is evenly divided between
those who were introduced by a friend, and those who married on
their own. Through movies, TV, and magazines, the Chinese gradu-   45
ally began to adopt some of the customs of other Westernized countries. In the 1960s couples began more and more to rely on their own
initiative in choosing a marriage partner. Statistics show that only
27% were married by a matchmaker, 35% by the family, 8% by a
friend, and 31% by themselves. A full one third of the couples were   50
then making their own decisions. The last decade has shown a further drop in arranged marriages with 21% being arranged by a
matchmaker, 33% by the family, 24% by a friend, and 23% by the
couple themselves.

4   In general, even though the processes of selecting a spouse are   55
complex and varied, it is quite clear that arranged marriages are
becoming less and less popular in China. It appears that marriage is

becoming more a matter of romance as opposed to convenience and obedience. Who knows? Perhaps in the near future, when children in China ask their parents how they met, parents will respond with   60 stories of love at first sight, engagement rings in cakes, and skating parties.

REVIEW | MOM, HOW DID YOU MEET DAD?

Comprehension

1. What two main causes led to the changes in courtship in China?

   _____

   _____

2. Sometimes the main idea is not always neatly packaged in one sentence, nor is it always placed in the introduction. In this reading, the thesis is clearly given in the first paragraph, but it is not contained in just one sentence. In the space below, write down the *entire* thesis.

   _____

   _____

3. The main idea about the thesis is summarized in the concluding paragraph. Write down this important idea.

   _____

   _____

Skill Review: Understanding Tables

In the preceding passage, percentages were given concerning the use of matchmakers, family, and friends in arranging marriages. For quick reference this information would probably be more useful in the form of a table. Look back at the reading and fill in the proper percentages in the table below.

	1950s	*1960s*	*1970s*
Matchmaker	48	27	21
Relative	29	35	33
Friend	14	8	24
Self	14	31	23

Textual Pattern: Comparison and Contrast

1. Of the two comparison patterns we have studied so far, which did the author choose?

Point - by - Point / *all of one / all of the other* *(The "Whole" Approach)*

before 1949 after 1949

2. In the chart below, list the characteristics of each topic discussed by the author. If an idea is mentioned in both paragraphs of the body of the selection, write them opposite each other in the chart. If a point is mentioned in one paragraph but not in the other, leave the appropriate side of the chart blank (empty).

In the old days . . .	*Nowadays . . .*
youth not involved in selection process	youth involved in a 57%
men and women separated	work together and go together to dances / of romance.
marriage primary instrument to continue the family	made by matchmakers,
marriage by matchmaker	families, themselves, and friends
families arrange / by convenience and obedience	they choose to marriage.

Understanding Bar Graphs

Tables are not the only common method of visually presenting information. Many types of graphs are also used. In this chapter we will study three of the most common types: bar, line, and pie graphs.

BAR GRAPHS

Look at the bar graph in Figure 3-1. It represents the marriage percentages for men shown in the table we studied earlier.

In this bar graph only one series of percentages—the percentages for married males in general—is entered. It is possible to represent more than one series of data by using another set of bars of a different shade or color. In the bar graph in Figure 3-2, the male and female percentages of divorce are represented side by side.

EXERCISE   Take the percentages of white and nonwhite males who are married (from the table on page 112) and show this information on a bar graph (Figure 3-3). Be sure to make the two sets of bars look different so readers can tell which set of bars represents each group.

Figure 3-1

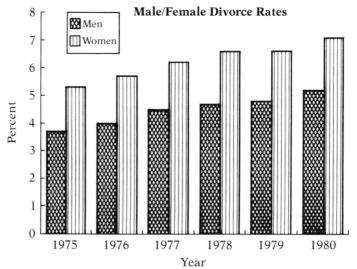

Figure 3-2

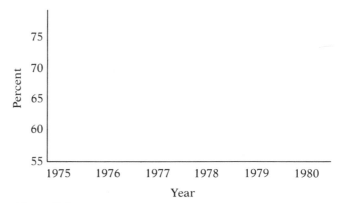

Figure 3-3

Comparison and Contrast—Pattern C: The "Same/Different" Approach

The next reading, "The Amish and the Kibbutzim," is an example of the third pattern we will discuss. It is called the "same/different" approach because the writer discusses first the subjects' similarities and then their differences, or vice versa, depending on the writer's emphasis. If the writer were trying to show that two seemingly similar things were really quite different, then the similarities would be discussed first.

On the other hand, if the writer were trying to show that the items were basically the same despite several obvious differences, then the paragraph order would be reversed (differences discussed first). Take a look at the Abdullah and Singh families again:

Religion in the Lives of Two Families
   I. Introduction
  II. Similarities: Abdullah vs. Singh
       Politically conservative
       Role and status of the women
 III. Differences: Abdullah vs. Singh
       Religious foods
       Holy Scriptures
       Traditional clothing
 IV. Conclusion

PREVIEW | THE AMISH AND THE KIBBUTZIM

Things to Think About

1. Are there any minority groups (ethnic or religious) in your country?

   Yes, gypsies

2. Are these groups trying to remain separate from the main culture or are they attempting to become a part of it?

   yes, the don't culture and fashions are not any to become a part of their culture.

3. How are their customs different from yours? *They live in* *coves, they have patriarcal clane families.* *They don't have the same law or regulations.* *The way of marriage is different.*

Vocabulary in Context

1. Another interesting group consists of those Jews in Israel who live on collective agricultural settlements called kibbutzim (plural for **kibbutz**).

   kibbutz *sistem of living on collective agricultural settlements*

2. The Amish could best be described as **apolitical**—that is, they emphasize hard work and family independence over particular political issues and parties.

   apolitical *not a political definition,*

Preview

1. Read the first paragraph of this essay and briefly define each group being compared.

   a. *Amish from Germany, a particular practice religion,*
   b. *Jews, in Israel, a particular way of living, in kibbuthzim,*
   a sistem of collective agricultural settlement

2. According to the order of comparison, is the author's emphasis on similarities or differences?

   Differences

READING THREE

THE AMISH AND THE KIBBUTZIM

1   Every country has at least one or two minority groups who represent traditions or principles that are not a part of the main-stream culture of that country. One such group is the Amish people of the Eastern United States, who came from Germany to practice their religion in the early days of America's colonial history. This   5
group of people has succeeded in remaining apart from the main culture and society of America. Another interesting group consists of those Jews in Israel who live on collective agricultural settle-ments called "kibbutzim" (plural for "kibbutz"). The kibbutz move-ment began in 1909 and has continued to exist as a viable lifestyle   10
for about 4 percent of the total population.

Amish father and children

2   The families of a kibbutz and of an Amish community share several characteristics in common. The most obvious similarity that these two groups share is their underlying religious heritage. Each community is quite homogeneous in its religious views and has   15 succeeded in preserving and handing these views down to the following generation. Both societies have strict laws concerning the statutes of their faith as well as the marriage of the youth within their faith.

3   The next most obvious similarity to most outside urbanized   20 observers is the central role given to agriculture and hard work. Both the Amish and the kibbutzim feel that family and society are most healthy when they live close to the land. Consequently, most of a member's life revolves around the long hours of work required for life on a farm. In addition, it must be pointed out that the women,   25 whether married or not, are expected to work just as hard as the men, though the roles are more distinct for the Amish women.

4   Respect for their elderly is common in both communities. The Amish frankly state that they are carrying on an old Jewish tradition, best summed up in the Bible, "Honor thy Father and thy   30 Mother, that thy days may be long upon the land which the Lord thy God giveth thee." Though the kibbutz system can be considered liberal in many ways, this is one traditional family principle that they continue to practice. The elderly hold active positions of responsibility and respect in both of these religious societies.   35

5   A quick look at these two communities would lead a person to think that they were much the same, especially given their general desires to remain separate from the rest of society in many ways, and their strong emphasis on religious customs and values. The similarity dissolves quickly, however, upon a closer study of these   40 two groups.

6   The kibbutz system is most famous for its collective method of raising children. The responsibility of child rearing is placed directly on the community almost immediately after birth. Parents spend only a small portion of the day with their children after working hours. Professional nurses and teachers are responsible for the upbringing and education of the children. In contrast, the Amish are much more individualistic, tending to do things as a family unit, instead of as a community. Children spend most of their day with their family members in Amish communities.

7   There is a great difference between the two groups in their views of women. The women of the kibbutz hold absolute equality with the men. Work assignments are handed out to both male and female without regard to one's sex. This is just the opposite for Amish women. Men's and women's roles are very distinct. In addition, females are not nearly the equals of their male counterparts. At the dinner table, for example, the Amish men and boys sit down first and are allowed to take what they want before passing the food to the female members of the family.

8   The life of the youth is quite different also. In a kibbutz, the children, male and female, mix together continually, from the time they are quite young. They work, eat, sleep, shower, and play together until they reach high school age. Premarital relations are seen as personal decisions and young couples in the kibbutz begin living together when they feel they wish to begin a stable, enduring relationship. They are assigned a room to share, and are formally married shortly before the birth of their first baby. This "marriage" is not to satisfy any internal moral code, but simply to avoid the problems caused by the laws of the land which state that a child born out of wedlock has no legal rights. On the other hand, young girls and boys are kept mostly separate in Amish communities. Their most common time to meet each other and mix is at "Sunday-evening singings," meetings specifically intended for the unmarried youth to have the opportunity to talk and get to know one another. The Amish courting and marriage customs would probably be considered conservative, even old-fashioned, by American standards, while those of the kibbutzim would seem quite liberal and ultra-practical.

9   These two groups also differ greatly in their philosophy. The Amish are very conservative in relation to the culture and philosophy of mainstream America, including their manner of dress, transportation and material possessions. Politics is not a common topic for discussion. The Amish could best be described as apolitical, preferring to emphasize hard work and family independence over particular political issues and parties. The kibbutz system, in contrast, was set up specifically as an answer to the political views of a number of young liberal Jews who were not satisfied with the "bourgeois" social customs of their respective countries, or of Israel. The kibbutz was an effort to implement an ideal socialist, communal style of living. It is quite liberal in its definition of the respective roles of males, females, and families in society.

10   It has been noted that the Amish are slowly following the path to modernization, especially in their outlying fringe communities. It must also be pointed out that in recent years, there has been a trend away from the complete collectivization of the family roles in the kibbutz society, toward a more traditional understanding of the roles of male and female. Even though these two groups, which represent the conservative and liberal ends of the spectrum, are slowly converging towards common ground, they will probably forever remain, geographically and philosophically, worlds apart.   100

95

REVIEW | THE AMISH AND THE KIBBUTZIM

Comprehension

1. Which group does not allow premarital relations? *Amish.*

2. In which system are the males and females considered basically equal?

   Kibbutzim

3. The Amish established "Sunday-evening singings" for what purpose?

   for unmarried youth to have the opportunity to talk and get to know one another.

4. Which of the two groups is considered culturally conservative?

   Amish

5. Where did the Amish people come from? Why did they come to the United States?

   From Germany — to practice their religion.
   in the early days of America.

Textual Pattern: Comparison and Contrast

1. By presenting the similarities first and then the differences, which is the author trying to emphasize? Explain.

   The differences

2. This selection is an example of the third type of comparison and contrast: "same/different." In the space below list the similarities and differences that the author used in his comparison.

Similarities	Differences
religios heritage central role to agriculturd both follow the principle of taking care for the elderly (Bible and tradition) active positions respect and responsabilitg.	collective method of raising children family, mothers the "same than ma views of women at home. youth join together separated philosophy {a political, conservative political, socialist, communa

Skill Review: Word Analysis

Separate the prefixes, suffixes, and stems and identify the meaning or function of each.

counterparts	premarital	ultra-practical
coun-ter-parts	pre-marital	ultra-practical
	indicates: before	indicates
	relating to marriage	beyond the range of
		practical.
		relating to practice

Questions for Further Discussion/Composition

1. Earlier you wrote about minorities in your country. Are these minority people becoming more like those in the mainstream culture of your country? Do you think this is beneficial or not?

2. What problems are these minority cultures facing in your country? Who is at fault?

3. What benefits do minority cultures offer to the nations in which they reside?

4. What do you think a government's role should be in relation to minority races or cultures within its borders?

Comparison and Contrast: Equality

In the first two readings of this chapter, the authors were comparing the same subject by looking at how that subject had changed over time. The author of the next reading is comparing two different items.

In evaluating comparisons in advertisements, editorials, consumer reports, and so forth, readers must determine whether the writer/company is comparing items of equal class or category. For example, comparison of a lemon and a lime would be possible, since each item is a single type of citrus fruit. A comparative study entitled "Bananas and Tropical Fruit" would not be a logical comparison.

EXERCISE   Place a check mark next to topics in the following list that represent legitimate comparisons.

___✓___ a. Rugby and football	___✓___ k. Biology and science
_____ b. My dog and John's fish	_____ l. My two dogs
___✓___ c. Boy George and Julio Iglesias	___✓___ m. A tiger and a lion
___✓___ d. Harvard and Oxford	_____ n. France and Africa
_____ e. The weather in Paris and Moscow	___✓___ o. Venus and Mars
_____ f. Country and city living	_____ p. The number of students at Harvard and Oxford
_____ g. My neighbor and Americans	_____ q. A French wine and a French cheese
_____ h. German and Japanese cassette recorders	_____ r. Jazz and punk rock
_____ i. Butterflies and caterpillars	_____ s. Elvis Presley and break dancing
_____ j. A knife and a pencil sharpener	_____ t. Beethoven and John Lennon
	_____ u. Elephants and giraffes

Understanding Line Graphs

As we mentioned before, there is more than one type of graph. The second type that we will focus on is the line graph. In this type of graph a series of points are connected in order to make the pattern clearer.

Let's go back to some familiar data—the percentages of married men and women for the years 1975 through 1980. We have seen these data represented in the form of a table. Now let's see the same information in a line graph.

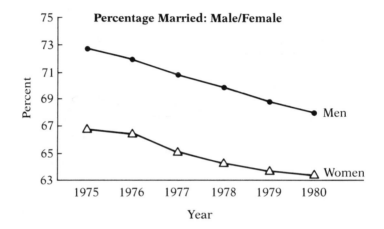

Notice that the two lines connect different types of points. This makes the data easier to read. It is the same principle we use when we shade different sets of bars in bar graphs. Bar graphs may be difficult to read if there are many points along the line of progression. In such cases researchers and business personnel use line graphs.

PREVIEW | MARRIAGE IN IRAN AND AMERICA:
A STUDY IN CONTRASTS

Things to Think About

1. Have you ever been to a marriage ceremony in your country? What was it like? If you've been to more than one, were they basically the same?

_____

_____

_____

2. What sort of preparation leads to the ceremony? Who is responsible for various aspects of the preparation?

_____

_____

_____

_____

3. Have you ever attended a marriage in another country? If so, how was it different from the ones you attended in your country?

_____

_____

_____

_____

4. What happens to newlyweds in your culture immediately after the marriage ceremony?

_____

_____

_____

_____

Vocabulary in Context

1. "I've lived in the U.S. for four years now, but I'm still not comfortable with the **courtship** customs here. In fact, what seems strange to me is that **courting** or dating is not always for the purpose of finding a husband or wife. Some people seem to do it as a hobby."

*to court*_____

2. "In Iran, courtship is more serious, and is performed strictly for the purpose of marriage. It is definitely not a part of the fun-filled years of growing up like it is here in America. It is the mother of the young man who **initiates** the process by visiting the home of a **potential** bride."

*to initiate*_____

*potential*_____

3. "Two **mullahs**, or Islamic religious leaders, stand outside the door to this room reading from the Koran."

mullah _____

Preview

1. The title of the reading announces the objects of comparison quite clearly. From the title, what seems to be the emphasis, similarities or differences?

    _____

    _____

2. Read the first sentence of each paragraph. Of the three patterns of comparison we have studied in this chapter, which one has the author used?

    _____

3. After reading the conclusion, what would you say is the personal opinion of the author?

    _____

    _____

    _____

READING FOUR

Marriage in Iran and America: A Study in Contrasts

1   Though marriage is practiced in almost all countries of the world, the customs surrounding this ritual are quite different from one culture to another. It is interesting for me to compare the customs of marriage in the United States with those in my country.

2   I've lived in the U.S. for four years now, but I'm still not comfortable with the courtship customs here. In fact, what seems strange to me is that courting or dating is not always for the purpose of finding a husband or wife. Some people seem to do it as a hobby.

3   Here in the United States, I have noticed that courtships are begun by the young couple themselves, and they seem to have a lot of freedom to decide and do what they want. Both young men and women date a number of different people. They do it without the knowledge or help of their parents. In fact, I have known several friends who got married without even telling their parents or other family members.

4   Once a couple is serious about marriage, however, the young man gives the girl an engagement ring (usually a diamond) if he can afford it. This ring makes their intentions "official." During this engagement period, the two usually agree not to court other people. The couple spends time planning for their wedding, sometimes with the help of their families.

5   At the actual wedding ceremony, the father of the bride sym-
bolically gives his daughter to the groom. It's only a custom, I think,
because the bride and groom already know each other quite well.
The bride and groom stand together in front of the religious leader   25
or government official to be married. The official reads from a short
prepared speech and then asks both the man and woman if they are
willing to be married to the other. If they both say "yes," and
nobody attending the wedding stands up to object, they are
declared "man and wife." It is interesting that the two families are   30
asked if there are any objections right during the ceremony. Perhaps
it is because the family members are not as involved in the wedding
preparations as they are in Iran.

6   Marriage is different in a number of ways in my country. In Iran,
courtship is more serious, and is performed strictly for the purpose   35
of marriage. It is definitely not a part of the fun-filled years of growing up like it is here in America. It is the mother of the young man
who initiates the process by visiting the home of a potential bride.
She goes to inspect the girl, and discover the position and wealth of
the girl's family. If she is pleased, then she will return another day   40
with her son. If her son is also pleased, then the two families get
together to talk about the dowry, the wedding ceremony, who they
will hire to perform the marriage, any festivities, and other matters.

7   Then begins what Americans would call the engagement period.
During this period, several gifts are sent by the groom's family to   45
the future bride. The first gift is usually a diamond ring, similar to
the American custom. After that follow other gifts. A beautiful illustrated copy of the Koran is given, as well as other expensive items
that represent the best of our culture and art, like delicately carved
silver candlesticks, chests, etc. Meanwhile, the bride spends her   50
time with her mother preparing the dowry.

8   The actual marriage ceremony is quite different however, from
the American wedding ceremonies I have seen. In Iran we follow
Islamic customs since we are all Moslems. The bride, dressed in
white, with a veil over her face, sits in another room alone. She sits   55
on a special piece of Persian silk which is surrounded on two sides
by very long pieces of flat bread. Two mullahs, or Islamic religious
leaders, stand outside the door to this room reading from the Koran.
Twice the bride must remain silent to the questions of the mullahs.
The groom's mother then presents a gift of gold, such as a pair of   60
bracelets, to show that her side of the family is serious. The bride
then responds to the mullahs in much the same manner as do Americans when they say "I do." There is much rejoicing and applause at
this point but the couple does not kiss in public as I have seen them
do here in America. The groom is allowed to go into the bride's room   65
and they are left alone behind a drawn curtain while the mullahs
take care of the official marriage papers.

9   One more difference between the marriage customs of the
United States and my country is that the bride does not immediately go to the home of her new husband. For several months, she   70
continues to stay at her own home preparing her dowry and receiving instructions from her mother on how to be a good wife and

mother. After a few months, the groom and his relatives come for
the bride and take her to his home along with the dowry.

10   Though I can certainly see the advantages of the freedom that is   75
given to American youths to choose whom they will marry and
when, I think I still prefer the customs of my home country. I suppose that's because there is not so much guessing and uncertainty.
In Iran families are so much more involved in helping us through
this difficult stage of life. I guess that's why I'm not married yet.   80

REVIEW | MARRIAGE IN IRAN AND AMERICA: A STUDY IN CONTRASTS

Comprehension

1. Who is "I" in this personal essay? _The author,_
    _____

2. According to the author, there is a fundamental difference between
    Iran and the United States in the purposes of courtship. Explain.
    Fun -

3. Though the customs of the United States and Iran seem quite dif-
    ferent, the author did mention some similarities. What are they?
    _____

    _____

4. What is the author's final opinion after making the comparison?
    the prefers his home country customs.

5. Is the author of this article male or female? _Male_

    How do you know this from reading the article? _Because_
    uses to be the man who decides to get married or not.

Skill Review: Detecting Sequence

Without looking back at the passage, try to recall the sequence of
events in a typical Iranian marriage ceremony and write it down in the
space provided below.

_____

_____

_____

_____

Skill Review: Vocabulary

Divide the following words into their respective parts and define the meaning or function of each part.

uncertainty   festivities

_____   _____

_____   _____

_____   _____

_____   _____

Textual Pattern: Comparison and Contrast

1. Did you answer the preview question correctly concerning which pattern of comparison and contrast the author used?

_____

_____

2. Why do you think the author chose this pattern to make the comparison?

_____

_____

3. Outline the respective customs of the two countries. Not all items will have counterparts on the other side of the chart.

Iran	United States

Questions for Further Discussion/Composition

1. A major difference that this author sees between the two countries is the amount of family involvement in courting. How much freedom or support do you personally feel is ideal?

2. In light of your answer to question 1, do you prefer the customs of your own culture or those of Iran or possibly the United States?

3. Compare courting customs in Iran to those in your country.

Understanding Pie Graphs

The third and last type of graph that we will look at is the pie graph. Pie graphs are used when one wishes to show how several parts make up the whole. Pie graphs are an effective way to show percentages. In the case of the percentages of married men during the years 1975 to 1980, a pie graph could not be used because these percentages do not represent parts of a whole. Percentages representing the age groups of the men who got married in any particular year could be converted into a pie graph.

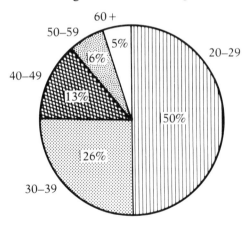

Age of Men at Marriage

Show the following information on the empty pie graph provided on page 133. Shade each category with a different color or design to make it easier for your readers.

Marital status of American men:

Single	Married	Widowed	Divorced
23.5%	68.6%	2.7%	5.2%

Marital Status of American Men

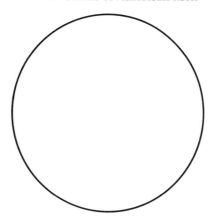

You will probably notice that you were not able to make the slices of the pie exactly accurate in terms of their percentages. They don't have to be, since the percentages are usually written in. The reader must realize that pie graphs are used to make the relative relationships between the various groups clearer through an appeal to the visual sense of the reader. At a glance we "understand" what would take quite a lot longer to read in table form.

PREVIEW | FAMILY LIFE IN THE PEOPLE'S REPUBLIC OF CHINA—THEN AND NOW

Things to Think About

Write two specific things that your family does that are different from what was done a generation ago when your parents were young. Here are some examples.

Your sister is allowed to go to college.

Your mother works outside the home.

Your grandparents do not live with you as grandparents often did a generation ago.

_____

_____

_____

Vocabulary in Context

1. "The new official ideal of one child per family is gaining in popularity. Pines (1981) reported that approximately 70 percent of the children in some Shanghai schools have no **siblings**."

   *siblings*_____

2. "Divorce in traditional China was rare and generally only a male **prerogative**. The 1950 Marriage Law gave women, as well as men, the right to divorce for quite liberal grounds similar to America's no-fault."

   *prerogative*_____

3. "... by 1953, the increased number of divorce and marital disputes generated considerable opposition and even violence, such that a more conservative policy was adopted.... Basically the policy stressed more **mediation** prior to divorce. By the late 1970's, local cadres and officials tried very hard to solve marital problems and preserve marriages through **mediation**, even when both partners wanted a divorce. Such **mediation**, along with pressure from community and friends, appears to be quite successful."

   *mediation*_____

4. "Distinctions between **gentry** and **peasantry**, urban and rural, are helpful in understanding the variety of family patterns within the concept of a traditional Chinese family. China has always been primarily rural and even today, 80 percent of the Chinese live in a rural setting. On the other hand, there was also an upper-class minority, the gentry, characterized by wealth and freedom from manual labor, who were the intellectuals, the landowners, and the officials."

   *gentry*_____

   *peasantry*_____

Vocabulary Study List

Study the following terms. They are important in the scientific study and description of types of family organization.

1. **nuclear family:** parents and children

2. **extended family:** family structure composed of several nuclear families and generations

3. **patriarchal:** father, or oldest male member, is the dominant member of the organization (**matri-**, mother)

4. **patrilocal:** married couple resides near or with husband's father's household (**matri-**, wife's)

5. **monogamy:** the custom of marrying only one spouse

6. **polygamy:** the practice of being married to more than one spouse

7. **stem family:** one married child and his or her nuclear family

8. **joint family:** several married children and their respective families living together in the same household

9. **betrothal:** formal acceptance, permission, or promise of marriage

10. **concubine:** a woman who lives with a man without being his legally married wife. (Some cultures allow a man to have one or more concubines in addition to his legal wife. The purpose is often to give the man more sons.)

11. **filial piety:** proper devotion or respect for one's parents

Preview

1. Read the abstract at the beginning of this reading selection. What exactly is the author going to compare?

   _____

   _____

   _____

   _____

2. What is meant by pre-revolutionary China?_____

   _____

3. What conclusions does the author make about the comparison in the abstract?

   _____

   _____

   _____

   _____

4. Read the major subheadings in the passage. Of the three forms of comparison that we have studied in this chapter, which pattern has the author used for this selection on family life in the People's Republic of China?

   _____

5. As you read the selection, underline helpful phrases of comparison and contrast used by the author.

   Note: The Revolution spoken of in this reading refers to the Communist Revolution of 1949.

READING FIVE

FAMILY LIFE IN THE PEOPLE'S REPUBLIC OF CHINA—
THEN AND NOW

Abstract

1   For nearly 2000 years, Chinese male-female relationships and family life were guided by a set of ideals supported by tradition, religion, and legislation. In more recent times, dramatic efforts have been made by the Communist government to change those tradi-   5 tional ideals and to bring about revolutionary changes in family life. This paper compares the male-female relationships and family life of traditional pre-revolutionary China with those of the contemporary People's Republic of China, and analyzes evidence of both continuity and change.   10

Introduction

2   Male-female relationships and family life in China have fascinated Western scholars since the time and travels of Marco Polo. Surely some of this fascination resulted from the geographical and

Adapted with permission from John W. Engel, *Changes in Male-Female Relationships and Family Life in the People's Republic of China* (Honolulu, Hawaii: College of Tropical Agriculture and Human Resources, University of Hawaii), Research Series 014. July 1982.

political insulation that kept China closed to the West for much of   15
recorded history. As China cautiously opened its door to Western
trade and concomitant scrutiny, observations of family life and
male-female relationships continued to interest Western social scientists, if for no other reason than that Chinese traditions and
customs appeared so different from those of the West.   20

3   With the victory of the Communist forces in 1949, the door to
China was effectively closed again. Nevertheless, refugees provided
evidence that the Communist revolution also involved revolutionary changes in male-female relationships and family life. The 1950
Marriage Law attempted to abolish the traditional Chinese family   25
system and establish in its place a new set of ideals for male-female
relations and family life. Social scientific investigations and documentation of revolutionary change in Chinese family life were made
more difficult, for the Chinese as well as for the West, by the
1966–1976 Cultural Revolution, when universities were closed and   30
social scientists were sent into the countryside to work as peasants.
Since the end of the Cultural Revolution and "normalization" of
relations with the West, however, the door to China is opening
again. Social scientists and scholars have new opportunities to
learn about contemporary Chinese family life, to identify con-   35
tinuities with the traditions of the past and to analyze the changes
that have accompanied the Communist revolution.

4   Recent observations of Chinese family life suggest that, while
there is much evidence of revolutionary change, the past pervades
the present. Revolutionary change in family life is an important   40
topic for social scientific inquiry and is receiving more and more
attention in the literature. Nevertheless, in the case of China, the
continuation of tradition in spite of governmental efforts to bring
about revolutionary changes is equally important and deserves
attention. Therefore, this treatise on male-female relationships and   45
family life in China begins with a description of family life and
ideals in traditional (prerevolutionary and feudal) China. The Com-
munists' ideals and attempts to bring about revolutionary change in
family life are summarized. And finally, contemporary male-female
relationships and family life in the People's Republic of China are   50
described and analyzed in terms of continuities with tradition as
well as in terms of revolutionary change.

I. MALE-FEMALE RELATIONSHIPS AND FAMILY
LIFE IN TRADITIONAL PRE-REVOLUTIONARY CHINA

5   The traditional Chinese family, from the perspective of someone   55
from the West, appears to be a model of strength and stability.
Indeed, scholars suggest that the Chinese family remained relatively unchanged for 2000 years. The concept of a "traditional Chinese family" requires qualification, however. Just as there is no
single family pattern in America that universally depicts "the Amer-   60
ican family," there is similarly no single "Chinese" family.

6   Distinctions between gentry and peasantry, urban and rural, are

helpful in understanding the variety of family patterns within the concept of a traditional family. China has always been primarily rural and even today, 80 percent of the Chinese live in a rural set- 65
ting. On the other hand, there was also an upper-class minority, the gentry, characterized by wealth and freedom from manual labor, who were the intellectuals, the landowners, and the officials. The gentry's family life and ideals were referred to in the literature, songs, laws, and official records of the time. Apparently there was 70
enough upward mobility for peasants to aspire to gentry status; and ᶠupper-class family patterns became the ideal for peasants as well, even though in reality the ideal could seldom be attained. Primarily, then, the concept of a traditional Chinese family refers to the family life of a gentry class in pre-revolutionary China. 75

7   The Confucian classic, the *Li Chi* (Book of Rites), provides a view of traditional ideals for family life, roles, and rituals. In general, the traditional (ideal) Chinese family was a large extended family with as many generations as possible living together. Several married sons lived with their parents in a joint family structure, which was 80
both patrilocal, that is, brides left their families to live with the families of their husbands, and patriarchal, in that the father was the dominant member who held the power within the family. . . .

Mate Selection and Marriage

8   Marriage, in the traditional ideal, was arranged by parents or 85
parental representatives such as a family elder, matchmaker, or go-between. Young people themselves had no choice in the matter, and sometimes met for the first time on their wedding day (referred to as "blind marriage"). Marriage was seen as a contract between families rather than between individuals. Its primary purpose was con- 90
tinuation of the family line. . . .

9   Because traditional Chinese marriage was a contract between families rather than between individuals, mate selection was based on family needs and interests rather than on the young couple's attraction, love, or emotional involvement. Personal attraction and 95
love between bride and groom were considered unnecessary if not harmful. . . .

10   The next step in the marriage process, betrothal, was typically accomplished through the transfer of gifts. Acceptance of the gifts was followed by the signing of a betrothal contract by family heads. 100

11   Following betrothal, a favorable date for the wedding was determined with the help of a fortune-teller. The wedding was primarily a ritualistic transfer of the bride from one family to another. . . .

Marital and Extramarital Relations

12   "The purpose of marriage is creation . . . the marriage is a 105
failure if it is childless." Productions of sons was a matter of filial piety. To continue the family line, men had to marry and have sons, who were responsible for continuance of the family's ancestor worship; this was the way a young man guaranteed being worshiped as an ancestor himself. Sons were necessary also to provide for parents 110
in their old age. Daughters were not necessary, since they would

leave the family at marriage. Women gained respect and prestige within the family and earned better treatment from their mothers-in-law by having sons. Each son, through marriage, expanded the family's size, resources, and wealth. Fertile couples tried to have 115 many sons to reach the traditional ideal of a large family.

13   Having concubines or mistresses was an acceptable and relatively common method of expanding the family in traditional China, particularly for the upper classes. Concubinage also served as a safety valve in the traditional Chinese family. It provided some 120 relief from the very carefully prescribed behaviors for men's roles in the family. The concubine was often chosen by the fellow himself on the basis of personal attraction and romance, in contrast to the mate-selection process in the arranged marriage. The relationships were characterized by love, romance, and eroticism. . . .   125

Divorce

14   Divorce in traditional pre-revolutionary China occurred in three different ways: by mutual consent, by initiative of the husband (rarely the wife), and under compulsion by the authorities. The interests of the family and clan were considered first and more 130 important than those of the individuals concerned. Divorce by mutual consent was hardly the no-fault divorce common in the United States today. Rather, in traditional China, marriages were dissolved through the mutual agreement of patriarchs or family heads and not by the couple themselves. In general, divorces were 135 relatively rare. They were perceived to be very tragic experiences, particularly for the women involved. . . .

II. MALE-FEMALE RELATIONSHIPS AND FAMILY LIFE IN CONTEMPORARY CHINA

15   A comprehensive view of male-female relationships and family 140 life in contemporary China includes evidence of continuity with the past as well as evidence of change towards something new. As in the description of the traditional Chinese family, where a distinction between the upper-class gentry and the lower-class peasants provided clarity, a distinction between rural and urban is helpful in 145 understanding contemporary forms of Chinese family life. The rural majority, approximately 80 percent, has maintained the greatest continuity with the ideals of the past, whereas more change has occurred within the cities.

Contemporary Chinese Family and Household Structure   150

16   The contemporary rural Chinese family can be seen as a mixture of both old and new. Parish and White's (1978) data on families in rural Kwangtung (Canton area) indicated that the traditionally ideal joint-family structure has become quite rare, whereas stem, nuclear, or stem and associated-nuclear family combinations are 155 more common. Patrilocal residence patterns still appear to be the norm in rural areas. Parents expect to be supported by their sons in

old age and continue to be highly motivated to have sons. Infant
mortality has decreased, however, with the advent of land reform,
collectivization, and birth control efforts to the extent that there is   160
no longer the need or motivation for many sons.

17   Aging parents still live with their sons and grandchildren, but in
a stem family (with one son and his wife and children) rather than
in a joint family (with several sons and their families). Other sons
and their nuclear families, while not living in the same household,   165
often live in the same compound or adjacent buildings, and maintain close associative and cooperative links. . . .

18   In the cities, change in family structure appears more dramatic.
A shortage of housing makes it very difficult for families to maintain
traditional household proximity as in rural areas. Birth-control   170
education and motivation efforts have been more imperative and
effective in urban areas. The new official ideal of one child per family is gaining in popularity. Pines (1981) reported that approximately 70 percent of children in some Shanghai schools have no
siblings.   175

Mate Selection and Marriage

19   In contrast to the mate selection of traditional China, in which
parents made arrangements without consulting the young people
themselves, mate selection in contemporary China is becoming
more like the free-choice system taken for granted in the West.   180

20   The other extreme, in which the young people take the initiative
and parents are not consulted, is also rare. More commonly, if parents take the initiative, their children are consulted and have veto
power. On the other hand, if the young couple takes the initiative,
their parents are usually consulted and have veto power. Very few   185
couples marry in defiance of their parents' wishes. Nevertheless,
extreme examples are occasionally reported in the popular
press. . . .

21   While there does appear to be a trend towards more free mate
choice, many of the traditional restrictions and taboos still exist,   190
and they severely limit the opportunities for meeting and having
contact with eligible partners. For example, in exogamy, the traditional taboo against marriage with someone of the same lineage is
often translated in terms of a taboo against marriage with someone
of the same village. Parish and White (1978) found that over 50   195
percent of their Kwangtung villages still maintained this taboo. In
such places, young people must look for and select an outsider. At
the same time, the opportunities for meeting and getting to know
young people from the other villages are very limited, because education is provided locally, work involves relatively small teams of   200
workers, and immigration to larger towns and cities is restricted.
Thus, the amount of free mate choice appears to be limited by the
lack of opportunities for meeting eligible partners. City dwellers
have many more opportunities in this regard, and thus the trend
toward free mate choice is stronger in the cities.   205

22   The trend toward free mate choice is also restricted by limited
opportunities to become acquainted with eligible partners once

they are introduced. In rural areas, the traditional taboos against pairing off and public displays of affection are still enforced through teasing, ridicule, and gossip. Urban young people have more ano- 210 nymity and, therefore, a bit more freedom to break taboos without suffering social consequences. . . .

23   Where opportunities to meet and develop relationships with eligible mates are limited, young people depend upon others to arrange a meeting. In 74 percent of Parish and White's (1978) 215 Kwangtung villages, professional matchmakers still provided services for a fee, although matchmaking for profit has been denounced by the authorities. During the Cultural Revolution of 1966–1976, matchmakers were singled out for criticism and confiscation of fees. Their survival is in itself evidence for the need for their services. 220 There appears to be a trend, however, towards decreased use of professional matchmaking services and a trend towards increased use of arranged introductions by friends and relatives. Friends or relatives who arrange such introductions are expected to do much of the work of the professional, including investigation of character, 225 honesty, and family background. Parish and White (1978) reported 80 percent of marriages in the Kwangtung sample had had some sort of arranged introduction. While this can be interpreted as continuing the traditional arrangement of marriage, it can also be interpreted in terms of change—a trend away from the time when 230 all marriages were arranged, toward less formal arrangements and towards more self- or independent selection. . . .

24   Marriages by purchase, concubinage, and child betrothal were prohibited by the 1950 Marriage Law. Parish and White (1978) suggested that concubinage and child betrothal have virtually disap- 235 peared in rural areas, although payment of the bride-price appears to be very common if not universal.

25   The Communist government tried to eliminate the bride-price custom for various reasons: it was considered feudal and capitalistic, as if a bride were being purchased, and it perpetuated 240 inappropriate class inequalities by basing mate selection on wealth or buying power. Despite government efforts, however, payment of bride-price is quite common. It appears to be even more difficult economically for the groom and his family than it was in the past. In traditional China, much of the bride-price was returned to the 245 groom's family as part of the dowry. In contemporary China, however, the bride-price is kept by the bride's family, to finance the marriage of a son, rather than returned as dowry. . . .

Wedding Rituals

26   Weddings in contemporary China show dramatic change as well 250 as aspects of continuity with the past. The official press in China depicts an ideal in which a couple falls in love, decides to marry, goes to the government office to register the marriage, and returns home to set up house with very little ceremony or expense. While such weddings may become more and more common in the cities, 255 they appear to be quite rare in the countryside.

27   Rural weddings tend to involve considerable ceremony and

expense. Both families have wedding feasts. Astrologers and for-
tune-tellers no longer have an important part. Bicycles have been
substituted for sedan chairs, but the bride is still fetched with some   260
fanfare and transported to her new home with her husband's family.
There is still some teasing on the wedding night by guests before
young couples can be alone together. Thus, while weddings exhibit
continuity within change, change is more dramatic in the cities
than in the countryside.   265

Divorce and Remarriage

28   Divorce in traditional China was rare and generally only a male
prerogative. The 1950 Marriage Law gave women, as well as men,
the right to divorce for quite liberal grounds similar to America's
no-fault. According to Parish and White (1978), by 1953, the   270
increased number of divorce and marital disputes generated considerable opposition and even violence, such that a more conservative
policy was adopted while the law itself was left unchanged.
Basically the policy stressed more mediation prior to divorce. By
the late 1970's, local cadres and officials tried very hard to solve   275
marital problems and preserve marriages through mediation, even
when both partners wanted a divorce. Such mediation, along with
pressure from community and friends, appears to be quite successful. In 1980 in Peking, of 2,131 applications for divorce in the
first seven months of the year, 923 were withdrawn after mediation.   280
While divorce in rural China appears to be infrequent, when it does
occur, the reasons are usually economic, and the woman demands
the divorce. . . .

Discussion of Limitations and Conclusions

29   Current information about male-female relationships and fam-   285
ily life in contemporary China is limited by the fact that China was
closed to Western science for nearly 30 years. . . .

30   In addition, any conclusions or generalizations about contemporary family life in China are seriously limited by the fact that China
is still undergoing dramatic change. A new marriage law and a one-   290
child family law are being tested. The population and related economic problems require immediate attention and drastic action.
Surely change will continue, while some continuity with traditions
will be maintained.

REVIEW | FAMILY LIFE IN THE PEOPLE'S REPUBLIC OF CHINA—THEN AND NOW

Comprehension

1. True or false? The 1950 Marriage Law has had less effect on urban areas than on rural areas. _____

2. True or false? Since the revolution, the rate of divorce has decreased slightly. _____

3. True or false? In general, pre-revolutionary China was characterized by small nuclear families living together or in closely related villages. _____

4. According to the reading, why was it important to have sons in traditional China? (Circle all correct responses.)

   a. To support the parents in their old age.
   b. To show respect and bring happiness to the wife's parents.
   c. Because so many died in the constant wars and famines.
   d. To guarantee a continual ancestor worship.
   e. To increase the wealth and power of a clan.
   f. Because of the high mortality rate in the rural areas.

5. True or false? The 1950 Marriage Law eliminated the bride-price customs because it was seen as capitalistic. _____

6. True or false? Like modernization, changes in family traditions have been most dramatic in urban areas. _____

Textual Pattern: Comparison and Contrast

1. What pattern of comparison did the author use? _____

   _____

2. Write a brief summary for each of the following aspects of family life in the People's Republic of China.

   Matchmaking_____

   _____

   _____

   Divorce_____

   _____

   _____

Wedding ceremony_____

_____

_____

Household structure_____

_____

_____

Urban vs. rural (pre-revolutionary times)_____

_____

_____

Urban vs. rural (modern times)_____

_____

_____

Questions for Further Discussion/Composition

1. Earlier you described two specific aspects of family life that have changed since your parents were young. In your particular culture are these changes for the better?

2. What further changes do you hope will take place soon?

3. If you were to recommend one custom of marriage or family life in your culture to others, what would it be?

Reminder: With each reading in this text so far, you have been given preview or prereading exercises and activities. These have been designed to make you aware of what you already know about a topic and how that may be related to your own life. Remember, increased awareness before reading makes a stronger foundation for comprehension. Learning in general is the process of relating new information to what we already know.

CHAPTER 4

*In nature
there are neither
rewards or punishments—
there are consequences.*

—Robert G. Ingersoll,
"Some Reasons Why"

ECOLOGY

It was during the 1960s that ecology, a small and relatively unimportant branch of biology, rose to the attention of the United States public. Science and medicine had made great advances in making human life easier, longer, and more comfortable. People became so reliant on technology that they were sure science could solve almost any problem. In the early 1960s, however, as populations became larger and open space less available, people started to realize that there was one problem technology didn't have a quick-fix solution for—the mistreatment of the environment.

The science of ecology studies the ways humans can live in harmony with their natural environment—ways humans can exist on this planet without destroying the very systems that sustain life. Nature abides by very strict laws and an extremely delicate check and balance system. When those laws and that system are upset, the results can be devastating. It is an ecologist's job to see to it that the laws and system are not violated.

The readings in this chapter discuss such ecological topics as pollution, the balance between nature and humans, the effects of pesticides on nature, and the effects of a natural disaster on our environment.

CAUSE AND EFFECT

Each of us has some concept of causes and effects because they are an unavoidable part of our lives. Almost everything we do is related to cause/effect, from turning on a light switch to parking our car in a no parking zone. Each action has a reaction.

Cause and effect is a very common pattern of discourse in scientific reporting and liberal art studies. The aim of science from its early beginning has been to understand natural causes and effects. Scientists are constantly trying to refine their understanding of natural causes and effects in order to make human existence better. It would be impossible to study ecology without some understanding of causes and effects.

Your understanding of how writers present cause/effect relationships in magazine articles, textbooks, and other reading sources will determine how well you understand what you read. The lessons in this chapter are intended to teach you some of the basic patterns found in cause/effect reading material.

MAIN IDEA

Being able to read a passage, no matter how large or small, and then retell in your own words what you have read is an essential reading skill. Such a skill is often referred to as "getting the main idea." The skill lessons and exercises in this chapter are intended to help you understand main ideas in sentences and paragraphs.

Cause/Effect: Distinguishing Between Causes and Effects

Before you study the cause-and-effect patterns used by writers, it is first necessary to be able to distinguish between causes and effects. A cause can best be identified as something that makes something else happen. For example, turning on a light switch will cause an expected event— the light comes on. A chemical company dumping waste products in a river will most likely cause a disruption of the river's ecological balance. An effect or result, on the other hand, is the thing or condition that results from the cause. In the case of the light switch, the electricity running to the bulb and the eventual light are the effects or results of turning on the switch. Some of the effects of the dumping of wastes in the river could be the contamination of drinking water and the deaths of fish and other aquatic life.

EXERCISE

A. One of the columns below is a list of causes and the other is a list of effects. Identify which column represents causes and which represents effects. Then draw lines connecting the related causes and effects.

_____	_____
Overuse of pesticides	Fish can no longer reach spawning grounds upstream
Building a dam across a river	Possible extinction
Destroying all predators of the deer population	Insects become resistant to chemicals
Allowing animals to overgraze grassland	Overpopulation of the herds
Allowing hunters to kill animals freely	More serious air pollution
Dumping toxic chemicals into freshwater lakes	Lakes become barren of fish
Factories burning coal without filters on the smokestacks	Serious land erosion

B. Each of the following passages has at least one cause and one effect; most have several causes and effects. In the space provided, list as many causes and effects as you can find.

1. Deadly chemical leaks are much more common in the United States than most people realize. According to recent reports from the government, there are at least four serious leaks each day in the United States. The direct effects of this escape of chemicals into the environment are devastating. In the last five years, because of toxic chemical leaks at least 135 deaths have occurred, an estimated

4,700 injuries have resulted, and nearly 200,000 people have been forced from their homes.

Causes	Effects
_____	_____
_____	_____
_____	_____
_____	_____
_____	_____

2. Pristine lakes far from civilization are dying. Certain rivers and lakes in Canada can no longer sustain the fish that they once could. Trees along the Camel's Hump in Vermont's Green Mountains are withering and dying. Many of the rivers and lakes in the Adirondacks are nothing but lifeless bodies of water. And the air quality in Boston and other eastern U.S. cities is getting worse almost daily. All of this destruction to the environment can be linked to acid rain—the highly toxic form of air pollution released by power plants, automobiles, and industrial smelters.

Causes	Effects
_____	_____
_____	_____
_____	_____
_____	_____

3. Dioxin, a man-made substance used in different forms of pesticides, is perhaps the most deadly toxic chemical known today. When this deadly substance is used even at extremely low levels (a few parts per billion or even per trillion), it has devastating effects on laboratory animals. The consequences of the presence of dioxins in the air have been obvious. Cancer, miscarriages, birth defects, and even death have all been attributed to the use of dioxin.

Causes	Effects
_____	_____
_____	_____
_____	_____
_____	_____
_____	_____

Cause/Effect: Author's Emphasis

Causes and effects are not easy to analyze. An error commonly made when analyzing causes and effects is to oversimplify. It is usually incorrect to assume that a single factor caused a single situation. For example, when fish in a river start to die, we speculate on the cause. Some say the flood last spring destroyed the fish food growing in the river; others may say the chemicals dumped in the river by the XYZ Chemical Company have killed the fish. Others may speculate that new roads and home development along the river have destroyed the natural habitat of the fish. The truth of the matter is that perhaps none, all, or a combination of these causes have resulted in the death of the fish. Very seldom is a condition the result of just one factor. Good authors realize that cause/effect relationships are difficult to analyze and even more difficult to write about. The reader has to be very careful not to oversimplify or overlook important causes and effects.

In short, the causes and effects of a situation can be reported by an author in many different ways. The way they get reported is determined by what the author chooses to emphasize. The variety of possibilities can be seen in the following situation:

John was walking home from the store with his arms full of packages when a car came around the corner and hit him. As a result, John was in the hospital for two weeks with a brain concussion and a broken leg.

If an author wanted to report on John's situation, there are several possible ways in which it could be reported. The writer could **emphasize the causes** of John's condition. An outline of a passage emphasizing causes only might look something like this:

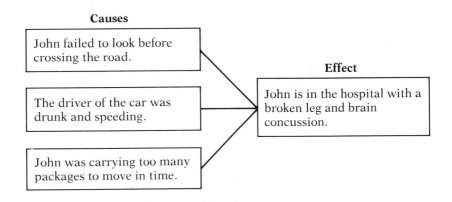

An author could likewise **emphasize only the effects** of John's situation. A diagram of the effects only might look like this:

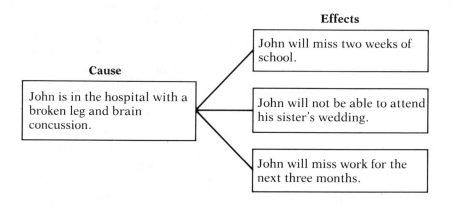

Both causes and effects of a situation could also be **emphasized** by an author.

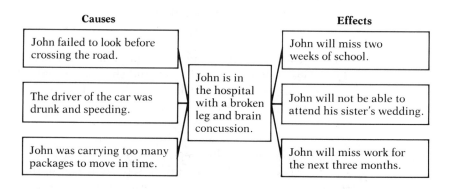

Perhaps the most common of all patterns is the **cause/effect chain** or **the causal chain.** This occurs when an author attempts to emphasize how one event or action causes another event or action which in turn causes another, and so forth. This is sometimes called the domino effect. One way of diagramming a cause/effect chain is shown below.

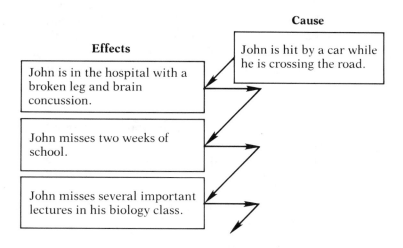

The cause/effect chain reaction is often used in conjunction with other patterns. For example, an author may be emphasizing the effects of John's accident but may still show how one of the effects led to other effects. This could be diagrammed in this way:

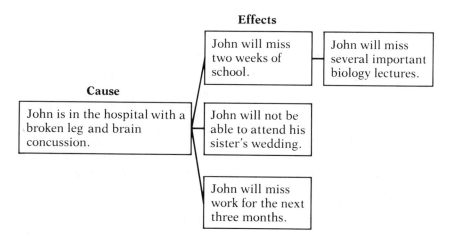

The way information gets presented and emphasized in a cause/effect passage depends on what the author's purpose is. For example, the third reading in this chapter, "Exploding Volcano: Full Impact Yet to Come," emphasizes the many effects of a single event—the eruption of Mount St. Helens. Another author might choose to write only about the causes of the fierce eruption. It is the author's purpose and focus that determine what gets emphasized.

EXERCISE The following paragraphs emphasize either the causes, the effects, the causes and effects, or the cause/effect chain reaction of a volcanic eruption. Read the paragraphs to determine what is being emphasized. Write your response in the blank provided. After you have determined the type of emphasis, read the paragraph again and list as many causes and effects as you can. Remember that one event can be both a cause and an effect if the author is emphasizing a chain reaction.

1. Volcanic eruptions brought about by groundwater coming in contact with volcanic heat are called phreatic eruptions. Such an eruption can happen in several ways. The most common occurrence is when magma that is working its way upwards encounters water in the rocks. Similarly, water can enter hot conduits of a volcano through cracks in the rocks. In both cases, the result is the same—a volcanic eruption.

   Cause/effect emphasis: _____

   Causes   *Effects*

   _____   _____

   _____   _____

   _____   _____

   _____   _____

   _____   _____

2. Many scientists are of the opinion that the eruption of Krakatoa, a small volcanic island near Jakarta, Indonesia, was a phreatic eruption. The volcano had been inactive for over two hundred years. For some unknown reason, however, the heat deep inside the volcano became extremely intense. The rise in temperature caused an increased flow of magma and fires throughout the arteries of the volcano. As this heat was driven outward, huge cracks began to open in the crater, allowing ocean water to pour in. The water and resulting steam forced the superheated magma further outward and upward. The steam and magma finally reached such an intense level of pressure that a release of some kind was necessary. The release of that pressure was the eruption and complete demolition of Krakatoa.

   Cause/effect emphasis: _____

Causes   *Effects*

_____   _____

_____   _____

_____   _____

_____   _____

_____   _____

3. When the small volcanic island of Krakatoa erupted, it unleashed some of the most destructive volcanic force ever recorded. The complete demolition of the island itself was only one of the many serious consequences of the eruption. The sound of the explosion carried over 5,000 kilometers. If the eruption had taken place in Hawaii, a person living in Chicago would have been able to hear it. There are reports of the sound being heard as far away as Australia, Manila, and Sri Lanka. In addition to the sound waves, atmospheric waves were altered worldwide. In Japan, for example, barometers registered pressure increases of 1.45 millibars. Perhaps the most devastating effects of the eruption were the enormous tidal waves that were generated. The largest of these waves swept across nearby islands in the Indian Ocean, killing an estimated 36,000 persons. The waves were of such force that they crossed both the Pacific and Atlantic Oceans. Tidal gauges as far as 17,000 kilometers away from Krakatoa registered the tidal waves. The gases and volcanic ash were far less destructive than the tidal waves. The gases and dust that were blown into the atmosphere lingered for nearly a year, producing spectacular sunsets. The heavy concentration of dust clouds in the Northern Hemisphere caused temperatures to drop as much as .8° Celsius below normal.

Cause/effect emphasis: _____

Causes   *Effects*

_____   _____

_____   _____

_____   _____

_____   _____

_____   _____

_____   _____

_____   _____

_____   _____

4. Many scientists today explain volcanic activity according to the theory of plate tectonics. Simply stated, the earth's crust forms the top layer of about twelve major plates, which range in thickness from 20 to 150 miles. These plates or sections are floating on a layer of partly molten rock. As the plates move in different directions they collide with each other, causing them to buckle against one another. As oceanic plates are buckled, they are driven down into a region of higher temperatures. These higher temperatures cause the rocks in the area to soften and melt. Also, as the plates are driven deeper, water may enter in behind, causing even greater pressure and more melting. The water and minerals unite with the melted rocks and form tear-shaped packets known as diapirs. Because they are more buoyant than surrounding rock, the diapirs float upward like bubbles. As these diapirs increase in frequency and intensity, the volcanic activity on the earth's surface also becomes more frequent and intense.

Cause/effect emphasis: _____

Causes   *Effects*

_____   _____

_____   _____

_____   _____

_____   _____

_____   _____

_____   _____

PREVIEW | A DELICATE BALANCE

Things to Think About

1. Where is the Nile River? _____

2. What possible effects would damming a river have on

   a. agriculture? _____

   _____

   b. animal and fish life? _____

   c. human habitat? _____

   _____

3. What would happen if an animal or insect had no natural enemies?

    _____

    _____

4. What is the meaning of *extinct*? _____

    _____

5. What are some of the factors that would cause a creature to become extinct?

    _____

    _____

6. What effect would a law prohibiting the killing of an animal have on

    a. that specific animal population? _____

    b. other animal populations? _____

    c. insect populations? _____

    _____

Preview

1. Quickly scan the reading for its length and structure.

2. The reading is divided into three major sections. What are they?

    _____   _____   _____

3. How might these three sections be related to the title? _____

    _____

    _____

4. Now scan the three sections for any clues to what the author is emphasizing (effects, causes, chain reaction, etc.).

    _____

Pete Seeger is the singer (folck)

READING ONE

A DELICATE BALANCE

1   In 1965 the American statesman Adlai E. Stevenson said, "We all travel together, passengers on a little spaceship, dependent on its vulnerable supplies of air and soil . . . we manage to survive by the care, work, and love we give our fragile craft." Our planet is indeed 5 fragile. Every living thing on this planet is part of a complicated web of life, for no organism lives entirely on its own. Every organism is affected by all that surrounds it whether living or nonliving. And in turn each organism has some effect on its surroundings.

metaphore

Earth - spaceship

2   Even the most elementary understanding of ecology requires knowledge of this cause/effect relationship all organisms have on 10 each other. Every thing we do to our environment will in one way or another affect the quality of life we experience on this tiny spaceship. If we want the quality of life to be high, we must be more aware that nature is a finely balanced mechanism and that it will not tolerate the abuse we have been giving it. Consider the following 15 examples of human ignorance concerning the delicate balance of nature.

main idea

Three examples of human ignorance

ASWAN AND OTHER FABLES

3   "Once there was a country that desperately needed food and energy for its growing population. It happened that one of the most 20 magnificent rivers in the world flowed through this country. Each year the river deposited tons of mineral-rich silt on its fertile floodplain before it reached the sea. Why not dam the river, said the country's leaders, and use the water to irrigate more land, control the annual spring flooding of the river, and provide hydroelectric 25 power all at the same time? The result of this modern-day fairy tale is known as the billion-dollar Aswan High Dam of Egypt, and not all Egyptians are living happily ever after.

4   "For one thing, as water backed up behind the dam, almost 100,000 Egyptians had to choose between giving up their family 30 homes or being submerged along with ancient and priceless temples that were part of Egypt's cultural heritage. But there have been far more devastating results. Now that the Nile River floodplain is deprived of its annual enrichment with silt, artificial fertilizer has

Paragraphs 3–5 from Cecie Starr and Ralph Taggart, *Biology: The Unity and Diversity of Life*, 2nd ed. (Belmont, Calif.: Wadsworth Publishing Co., 1981), pp. 532–534, © 1981 by Wadsworth, Inc. Reprinted by permission of the publisher.

Paragraphs 10 and 11 from *Extinction: The Causes and Consequences of the Disappearance of Species* by Paul R. and Anne H. Ehrlich. Copyright © 1981 by Paul R. and Anne H. Ehrlich. Reprinted by permission of Random House, Inc.

to be trucked in at a cost of 100 million dollars a year—a cost 35
carried by the subsistence farmers who make, on the average, less
than a hundred dollars a year each. Furthermore, now there is
nothing to wash away the previous year's silt buildup in the soil.
And with silt deposits no longer compensating for erosion, the fertile river delta is shrinking—and an alarming part of what remains 40
has completely dried up. Restoring the delta with pumps, drains,
and wells may cost more than the dam itself.

5   "Ironically, evaporation as well as bottom seepage from the new
lake filling in behind the dam is so great that the lake basin may
never fill up to predicted levels. So nobody can live around the lake 45
because nobody knows for sure where the shoreline will be. More
seriously, there is less water to go around than there was before.
And even though some 700,000 new acres (about 1.6 million hec-
tares) have been opened up for agriculture, the population outgrew
the potential food increase even before the dam was finished. At the 50
same time, with the nutrient-rich flow of the Nile turned off,
another major food source—the sardines, shrimp, and mackerel
that flourished in the enriched waters off the delta—has declined
catastrophically. Worse yet, the lake and the irrigation networks
have so accelerated the spread of blood flukes that half the Egyptian 55
populace are now carriers of schistosomiasis. In irrigated areas,
where eight out of ten humans live, women can expect to live only to
age twenty-seven, men to age twenty-five."

THE HAWAIIAN GOOSE

6   Another clear example of human ignorance of nature's delicate 60
balance is seen in the near extinction of the Hawaiian Goose or

*The tame, land-living Hawaiian goose or
Nene was driven to near extinction because
of human ignorance.*

Nene. It was estimated in the late eighteenth century that the population of Hawaii's unique variety of goose stood at about 25,000. In a matter of fifty years the population had dropped to approximately thirty birds. There were undoubtedly multiple causes for the decline 65 in the Nene population, and virtually all of them resulted, either directly or indirectly, from humans.

7   The most disastrous activities of humans included hunting with firearms, ranching activities, and the building of beach resorts. There is little doubt that the Nene's near extinction was hastened 70 after shotguns were brought to Hawaii. It seems reasonable to assume that many more Nene were killed when guns became common. In a similar fashion, as people moved further inland on the islands they began to open more and more land for the development of ranches and beach resorts. These developments forced the geese 75 out of their natural nesting and breeding ranges. As these ranches and resorts became more plentiful, the Nene population accordingly decreased.

8   The most harmful indirect effect of humans' activities was the introduction of animals such as cattle, goats, mongooses, and game 80 birds. When cattle were first brought to the islands, King Kamehameha proclaimed a ten-year protection of the animals. They were allowed to roam the islands unrestrained. They multiplied rapidly, and as they did they moved further and further into the virgin forests, destroying many of the plants that provided food 85 and shelter for the Nene. The goats that were introduced to the islands were even more destructive to the Nenes' natural habitat. Because the goats were more agile, not only could they reach the plants at the lower elevations, but they also moved into the highlands. In 1882, the mongoose was introduced to Hawaii in hopes 90 that it would control the rats that were doing great damage in the sugar cane fields. The mongoose neither solved the rat problem nor remained in the sugar cane fields. As it moved out of the cane fields, it did what it does naturally: it became a predator of ground-nesting birds—including the Nene. The game birds introduced to Hawaii 95 (pheasant, quail, guinea hen, turkey, and peafowl) all encroached on the Nene's already severely limited natural range. With the limited land space that an island has, the Nene had no escape route and no time to build defenses against these rapidly arriving unnatural opponents. 100

9   By the 1940s, the Nene population had dwindled to a number so low that almost nothing could be done to save this unique, tame, land-living goose. It had become a classic example of our unconscious destruction of nature.

MOSQUITO PLAGUE   105

10   "Still another famous incident drives home the intricate relationships within our ecosystem. Some years ago, large quantities of DDT were used by the World Health Organization in a program of mosquito control in Borneo. Soon the local people, spared a mos-

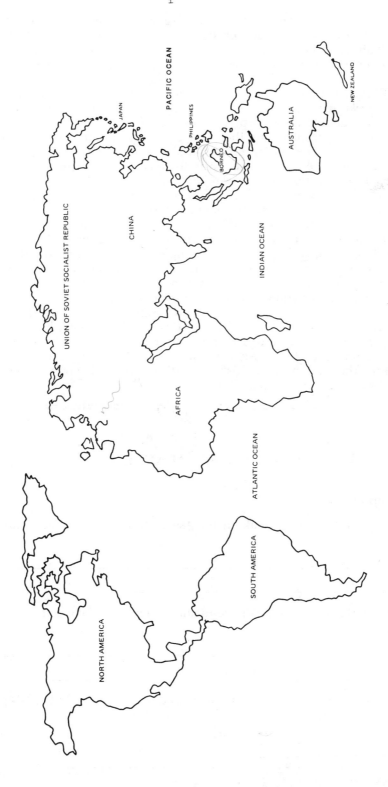

HAWAII

PACIFIC OCEAN

JAPAN

PHILIPPINES

BORNEO

AUSTRALIA

NEW ZEALAND

UNION OF SOVIET SOCIALIST REPUBLIC

CHINA

INDIAN OCEAN

AFRICA

ATLANTIC OCEAN

NORTH AMERICA

SOUTH AMERICA

quito plague, began to suffer a plague of caterpillars, which 110
devoured the thatched roofs of their houses, causing them to fall in.
The habits of the caterpillars limited their exposure to DDT, but
predatory wasps that had formerly controlled the caterpillars were
devastated.

11   "Further spraying was done indoors to get rid of houseflies. The 115
local gecko lizards, which previously had controlled the flies, continued to gobble their corpses—now full of DDT. As a result, the
geckos were poisoned, and the dying geckos were caught and eaten
by house cats. The cats received massive doses of DDT, which had
been concentrated as it passed from fly to gecko to cat, and the cats 120
died. This led to another plague, now of rats. They not only
devoured the people's food but also threatened them with yet
another plague—this time the genuine article, bubonic plague. The
government of Borneo became so concerned that cats were para-
chuted into the area in an attempt to restore the balance." 125

12   These are only three of many examples of our misunderstanding
and mistreatment of the environment. Every thing we do to the
environment will in one way or another affect other living things
around us. Every time a factory dumps chemicals, a power plant
burns coal, a corporation builds a new resort, or hunters overkill a 130
species of animal, a chain reaction is started that may have harmful,
long-range consequences. The more we try to understand, control,
and compensate for those consequences before they are set in
motion, the more harmoniously we will be able to live on this delicately balanced "tiny spaceship." 135

REVIEW | A Delicate Balance

Comprehension

1. True or false? The story about the Aswan Dam did not really happen.

_____False_____

_____

2. Why didn't the Egyptians have to ship in fertilizer before the dam
was built?

_____Because the River no longer deposit___

_____silt._____

3. Why is shipping fertilizer into their land such a financial hardship
for the farmers?

_____Because the farmer has to pay for__

_____the trucks. Al_____

4. Why is the delta shrinking?

Because the natural erosion was no longer restored with silt.

5. If you had to select the most important cause of the Nene's near extinction, what would it be? Why?

The worse effect that caused it were the human activity — the introduction of animals. [parg. 8]

6. In what way did imported birds contribute to the decline in the Nene population?

They crowded the designated area for the Nene.

7. Why was resort and ranch development harmful to the Nene?

They occupied space and forced the Nene to move and restrict their natural nesting.

8. Why were the mosquitos in Borneo killed by the DDT but the caterpillars weren't?

Because of caterpillars habits limited their exposure to DDT, and DDT killed wasps which controlled the caterpillars.

9. DDT was sprayed twice in Borneo. What were the two sprayings supposed to kill?

First time mosquitos
Second one flies

10. What had to be done in order to bring the ecosystem back into balance in Borneo?

The Government of Borneo had to parachute cats to restore in an attempt to restore balance.

Textual Pattern: Cause/Effect Emphasis

1. Each of the three sections of the reading "A Delicate Balance" was written with a different cause/effect emphasis. Which emphasis was used for each? (Review the lesson on page 149.)

"Aswan and Other Fables": _____

"The Hawaiian Goose": _____

"Mosquito Plague": _____

2. Complete the following diagrams with information given in the three major sections of "A Delicate Balance." The diagrams below are only one of several ways the cause/effect information given can be diagrammed. You may add boxes of your own or use only part of those provided.

"Mosquito Plague":

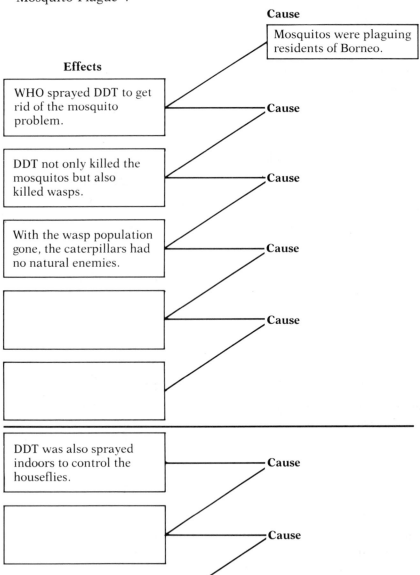

Cause

Mosquitos were plaguing residents of Borneo.

Effects

WHO sprayed DDT to get rid of the mosquito problem.

Cause

DDT not only killed the mosquitos but also killed wasps.

Cause

With the wasp population gone, the caterpillars had no natural enemies.

Cause

Cause

DDT was also sprayed indoors to control the houseflies.

Cause

Cause

"Aswan and Other Fables":

Effects

Cause	Effects

Cause

Building the Aswan Dam on the Nile River in Egypt

Water backed up so far behind the dam that 100,000 Egyptians had to move or be submerged along with priceless temples.

The flood plain is now deprived of its annual enrichment of silt.

Fertilizer has to be shipped in.

Farmers have to pay extra expense.

Half of the population are carriers of schistosomiasis.

Inhabitants of some areas have a shorter life span.

163

"The Hawaiian Goose":

Causes

Effect

The Nene nearly becomes an extinct species of bird in Hawaii.

Humans introduce into the Nene's environment animals and birds that the Nene cannot cope with.

Questions for Further Discussion/Composition

1. Adlai Stevenson compared our planet to a fragile spaceship. Do you agree with his comparison? Is it accurate?

2. Suppose a certain city needed to build a large new factory to help supply jobs and needed products. Building the factory would require the destruction of untouched land and streams. What precautions would you suggest the city take before going ahead with the project?

PREVIEW | HISTORIC EXTINCTIONS

Things to Think About

1. Who is John James Audubon?
   An American ornithologist, he was confounded of American Ornithology

2. What near-extinction did you read about in the last reading?
   The Nene have past from 25 000 to 35 just in only fifty year

3. List some of the causes of that near-extinction (question 2).
   Hunting guns.
   Introduction of different animals: cattles, goats, mongoose.
   The reduction of ability to adapt.

4. Why is it important for a species to be able to adapt to new conditions?

    Because their environmental change

5. Do you think we should pass legislation protecting species of wild animals, or should we just let nature take its course? Explain your answer.

    We should pass legislation protecting, species of wild animals because human behavior is breaking nature course.

Preview

1. How many different extinctions will this reading discuss? What does the title imply?

    As much as eras had been in History.

2. Scan the reading for the following information:

    What has become extinct? _Passanger Pigeon._

    When did it become extinct? _In 1914._

    Where did the extinctions take place? _After civil war_

3. Scan the reading for any indication of what the author emphasizes—causes, effects, etc. Does the title give any indication of the author's emphasis? Explain your answer.

READING TWO

HISTORIC EXTINCTIONS

1   Historic extinctions of exploited species seem to have followed a
pattern resembling at least some of the prehistoric ones. Hunting
has played an important role in reducing numbers, as has environmental change, but the final push over the brink has come from a
reduction in some way of the species' ability to adapt. The complex-   5
ity that may characterize the path leading to extinction is well illustrated by the most famous historic extinction of all—that of the
Passenger Pigeon in North America.

wild high cr

2   The Passenger Pigeon was a fascinating creature. A pretty,
graceful pigeon with a slate-blue back and deep pink breast, it   10
didn't coo like a dove, but produced "shrieks and chatters and
clucks." Its greatest claim to fame was the gigantic size of its populations; it may have been the most abundant bird ever to exist.
Audubon observed a flock of passenger pigeons passing over a
period of three days. Sometimes, he estimated, they went by at a   15
rate of over 300 million birds an hour. The passage of large flocks
created a roar of wings that could be heard a half-dozen miles away.
Alexander Wilson, who with Audubon founded American ornithology, estimated another flock to contain 2 billion birds. The pigeons
nested in long narrow colonies that could be forty miles long and   20
several miles across. Their droppings in favorite roosting areas
piled inches thick, killing all herbs and shrubs and eventually the
trees themselves.

3   The birds occurred throughout eastern North America, where
they fed on the fruits of forest trees—especially acorns and   25
beechnuts. The reason for their flocking behavior is not known for
certain. It may have helped them to find food; it may also have been
a predator defense.

4   Early settlers in the United States, though, had no trouble
adding the Passenger Pigeon to their diets. The nesting grounds   30
were so crowded that the adults were always being injured or killed
and the succulent squabs knocked out of the nests. All that was
required was to wander through the colony picking up dinner. As
the human population increased, however, two things began to happen. Railroads pushed through the wilderness, opening avenues for   35
market hunters to ship the birds to centers like New York, and the
great oak and beech forests in which the birds nested began to be
cleared.

5   The market hunters devised ingenious ways of killing large
numbers of the birds. The pigeons were suffocated by burning grass   40
or sulfur below their roosts; they were fed grain soaked in alcohol

[handwritten margin notes: "Low soft cry. a type of pigeon", "low, short noise of a hen calling her chickens."]

From *Extinction: The Causes and Consequences of the Disappearance of
Species* by Paul R. and Anne H. Ehrlich. Copyright © 1981 by Paul R. and
Anne H. Ehrlich. Reprinted by permission of Random House, Inc.

and picked up dead drunk, batted down with long sticks, blasted with shotguns, or netted (after which their heads were crushed with a pair of pincers). One ingenious trapping device depended on a decoy pigeon with its eyes sewn shut, tied to a perch called a stool. "Stool pigeon" thereby became part of the language.

6   The demise of the pigeons was startlingly rapid. After the Civil War, many millions were shipped from the Midwest to New York—so many that live birds were used as targets in shooting galleries. But the huge flocks were by then gone from the coastal states, and by the 1880s they were dwindling everywhere. In 1878 one hunter shipped some three million birds from Michigan, the Passenger Pigeon's last stronghold. The last wild bird was seen in that state just eleven years later, and the last captive bird died in the Cincinnati Zoo in 1914. Her name was Martha.

7   Economic extinction preceded biological extinction. The last birds in the wild were not killed by hunting, which became unprofitable as soon as the great flocks were gone. And there are still large areas of forest extant in the eastern United States that would serve as suitable habitat. But apparently the ability to form huge flocks was essential to the survival of the pigeons. When their population sizes became too small to maintain sufficiently large breeding colonies, nesting failures, inbreeding, and mortality from predation must have escalated and pushed the species to extinction.

8   The fate of the Passenger Pigeon illustrates very clearly that enormous numbers do not guarantee the safety of a species. Under the right circumstances, species can move from superabundance to extinction with astonishing speed. The fate of the American Bison (inaccurately called the buffalo) is another example. The eastern U.S. populations, sometimes considered a separate race, were hunted to extinction by the early 1830s, and the Oregon race by midcentury. The northern Wood Bison still lives in relatively large numbers in the forests of Alberta and the Northwest Territories of Canada.

9   The prairie populations of bison were huge almost beyond belief. In vast numbers they blackened the plains, an estimated 30 to 40 million individuals. They showed clearly that at least part of the megafauna could thrive in the presence of skilled hunters. Native Americans made little use of bison until they obtained horses from the Spaniards. Once mounted, some tribes based their economies on the shaggy beasts—eating their meat and making multiple use of their hides. But they made no discernible dent in the bison population; apparently the number they took each year was less than the annual production.

10   The arrival of the settlers from Europe, and especially of the railroads in the 1860s, signaled the start of the great bison slaughter. Professional hunters shot the animals primarily for their tongues and hides, leaving the carcasses to rot. Later, others collected the bleached bones that whitened the plains and shipped them east for use as fertilizer. Perhaps 2.5 million bison were killed annually between 1870 and 1875 by white hunters, and in 1883 the

The American bison (buffalo) was very nearly hunted to extinction.

last significant herd, numbering perhaps 10,000 bison, was slaughtered. At the turn of the century only about 500 Plains Bison remained—finally under legal protection.

11   The bison was luckier than the Passenger Pigeon—it was pulled   95
back from the brink. Today there are perhaps 25,000 in North America, scattered through parks and in private herds, but no prairie bison exist "in the wild." Humanity may have been lucky, too. A fertile hybrid has now been produced between cattle and bison by a California rancher. The hybrids, called "beefalo," are reported to be   100
very tasty, leaner, and more productive than beef. Beefalo are easier to raise than cattle, grow faster, and require no grain feed. At best, if accepted, beefalo could make meat cheaper and healthier, with less fat; at the least it could add variety to human diets.

REVIEW | HISTORIC EXTINCTIONS

Comprehension

1. What did the passenger pigeon look like? *It was a pretty pigeon with slate-blue back and deep pink breast.*

2. How was it different from doves and other types of pigeons? *because it did not coo, but shrieks and chatter and [clucks]*

3. Passenger pigeons were most famous for *the gigantic size of the popopulation*

4. The pigeons killed the plants and trees where they roosted because *they were*
millions and too heavy.
_____

5. It is believed that passenger pigeons flew in big flocks because
a. *maybe it helped them to feed*
b. *and also may have been a predator defense.*

6. Why was it so easy for early settlers to make pigeons part of their daily diet?
because they were so abundant that were easy to catch them.

7. What two effects did the railroad have on the passenger pigeons? Draw your answer in the form of a cause/effect diagram.

Causes | *Effects*
open avenues | *pigeons were sent to New York*
for market hunters | *oak and beech forests began*
and build houses | *to be cleared.*
for living |

8. What are some of the ways passenger pigeons were killed? *their roots.*
suffocated with burning grass, or sulfur below
fed grain soaked in alcohol & picked up dead drunk

9. Who was Martha? *The last captive pigeon died in Cincinnati.*

10. Hunting did not finally cause the extinction of the passenger pigeons. What did?
The decrease of pigeons in the flocks and they not
to be able to adapt.

11. The authors talk about three separate herds of bison. Two herds were hunted into extinction, and one still exists today. What two were destroyed and which one is still in existence? *in protection*
American Bison and Oregon race extinct. Wood Bison still lives

12. What two factors started the slaughter of the bison?
The railroads
The arrival of settlers from Europe.

13. The authors tell us that the bison was luckier than the passenger pigeon. What do they mean?
unlike the passenger pigeon, the bison
still remain, under legal protection.

Textual Pattern: Cause/Effect Emphasis

Which are the authors emphasizing—causes or effects? Give examples from the reading in support of your answer.

_____

_____

_____

The causes and effects of the two extinctions discussed in this reading have been partially diagrammed below. Fill in the missing information in the diagrams. You may need to turn back to the reading to complete this assignment.

American Bison

_____

Cause or effect?

cause

| Railroads pushed into the bisons' territory, making it possible to ship the dead bison to the East Coast. |

_____

Cause or effect?

| The American bison were pushed to near-extinction. | *effect.*

Passenger Pigeon

Causes

the rail roads pushed through the wilderness avenues for market hunters to ship the birds to N.Y.

Effect

| Extinction of the passenger pigeon in North America in the late 1800s. |

Questions for Further Discussion/Composition

1. Is it really necessary to protect all forms of life from extinction? Why or why not?

2. Which would be more important—jobs for 500 people or saving a species from extinction?

Understanding the Main Idea: Sentences

To a certain extent, the success of a reader can be measured by his or her ability to read a passage, synthesize all the information given, and make a general statement of the author's main ideas. If you cannot express the main point of what you have read, it is very likely you have not understood what you read. The purpose of this lesson is to help you understand main ideas.

Writers have specific ideas and information they want their readers to know. Good writers, therefore, select words, sentences, and paragraphs very carefully; exactness in communication is a writer's business. Being able to interpret that communication, those ideas, is your business as a reader. In writing, sentences build paragraphs which in turn build articles, short stories, essays, chapters, or entire books. At each of these levels (sentence, paragraph, entire piece), it is possible to pick out an author's main ideas.

MAIN IDEAS IN SENTENCES

Every complete sentence in English has a subject—who or what the sentence is about—and a predicate (verb)—what the subject is doing. Although sentences offer additional information, they must include at least a subject and a predicate (the subject and predicate of a sentence can sometimes be implied by the context). These two elements form the heart of a sentence's meaning. To find the main idea of a sentence you need to know who or what the sentence is about and what that person or thing is doing.

To find this information try asking the following three questions:

1. Who or what is this sentence about?
2. What is the person or thing (the subject) doing or what is happening to the person or thing?

Consider this example:

The use of pesticides has been practiced extensively over the last 25 years in the United States in an attempt to protect crops from insects and fungi.

Who or **what** is this sentence about? _____

What is the person or thing **doing**, or what is **happening** to the person or thing? _____

Once you have located the subject and predicate, you can then ask the third question:

3. Ask the journalistic questions (*who, what, when, where, why, how*) about the subject and verb of the sentence.

Where was the use of pesticides practiced? _____

Why was the use of pesticides practiced? _____

When was the use of pesticides practiced? _____

How (much) was the use of pesticides practiced? _____

By adding to "the heart" of the sentence the additional details provided by these journalistic questions, the sentence becomes much more meaningful.

| subject | predicate | detail—when |
(The use of pesticides) (has been practiced extensively) (over the last 25 years)

| detail—where | detail—why |
(in the United States) in an attempt (to protect crops) from insects and fungi.

In an attempt to reduce industrial smog in 1970, the Environmental Protection Agency hastily ordered industrial plants to increase the height of their smokestacks.

| detail—why | detail—when | subject |
(In an attempt to reduce   (in 1970),   (the Environmental Protection Agency)
industrial smog)

| predicate | detail—who | detail—what |
(hastily ordered) (industrial plants) (to increase the height of their smokestacks).

Being able to sort out the main idea of a sentence is a useful skill especially when you are reading complex sentences. The three questions taught in this lesson will not work for every sentence, but they will work for a majority of the sentences you read. Also keep in mind that not all sentences need to be analyzed in this way. Good readers realize when a sentence is too complex to understand in a quick reading. Effective readers will take time to analyze carefully a difficult but important sentence for its full meaning.

EXERCISE   Use the three questions discussed in this lesson to identify the main ideas of each of the following sentences. Write the subject and predicate in the blank provided. Write a "D" above each detail in the sentences.

1. Serious concern about the effects of pesticides on other organisms has been expressed in the last ten years.

   Subject: _____ Predicate: _____

   Main idea: _____

2. Before we realized just how much we could influence natural systems and how much destruction we could produce through our interference, serious inbalances in nature occurred.

   Subject: _____ Predicate: _____

   Main idea: _____

3. The accidental introduction of the chestnut blight fungus from China virtually eliminated the American chestnut.

   Subject: _____ Predicate: _____

   Main idea: _____

4. In most natural ecosystems a balance is generally achieved between the living populations and the environment, with certain limits providing the pivotal points for this balance.

   Subject: _____ Predicate: _____

   Main idea: _____

5. In the future the human race must be more concerned with adequate waste-disposal systems and control of air pollution (produced particularly by industry and automobiles), water pollution, and even noise pollution.

   Subject: _____ Predicate: _____

   Main idea: _____

6. Our ability ultimately to provide adequate food and shelter and to withstand the psychological and sociological effects of overcrowding must be questioned.

   Subject: _____ Predicate: _____

   Main idea: _____

7. Although our ability to provide adequate food and shelter poses great dilemmas to humans (especially in underdeveloped countries), perhaps of even greater magnitude is the problem of pollution of the total environment.

   Subject: _____ Predicate: _____

   Main idea: _____

PREVIEW | Exploding Volcano: Full Impact Yet to Come

Things to Think About

1. What effects would a volcanic eruption have on the following?

    Animal life: _would be killed ..._

    Weather: _Change_

    The economy: _crash_

    Air quality: _deteriore_

    Water quality: _no pure (clogged)_

2. What is the most serious volcanic eruption you have heard of? What were the consequences of that eruption?

    Vesubio and Etna, Pompeya city desappeared, Mexico, Alaska

3. Where and when was the most recent, serious volcanic eruption? What effects did it have? (Use the items listed in question 1 for discussion.)

    Mount St Helen, Washington

Preview

1. When and where did this reading first appear? Where will the most concise information be given? (Remember the lesson you studied on reading newspapers in Chapter 2.)

    U.S. News and World Report June 2, 1980

2. Scan the reading for titles, subtitles, maps, photos, etc.

3. Now scan the reading for any indication of which cause/effect emphasis is used in the reading.

    effects

4. Does the title give any indication of which emphasis might be used? Explain your answer.

    The impact is (a m) effect of explosion means

5. What is the meaning of *impact*? _____

_____

6. Scan for dates and locations. When and where did the volcano explode?

May 18, 1980 / Mount St. Helen (Vancuver, Washington)

7. Use the context provided to determine the meanings of the boldface words. Write a definition of, synonym for, or description of each of the vocabulary items in the space provided.

   a. Many of the problems from the eruption could be **aggravated** considerably if Mount St. Helens continues to erupt periodically.

   aggravated _____

   b. Even without further emissions of ash, the cost of repairing damage **inflicted** by the eruption may exceed 1 billion dollars.

   inflicted _____

   c. At present, the lumber industry is working at far less than capacity because so little new housing is being built. The **impact** of the destruction of timber may be felt, however, when home building **revives**.

   impact _____

   revives _____

   d. Over a long period of time **agronomists** say there is a possibility of damage to crops in a wide area resulting from acid rain from the ash cloud.

   agronomists _____

— *Title: Exploding Volcano*

READING THREE

Exploding Volcano: Full Impact Yet to Come

*Weather, crops, fishing and timber industries—and
taxpayers, too—will feel the fury of nature's attack at
Mount St. Helens.*

1   The impact of the devastating eruption of Mount St. Helens in
Washington will be felt for months—and perhaps years—to come.

2   • Crops such as wheat and apples have been badly damaged by
the volcanic fury, and later growth also may suffer.

3   • The timber industry in the Northwest could require years to   5
recover.

4   • Weather will be affected over much of the earth, especially in
the Northern Hemisphere.

5   • Water supplies in some Northwestern communities have
become so clogged that a major cleanup effort is necessary.   10

6   • Fish in nearby streams were killed by the millions, and shortages of some species appear likely in future years.

7   • Electrical power in parts of the Northwest may face disrup-
tions.

8   • Transportation routes—from river shipping to highways—will   15
require extensive repairs.

9   • Long-term—but as yet undetermined—health problems may
have been created.

10   Many of these problems could be aggravated considerably if
Mount St. Helens continues to erupt periodically, as it has in the   20
past. Agricultural experts are particularly worried that the spread
of more ash could kill much of the Northwest's wheat crop.

11   Even without further emissions of ash, the cost of repairing
damage inflicted by the eruption may exceed 1 billion dollars—with
much of that to be paid for by local, state and federal taxpayers.   25

12   **Bomblike blast.** The devastation began on May 18, when an
explosion, estimated at 500 times the force of the atomic bomb that
destroyed Hiroshima, ripped off the top 1,200 feet of the 9,700-foot
volcano near Vancouver, Washington. In less than seven days, a
cloud of volcanic gas containing some toxic chemicals and minute   30
particles of radioactive substances spread over most of North
America.

13   Scientists say that within several months the cloud—invisible to
the naked eye in most regions—will cover the Northern Hemisphere
in the stratosphere above 55,000 feet. It is expected to last about two 35
years before completing its fall to earth.

14   The environmental effects are considerable, although they tend
to decrease as distances from the volcano increase. The greatest

aserradero
to cut wood

economic impact is expected to be to the agriculture and timber industries in Washington and Idaho.   40

15   The logging industry in central Washington suffered the greatest initial economic damage—estimated at 500 million dollars or more. Officials say that some small logging companies may never recover from the loss of equipment—and enough trees were lost to build 200,000 single-family homes, roughly a fifth of the number of   45 housing units to be started this year throughout the U.S.

16   Forest companies have not completed surveys of the damage, but many experts believe the destruction will not appreciably affect the price of lumber to consumers in the long run. At present, the lumber industry is working at far less than capacity because so little   50 new housing is being built. The impact of the destruction of timber may be felt, however, when home building revives.

17   cultivated produce   Another consequence of the explosion is a possible shortage of some crops. Researchers at Washington State University are concerned that the state's 460-million-dollar wheat crop will not survive if the ash cover becomes greater than 2 inches—thus choking   55 the plants. In a few places, deposits measured more than a foot, burying uncut alfalfa and hay, but officials say that most affected farmlands are covered by an inch or so.

18   Over a longer period of time, agronomists say there is a possibility of damage to crops in a wide area resulting from acid rain   60 from the ash cloud. Scientists fear that toxic materials emitted by the volcano, such as sulfur oxides, hydrogen sulfides and nitrogen oxides, will fall to the ground in precipitation as the volcanic cloud disperses over North America.   65

19   Still undetermined is the status of fruit crops important to the region. Robert Mickelson, chief of the Washington State Agriculture Department, says Yakima County, where apples, cherries and peaches are economic mainstays, is among the hardest-hit areas. He is most worried about the cherries because that crop, valued at   70 nearly 50 million dollars, was near harvest and at a vulnerable stage. About a third of the nation's supply of sweet cherries is grown in Washington.

20   Also victimized by the blast is the fishing industry, another mainstay of the economies of Washington and Oregon. Fishermen   75 could suffer for many seasons because millions of young salmon and other fish may not survive the high temperatures created by the blast. The resulting scarcity could drive up the price of salmon.

21   Effects of the eruption on weather also are a matter of widespread concern. Some authorities are convinced that volcanic   80 explosions in the past have been responsible for substantial cooling trends. New England, for example, for a short time was subjected to unseasonably cold winters and summers after an immense eruption in Indonesia in 1815.

22   **Changes in temperature.** Scientists say there will probably be   85 no drastic changes resulting from the Mount St. Helens blast— assuming there are no more eruptions. Still, a temporary lowering of temperature—less than 1 degree—can be expected across much of the Northern Hemisphere. Reason for the drop: Dust particles in the

NOAA

atmosphere deflect a bit of the sun's warming rays. Meteorologists 90
say the lowering could make the difference between rain and snow
in some regions.

23   Observes Lester Machta, director of the federal government's
Air Resources Laboratories: "These microscopic particles can
remain in the stratosphere for months or years." 95

24   Officials of the National Oceanic and Atmospheric Administration say a more noticeable effect will be spectacular sunsets and
sunrises during the next year or two. These will be caused as solar
rays strike microscopic particles of silicon, turning the light into
brilliant rose-colored hues. 100

25   Of greater concern is the possible disruption of mountain snow-
packs, vital sources of water throughout the West. NOAA scientists
say volcanic ash falling on high-altitude snowfields—particularly in
the Rocky Mountains—could cause an earlier-than-normal melt-off,
leaving little stored water for late summer and early fall. 105

26   The ash also is worrying doctors studying the effects of fallout
on people within a few hundred miles of the volcano. Medical
researchers don't believe there is an immediate health threat, but
say long-term problems could occur from the ash.

27   Says Idaho health officer Russell Schaff: "It can be respired 110
deep into the lungs. There may be no acute symptoms now, but
problems could occur years later."

28   Widespread effects also have been felt by operators of machin-
ery—ranging from air-conditioning units to gas pumps. The
powderlike fallout clogged machines in Washington, Idaho and 115
Oregon, and covered farm animals and crops over a wide area. In
some sections of western Idaho, ash drifts of 1 foot or more were
reported.

29   Other damage resulted from mudslides and floods caused by
material dislodged by the mountain. Many homes, bridges and 120
highways were devastated, and shipping channels were clogged by
silt.

30   More than two dozen vessels were trapped in the harbors in or
near the Columbia River—the major port of Portland, Oregon, in
particular. Officials said it could take a year or more to clean up 125
Portland's shipping channel. Damage to water routes was estimated
at 15 million dollars.

31   The explosion also took its toll of roads and communication
lines, which were disrupted over wide areas of Washington and
Idaho, leaving thousands of persons stranded. 130

32   Still another worry: Blowing and shifting ash will clog electrical
generators or transformers, disrupting electrical supplies in large
portions of the Northwest.

33   Geologists have redoubled their studies of the mountain to try to
determine whether any more big eruptions are imminent. They 135
hope instruments will reveal considerably more about origins of the
spectacular explosion of Mount St. Helens that occurred 8 minutes
after a moderate earthquake.

34   **Blowing its top.** Some scientists think the tremor may have
triggered the eruption. Geologists say the peak exploded following 140

the buildup of pressure from gas and magma—molten rock—inside the mountain, which had lain dormant for 123 years.

35   The blast emitted thousands of tons of volcanic ash into the atmosphere, and its aftereffects were responsible for at least 30 deaths. Another hundred or so residents and campers who had decided to remain near the mountain despite previous upheavals were still missing in late May. . . .   145

36   No one is sure what Mount St. Helens will do next. As Sam Frear, a Forest Service official in Washington, pointed out, "We're entirely at the mercy of the mountain."   150

REVIEW | EXPLODING VOLCANO: FULL IMPACT YET TO COME

Comprehension

1. When did Mount St. Helens erupt? ___May 18 - 1980___

2. The force of Mount St. Helens' eruption was compared to what other force? How did Mount St. Helens compare?
   ___500 times Hirosima atomic bomb.___

3. How far into the future will the effects of this eruption be felt?
   ___At least two years.___

4. Was the elevation of Mount St. Helens over or under 9,000 feet after the eruption? Explain your answer.
   ___It was 9,700. The explosion ripped out 1200. The volcano is now 8,500 under 9,700.___

5. What industries will suffer the greatest economic setback from the eruption?
   ___agriculture and timber in Washington and Idaho.___

6. True or false? The eruption destroyed 200,000 trees. ___F.___

7. What effect did the eruption have on nearby farms?
   ___fruits, animals will be cover by ash. (1 inche or more caused___

8. Why are officials concerned about volcanic ash falling on high altitude snowfields?

It could cause an earlier melt-off snow leaving little storequater for late summer and early fall (handwritten)

ashma (handwritten margin)
lung tumors (handwritten margin)
euphysema (handwritten margin)

9. Why are medical officials concerned about the volcanic ash?

Because this ash could be respired deep into lungs and cause later health problems (handwritten)

10. When will the volcano stop emitting ash? _No one knows._ (handwritten)

Skill Review: Main Ideas in Sentences

In your own words, write what you think the main idea is for the following sentences.

1. Over a longer period of time, agronomists say there is a possibility of damage to crops in a wide area resulting from acid rain from the ash cloud.

    Main idea: _Possibly in future, acid rain from the ash cloud will cause damage to crops._ (handwritten)

2. Also victimized by the blast is the fishing industry, another mainstay of the economies of Washington and Oregon.

    Main idea: _The important fishing industry of Oregon and Wash. had been damaged by the blast._ (handwritten)

3. Forest companies have not completed surveys of the damage, but many experts believe the destruction will not appreciably affect the price of lumber to consumers in the long run.

    Main idea: _The price of lumber would not be affected._ (handwritten)

4. Many of these problems could be aggravated considerably if Mount St. Helens continues to erupt periodically, as it has in the past.

    Main idea: _Mount St. Helens used to erupt periodically and if it continues the damage could be aggravated._ (handwritten)

5. The blast emitted thousands of tons of volcanic ash into the atmosphere, and its after-effects were responsible for at least 30 deaths.

    Main idea: _30 people dead from the volcanic ash_ (handwritten)

natural cause (handwritten margin, vertical)

Textual Pattern: Cause/Effect Emphasis

1. What does the author emphasize—cause, effect, or a chain reaction—in "Exploding Volcano: Full Impact Yet to Come"?

    effects (handwritten)

2. The diagram below outlines the major points presented in the reading. Some parts have been filled in for you. Identify in the space provided which is the cause(s) and which is the effect(s) side of the diagram. Then fill in the missing information. You may not need all the blanks that have been provided, or you may add more of your own.

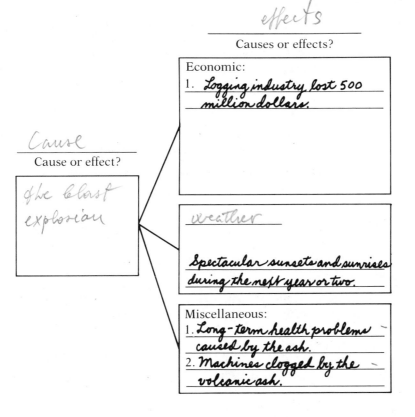

effects

_____

Causes or effects?

> Economic:
> 1. *Logging industry lost 500 million dollars.*

Cause

_____

Cause or effect?

The blast explosion

> *weather*
>
> *Spectacular sunsets and sunrises during the next year or two.*

> Miscellaneous:
> 1. *Long-term health problems caused by the ash.*
> 2. *Machines clogged by the volcanic ash.*

Questions for Further Discussion/Composition

The eruption of Mount St. Helens took very few human lives. It did, however, affect human life. How were the lives of the following people living near the volcano affected by the eruption?

A wheat farmer   A person with respiratory disorders
A fruit farmer   Sawmill owner
Owner of a fish market Home builder

Understanding the Main Idea: Paragraphs

One of the first rules a writer learns is that a paragraph develops one and only one main idea. Every sentence in a paragraph should serve a purpose—to support, add detail to, or further develop the main or central idea of the paragraph. In other words, if there is no main idea, there is no paragraph. If there is no main or central idea, all that exists is a group of sentences without a purpose or direction. This basic rule of writing can be helpful to you as a reader. Knowing that a writer focuses on one topic in a paragraph can help you focus your attention on a main idea when reading a paragraph.

Read the following sentences:

There is little doubt that the Nene's near-extinction was hastened after shotguns were brought to Hawaii.

It seems reasonable to assume that many more Nene were killed when guns became common.

In a similar fashion, as people moved further inland on the islands they began to open more and more land for the development of ranches and beach resorts.

These developments forced the geese out of their natural nesting and breeding ranges.

As these ranches and resorts became more and more plentiful, the Nene population accordingly decreased.

It is possible to guess what the main idea holding these sentences together is; however, it is not as clear as it could be. Try reading the same sentences now with the addition of one more sentence.

The most disastrous activities of humans included hunting with firearms, ranching activities, and the building of beach resorts.

There is little doubt that the Nene's near-extinction was hastened after shotguns were brought to Hawaii.

accelerated

It seems reasonable to assume that many more Nene were killed when guns became common.

In a similar fashion, as people moved further inland on the islands they began to open more and more land for the development of ranches and beach resorts.

These developments forced the geese out of their natural nesting and breeding ranges.

As these ranches and resorts became more and more plentiful, the Nene population accordingly decreased.

It is now much clearer why these sentences have been put together. The author's main idea is explicitly stated in the first sentence. It is a common practice for writers to state a main or central idea of a paragraph in a single sentence. Usually, that sentence is at the beginning of the paragraph. It can, however, be placed in the middle or at the end of the paragraph. Occasionally, a main idea is only implied, not expressly stated. Nevertheless, there must be a main idea or there is no paragraph.

In order to determine the main idea of a paragraph, you should ask yourself: (1) What subject do all the sentences in the paragraph support? What are they all related to? In the example just given all the sentences help clarify what disastrous effects humans had on the Nene. Another guideline that will help when trying to form a summary statement of a main idea is: (2) The restatement of a main idea should be general enough to include every significant detail in the paragraph. Similarly, it should be narrow enough to include only the details in the paragraph.

EXERCISE Read the following paragraphs. Then select the best main idea for each paragraph. In the space provided give a brief explanation for the choice you make. Be sure to study the example paragraph before you do the exercise. For example, which of the following statements would best summarize the main idea of the preceding paragraph about the Nene?

  a. Hotel and resort development caused the Nene's near-extinction.
  b. Shotguns were used widely in Hawaii to hunt birds.
  c. The Nene nearly became extinct in Hawaii.
  d. Several factors directly related to humans caused the near-extinction of the Nene.

Explanation: If you chose sentence (a) you selected a statement that is true, but it is too specific to be the main idea of the entire paragraph. Hotels and resorts are only part of the cause. If you selected sentence (b), you have made the same mistake as those who selected sentence (a). It is too specific. Sentence (c) is not the correct answer either because it is too general to be the main idea. Sentence (d) is the best choice for a restatement of the main idea of the paragraph. All the sentences in the paragraph support the idea expressed in sentence (d), and it is not too general or too specific to be a restatement of the main idea of the paragraph.

1. "The most harmful indirect effect of human's activities [on the Nene] was the introduction of animals such as cattle, goats,

mongooses, and game birds. When cattle were first brought to the islands, King Kamehameha proclaimed a ten-year protection of the animals. They were allowed to roam the islands unrestrained. They multiplied rapidly, and as they did they moved further and further into the virgin forests, destroying many of the plants that provided food and shelter for the Nene. The goats that were introduced to the islands were even more destructive to the Nene's natural habitat. Because the goats were more agile, not only could they reach the plants at the lower elevations, but they also moved into the highlands. In 1882 the mongoose was introduced to Hawaii in hopes that it would control the rats that were doing great damage in the sugar cane fields. The mongoose neither solved the rat problem nor remained in the sugar cane fields. As it moved out of the cane fields, it did what it does naturally: it became a predator of ground-nesting birds—including the Nene. The game birds introduced to Hawaii (pheasant, quail, guinea hen, turkey, and peafowl) all encroached on the Nene's already severely limited natural range. With the limited land space that an island has, the Nene had no escape route and no time to build defenses against these rapidly arriving, unnatural opponents."

Select the statement that is the best restatement of the main idea.

a. Cattle played an important part in the early development of Hawaii.
b. Animals played a necessary part in human activities in Hawaii.
c. Humans were indirectly responsible for the near-extinction of the Nene.
d. The Hawaiian Goose almost became extinct because of the introduction of unnatural predators.

Explanation for your choice: _____

_____

2. "The arrival of the settlers from Europe, and especially of the railroads in the 1860s, signaled the start of the great bison slaughter. Professional hunters shot the animals primarily for their tongues and hides, leaving the carcasses to rot. Later, others collected the bleached bones that whitened the plains and shipped them east for use as fertilizer. Perhaps 2.5 million bison were killed annually between 1870 and 1875 by white hunters, and in 1883 the last significant herd, numbering perhaps 10,000 bison, was slaughtered. At the turn of the century only about 500 plains bison remained—finally under legal protection."

Select the statement that is the best restatement of the main idea.

a. The plains bison had to be put under legal protection at the beginning of the twentieth century.
b. Bison tongues and hides were the primary reason hunters killed the animals.
c. The rapid arrival of people on the plains was the real cause of the destruction of the bison herds.

Explanation for your choice: _____

_____

3. "Still undetermined is the status of fruit crops important to the region. Robert Mickelson, chief of the Washington State Agriculture Department, says Yakima County, where apples, cherries and peaches are economic mainstays, is among the hardest-hit areas. He is most worried about the cherries because that crop, valued at nearly 50 million dollars, was near harvest and at a vulnerable stage. About a third of the nation's supply of sweet cherries is grown in Washington."

Select the statement that is the best restatement of the main idea.

a. Yakima County was the hardest hit by the volcanic eruption.
b. Mount St. Helen's eruption did a great deal of economic damage.
c. Though the damage of the fruit crop is still undetermined, it is very likely quite great.
d. The cherry crop in Yakima County was most likely ruined by the volcanic eruption.

Explanation for your choice: _____

_____

4. "The Passenger Pigeon was a fascinating creature. A pretty, graceful pigeon with slate-blue back and deep pink breast, it didn't coo like a dove, but produced 'shrieks and chatters and clucks.' Its greatest claim to fame was the gigantic size of its populations; it may have been the most abundant bird ever to exist. Audubon observed a flock of passenger pigeons passing over a period of three days. Sometimes, he estimated, they went by at a rate of over 300 million birds an hour. The passage of large flocks created a roar of wings that could be heard a half-dozen miles away. Alexander Wilson, who with Audubon founded American ornithology, estimated another flock to contain 2 billion birds. The pigeons nested in long narrow colonies that could be forty miles long and several miles across. Their droppings in favorite roosting areas piled inches thick, killing all herbs and shrubs and eventually the trees themselves."

Select the statement that is the best restatement of the main idea.

a. The passenger pigeon was perhaps one of the most abundant birds ever to exist.

b. The huge size of the pigeon's flocks was almost beyond belief.

c. Passenger pigeons were not only known for their extreme beauty, but for their unusual clucking sounds as well.

d. Passenger pigeons were a rare breed of bird in many ways.

Explanation for your choice: _____

_____

5. "The prairie populations of bison were huge almost beyond belief. In vast numbers they blackened the plains, an estimated 30 to 40 million individuals. They showed clearly that at least part of the megafauna could thrive in the presence of skilled hunters. Native Americans made little use of bison until they obtained horses from the Spaniards. Once mounted, some tribes based their economies on the shaggy beasts—eating their meat and making multiple use of their hides. But they made no discernible dent in the bison population; apparently the number they took each year was less than the annual production."

Select the statement that is the best restatement of the main idea.

a. The bison population remained strong and healthy despite being hunted by the American Indians.

b. The bison populations were extremely large.

c. The American Indians depended a great deal on the bison for their survival.

d. It wasn't until the American Indians obtained horses that they could base their economies on the bison.

Explanation for your choice: _____

_____

Argument/Controversy about acid rain

PREVIEW | Storm Over a Deadly Downpour

Things to Think About

1. What happens to the chemicals and tiny particles put into the atmosphere by industrial smokestacks?

   They cause pollution, acid rain
   They suffer a chemical reaction and become acid rain. They
   became acid/sulfur and nitrogen compounds

2. What is acid rain? _acid falling to the earth from pollution (fog, rain, snow or dry particles._

3. What does the diagram on page 188 tell you about acid rain?
That the pollutants from coal-fired and fossil-fuel burning are carried by the wind, into the atmosphere and later on deposited back on the earth again in the form of snow, solid, rain fog or dry particles.

4. What is the meaning of *downpour*? _rain heavily down_
_____

5. What is the meaning of *acidic* and *alkaline*? If you don't know, look the definitions up in the dictionary.
acidic _acid, containing the characteristics of acid. a compound containing hydrogen which, disolved in water provides hydrogen ions._
alkaline _alkali, usually a soluble hydroxide or carbonate of the alkali metals_

6. Who would suffer the most from the effects of industrial air pollution: the people who live five hundred yards away from a smoke-stack or the people who live fifty miles downwind from the stack? Explain your answer.
The people living fifty miles downwind from the stack. Because the pollution is pushed up in the atmosphere and it remains there long enough to start a chemical reaction that provides acid sulphure and nitrogen compounds which are transported by the wind and redeposited to earth far from the smokestacks.

Preview

1. Turn to page 188 and read the supplementary reading "A Hard Look at Acid Rain."

2. Now scan the reading "Storm Over a Deadly Downpour" for the following information:

    the source of the reading, _Time December 6, 1982_

    any and all dates, _____

    any charts and/or graphs that might help you better understand the reading.

3. Quickly read paragraph 3 and then give your own definitions of *acidity* and *alkalinity*.

    acidity_____
    _____
    _____

    alkalinity_____
    _____

West - less acid rain/ East more
hydroelectric / coal-fired utility plants.

electricity

Pollutants from coal-fired utility plants and auto emissions are transported
by wind and redeposited back to earth in the form of rain, snow, fog or dry
particles—all forms of acid rain.

SUPPLEMENTARY READING

A HARD LOOK AT ACID RAIN

1   Acid rain is rain, snow, or fog that contains high amounts of
sulfuric or nitric acid. To some extent, acidic rain occurs naturally
and can have a beneficial effect—for instance, serving as fertilizer.

2   But, when the acidity of the precipitation is abnormally high
over a prolonged period, it can overwhelm the ability of water and   5
woods (and buildings, statues, car finishes, fish, game, and humans)
to accommodate it. When this happens, lakes and trees may die,
game species may weaken, and human health may be endangered.

3   Those who have studied the current crisis believe it to be the
result of acid overload caused primarily by sulfur dioxide emissions   10
from coal-fired utility plants and nitrogen oxide emissions from
automobiles. These pollutants are either transformed to acid in the
air or deposited on the ground in dry form, combining with ground
water to form sulfuric or nitric acid.

4   Transported by the wind, pollutants can travel hundreds of   15
miles through the air before falling to earth as acid rain. That's why
"pristine" lakes far from civilization are dying. Thus, power-plants
in Ohio are believed to have killed lakes in New York. Waters in
Canada apparently are dying as a result of autos and industries in
the U.S.   20

Adapted with permission from "A Hard Look at Acid Rain," *Field and
Stream*, December 1984, p. 78.

5   Acid rain doesn't treat all lakes equally. Some lakes enjoy natural buffers provided by underlying rocks and surrounding soils,
which keep the water's pH value high (less acidic). Others, like
many in the Adirondacks, lie in impervious granite bowls surrounded by a thin soil layer and so are highly vulnerable to acid-   25
ification. The death toll mounts first in areas receiving the most
rain.

6   Just because your favorite fishing and hunting grounds lie far
from the northeastern United States and Canada, don't think you're
not affected. Acid-sensitive areas are spread across the continent,   30
North, South, Midwest, Southwest, Rocky Mountains, West Coast—
all parts of the country have areas showing damaging levels of acid
rain.

READING FOUR

a loud and vigorous expression

Storm Over a Deadly Downpour   _Summary_

heavy shower of rain

Acid rain is shaping up as the ecological issue of the decade.

1   A uniquely modern, postindustrial blight, acid rain is as widespread as the winds that disperse it. In the northeast U.S. and in
Canada and northern Europe, it is reducing lakes, rivers and ponds
to eerily crystalline, lifeless bodies of water, killing off everything
from indigenous fish stocks to microscopic vegetation. It is sus-   5
pected of spiriting away mineral nutrients from the soil on which
forests thrive. Its corrosive assault on buildings and water systems
costs millions of dollars annually. It may also pose a substantial
threat to human health, principally by contaminating public drinking water. Says Canada's Minister of the Environment John   10
Roberts: "Acid rain is one of the most devastating forms of pollution
imaginable, an insidious malaria of the biosphere. . . ."

2   Such natural processes as volcanic eruptions, forest fires and the
bacterial decomposition of organic matter produce some of the
damaging acidic sulfur and nitrogen compounds. But most experts   15
believe that the current problem is directly traceable to the burning
of fossil fuels by power plants, factories and smelting operations
and, to a lesser extent, auto emissions. When tall smokestacks vent
their fumes, sulfur dioxide, nitrogen oxides and traces of such toxic
metals as mercury and cadmium mix with water vapor in the   20

Adapted with permission from Frederic Golden, "Storm Over a Deadly
Downpour," _Time_, December 6, 1982, pp. 84–86. Copyright 1982 Time Inc.
All rights reserved. Reprinted by permission from _Time_.

atmosphere. Chemical reactions follow that form dilute solutions of nitric and sulfuric acids—acid rain.

3   The acidic "depositions," as scientists call them, can come down in almost any form, including hail, snow, fog or even dry particles. On the standard chemical scale for measuring acidity or alkalinity, they are defined as having a pH level under 5.6 (a neutral solution has pH 7). Despite the use of tracking balloons and other sophisticated techniques, it is difficult to link acidity with a specific smokestack. But there is little doubt about the damaging effects of acid rain. Absorbed into the soil, it breaks down minerals containing calcium, potassium and aluminum, robbing plants of nutrients. Eventually the acid enters nearby bodies of water, often with a delay burden of toxic metals that can stunt or kill aquatic life.

4   As successive rainfalls make the water increasingly acidic, lakes and rivers turn oddly clear and bluish. Their surviving microorganisms are trapped beneath layers of moss on the bottom; the afflicted water cannot support any but the most primitive forms of life. Some areas, rich in alkaline limestone, are able to resist the assault by "buffering" or neutralizing acid precipitation. But much of New York, New England, eastern Canada and Scandinavia is covered with thin, rocky topsoil left by glaciers long ago, and is particularly vulnerable to acid rain.

5   In New York's Adirondack Mountains, 212 of the 2,200 lakes and ponds are acidic, dead and fishless. Acid rain has killed aquatic life in at least 10% of New England's 226 largest fresh-water lakes. On Cape Cod in Massachusetts, fishery biologists have stopped restocking eight of the area's top ten fishing ponds because the waters are too acidic for young trout to survive in; the onslaught has spurred experimentation with new breeds of acid-resistant fish.

6   In the mid-'70s, the Quabbin Reservoir in central Massachusetts became so acidic that it dissolved water conduits and fixtures, producing unhealthy levels of lead in drinking water. Cost since that time for neutralizing chemicals: $1 million annually. In Maine, where the measured acidity of rainfall has increased 40 times in the past 80 years, high levels of toxic mercury, lead and aluminum in acidified streams have killed or deformed salmon embryos. The problem is spreading to other parts of the country. Damage from acid rain has been reported in Minnesota, Wisconsin, Florida and California.

7   But Canada suffers most severely. Environmental officials project the loss of 48,000 lakes by the end of the century if nothing is done to curb acid rain. Already, 2,000 to 4,000 lakes in Ontario have become so acidified that they can no longer support trout and bass, and some 1,300 more in Quebec are on the brink of destruction. In Nova Scotia, nine rivers used as spawning grounds by Atlantic salmon in the spring no longer teem with fish.

8   To some extent, environmentalists can blame themselves. In an attempt to reduce industrial smog in 1970, the fledgling Environmental Protection Agency hastily ordered industrial plants to increase the height of their smokestacks. As a result, winds carried

pollutants farther afield. The pollutants are now injected so high into the atmosphere that they remain there long enough for the critical chemical reactions to take place. Ironically, the tallest of these smokestacks is in Canada, a 1,250-ft. monster that belches fumes from a nickel smelter in Sudbury, Ontario. The area is so 75 bleak and lifeless that U.S. astronauts practiced moon walking there in the late 1960's.

9   Ottawa admits that Canada may be responsible for as much as 25% of the acid rain in the U.S., but adds that it is on the deficit side of this unhappy balance of trade. It contends that about 70% of the 80 acidic sulfates that fall on Canada come from the U.S., wafted by winds from areas like the industrialized Ohio Valley. Says Environment Minister Roberts: "We are at the end of a gigantic geographical exhaust pipe. . . ."

10   The U.S. government modestly stepped up its funding for acid- 85 rain research, from $18 million in 1982 to $22 million in 1983. It is the only area outside the defense budget where an increase is planned. The money is beginning to produce results. New research in the U.S. and West Germany strongly suggests that acid rain combines with traces of toxic metals emitted into the atmosphere by 90 fossil fuel-burning plants to leach away nutrients that sustain trees. *wash away* In addition, scientists believe the mixture of acid rain and aluminum trace elements in the soil is absorbed by roots and can choke off a tree's water supply.

11   "It's as if we were 80% of our way through reading a book," says 95 Chicago Meteorologist Walter Lyons. "We may have to read the last 20% just to make sure there's not a surprise ending." Lyons contends, along with some spokesmen for major U.S. utilities, that waiting for more research is not "going to make that much difference." Because the acid-rain problem involves so many different 100 disciplines and so much poorly understood data, he says, "we're like a lot of blind men grabbing at an elephant."

12   With an increasing number of areas classified by scientists as "sensitive" to acid stress in both North America and Europe, some environmental experts fear that an even more alarming and often 105 irreversible deterioration may take place before corrective measures are taken. The concern of environmentalists is that industrialists will continue to use delaying tactics to put off costly capital improvements necessary to reduce emissions. Says Richard Ayres, chairman of the National Clean Air Coalition: "The costs [for clean- 110 ing up emissions] aren't trivial. But neither is the damage. A nation that can afford to spend $5 billion a year on video games can afford the same amount to save its lakes and forests."

REVIEW | STORM OVER A DEADLY DOWNPOUR

Comprehension

acid rain

1. Why is acid rain associated with industrialization? *Because is primary caused from the burning of fossil-fuel industry use.*

2. What do scientists think is the largest cause of acid rain? *The fossil fuel-burning plants /coal-fired utility plants oil or gasoline from cars.*

3. Why are certain lakes more seriously affected by acid rain than others?
   Because they have a thin rocky soil layer

4. What effects did building taller smokestacks have on air pollution? List as many effects as you can. *and far away*
   the pollutant is carried so high into the atmosphere that it remains there longer enough for the critical chemical reaction take place. The area is bleak and lifeless.

5. Why is acid rain causing such a dispute between environmentalists and industrialists?
   Because industrialists should use taches to make improvements to reduce emissions but they delay to do because the casts is to high.

6. How are the terms *acidity* and *alkalinity* related to acid rain?
   If the lake's water is provided by alkalini minerals, it is stronger resistant to acid rain. It water has more acid its more vulnerable to acid rain.

Skill Review: Main Ideas in Sentences

A. Write a statement that summarizes the main idea of the following sentences.

1. A uniquely modern, postindustrial blight, acid rain is as widespread as the winds that disperse it.

   Main idea: *Acid rain is as wide spread as wind.*

2. Such natural processes as volcanic eruptions, forest fires, and the bacterial decomposition of organic matter produce some of the damaging acidic sulfur and nitrogen compounds.

   Main idea: *Natural processes and the bacteriol decomposti tion of organic matter produce acid sulfur and nitrogey compound*

3. The acidic "depositions," as scientists call them, can come down in almost any form, including hail, snow, fog, or even dry particles.

   Main idea: *The acidic depositions can come down in any form; hail, fog or dry particles.*

4. With an increasing number of areas classified by scientists as "sensitive" to acid stress in both North America and Europe, some environmental experts fear that an even more alarming and often irreversible deterioration may take place before corrective measures are taken.

Main idea: *Some experts fear that more alarming and irreversible deterioration may take place*

B. Reread paragraphs 2, 8, and 10 for main ideas. Write the main idea of each paragraph in the space provided below.

Main idea of paragraph 2: *Chemical reactions produced in the atmospher by mixing tall smokestacks toxics fumes and vapor diluting solution of acid rain.*

Main idea of paragraph 8: *The increasing of the high of the tall smokestacks has produced a worse problems. The pollution in now injected into the atmosphere and remains there longer.*

Main idea of paragraph 10: *The US government has planned to raise funds for acid rain research (scientific investigation)*

Textual Pattern: Cause/Effect Emphasis

Paragraphs 2 and 3 have been partially diagrammed for you. Complete the diagrams and then draw a diagram of your own for paragraph 8.

Paragraph 2

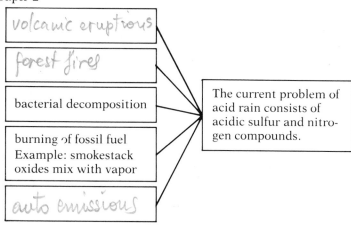

Paragraph 3

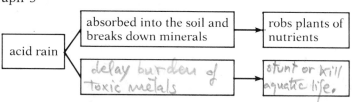

Paragraph 8

increase the high of → wind carries pollectant
smokes tasks   farther afield

pollatants injected → remain there enough for
higher into atmosphere   the chemical reaction take
                          place

Questions for Further Discussion/Composition

1. The reading indicated that we are not sure exactly what effects acid rain has on the environment. Do you think we should pass laws restricting industrial air pollution, or should we wait until we know more about the effects of that pollution?

2. Is there any similarity between the extinction of animal life as discussed in previous readings and the damage caused by acid rain?

PREVIEW | THE SILENT SUMMER

Things to Think About

1. What is a greenhouse? _____

_____

2. In what ways is our earth's atmosphere similar to a greenhouse?

_____

How is it different?_____

_____

3. Why doesn't the earth become steamy and hot like a greenhouse?

_____

_____

4. How would weather conditions be affected if our atmosphere were damaged?

_____

_____

Preview

1. Read the supplementary reading "A Warmer Globe Just Around Corner" on page 196. What information do the reading and the drawing give you about the causes of the greenhouse effect?

   _____

   _____

   _____

2. Read the first and last paragraphs of "The Silent Summer." What does the author mean by "chemicals are not innocent until proven guilty"?

   _____

   _____

3. What are the boldface sideheadings in this reading?

   _____

4. After previewing this reading, what do you think the author is emphasizing most—"causes" or "effects"? (If you are not sure, look at the boldface sideheadings once again.)

   _____

5. Use the context given to determine the meaning of the boldface words. Write your response in the blank space provided. Remember, an exact meaning is not necessary.
   a. Since 1974, when two chemists suggested that the chemicals chlorofluorocarbons destroy **ozone** in the atmosphere, industries that produce CFCs have refused to stop production.

      ozone _____

   b. The industries that make chlorofluorocarbons have argued for definitive research showing that the chemicals destroy the atmosphere before **curbing** their production.

      curbing _____

   c. Ultraviolet light from the sun causes skin cancer; indeed the U.S. Environmental Protection Agency now says a 2.5 percent destruction of ozone might mean 15,000 additional victims of deadly **melanoma** each year.

      melanoma _____

SUPPLEMENTARY READING

A WARMER GLOBE JUST AROUND CORNER

1   A slow but steady warming of the world's air—the "greenhouse effect"—may trigger changes within 10 years that could have dramatic results on life in the next century.

2   That conclusion came in two late-October reports from the government confirming what many scientists have said for years: The burning of coal and oil and the reduction of the earth's plant life as human population grows are causing the planet to get hotter.

3   What is new is the finding that the changes may be noticeable by the 1990s, much sooner than previously expected.

4   The greenhouse effect occurs when gases accumulate in the air. These gases, like the glass in a greenhouse, let the sun's warming rays reach the earth while reducing the heat that escapes.

The Greenhouse Effect. *How it starts: Use of oil and other fossil fuels, clearing of forests, and industrial and urban growth cause carbon dioxide and other gases to accumulate in the atmosphere. Results: The gases prevent infrared heat from sunlight from escaping the earth's atmosphere. This causes temperatures to rise, with possibly disastrous effects on sea levels, climate, and crops.*

5   The detailed studies by the Environmental Protection Agency and the National Academy of Sciences made these points:

6   • By 2050, buildup of greenhouse gases will be twice what it was   15
in 1900.

7   • Global temperatures will climb an average of 3.5 degrees Fahrenheit by 2040 and as much as 9 degrees by 2100. Never in recorded history has the earth experienced such a rapid warming.

8   • Farmland in the U.S. Southwest may eventually dry up and   20
become useless. Some areas to the north, however, may have longer growing seasons.

9   • Coastal waters may rise 2 feet over the next century, forcing people to migrate or erect dams along shorelines.

10   The Environmental Protection Agency report, the more pessi-   25
mistic of the two, warned of "catastrophic" results unless plans are made with "a sense of urgency" to do such things as reforest vast tracts of land and sharply curtail the use of fossil fuels. The academy's report, however, saw none of the problems as insurmountable and said there is plenty of time to adjust.   30

11   "A program of action without a program of learning could be costly and ineffective," said William Nierenberg, director of California's Scripps Institution of Oceanography and head of the academy's study. "Rather, the watchwords should be research, monitoring, vigilance and an open mind."   35

READING FIVE

THE SILENT SUMMER

Ozone loss and global warming: A looming crisis

1   Chemicals don't have constitutional rights, conservationist Russell Peterson once observed; "[They] are not innocent until proven guilty." It was a point underlined last week with the revival of an almost-forgotten scientific controversy: are the gases called chlorofluorocarbons hazardous to the earth's health? Since 1974,   5
when two chemists suggested that chlorofluorocarbons (CFC's) destroy ozone in the atmosphere, the industries that make these chemicals have argued for definitive research before curbing production. Ozone depletion, they said, was only a theory. As a result, despite a 1978 U.S. ban on using the gases in aerosol sprays, more   10
than 700,000 tons of CFC's continue to leach into the atmosphere

each year—the byproduct of their use as refrigerants, industrial solvents and components of plastic foams, as well as in spray propellants manufactured in other countries.

2   But the world may no longer have the luxury of further study. As   15
Sen. John Chafee put it last week, at hearings of his Subcommittee on Environmental Pollution, "There is a very real possibility that we humans—through ignorance or indifference or both—are irreversibly altering the ability of our atmosphere to [support] life."

3   Twelve years ago, when Sherwood Rowland and Mario   20
Molina—then both at the University of California at Irvine—announced computer-model calculations that CFC's threatened the ozone layer, their main concern was over the increased amount of ultraviolet (UV) light that would reach the ground. Ozone, a molecule made of 3 atoms of oxygen, screens out about 99 percent of the   25
UV rays falling on the stratosphere, the layer of atmosphere 9 to 30

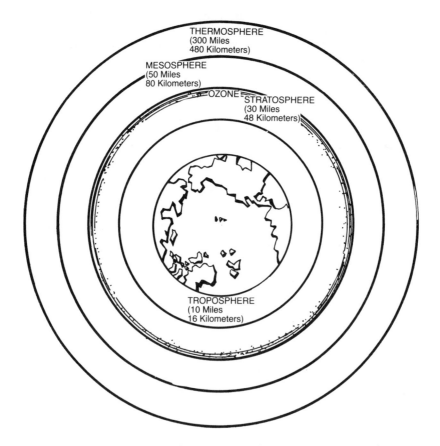

Ozone, a molecule made up of three atoms of oxygen, screens out about 99% of the ultraviolet rays falling on the stratosphere, the layer of the atmosphere ten to thirty miles above the earth's surface.

miles above the earth's surface. UV light causes skin cancer; indeed, the U.S. Environmental Protection Agency now says a 2.5 percent depletion of ozone might mean 15,000 additional victims of deadly melanoma each year.

4   Now researchers envision even more dire consequences. The same CFC's that destroy ozone are like a chemical version of a down jacket: they trap heat radiated from the ground. As the atmosphere warms, polar ice and glaciers begin to melt. Eventually, perhaps within 100 years, the rising oceans could drown much of the world's coastal plain, devastating low-lying countries like Bangladesh. This greenhouse effect, according to a parade of witnesses at last week's hearings, is no longer a matter of scientific debate, but a frightening reality. "Global warming is inevitable—it's only a question of magnitude and time," concluded Robert Watson of the National Aeronautics and Space Administration, the agency whose satellites monitor the upper atmosphere.

5   **Coastal erosion:** The EPA now projects that sea levels will increase somewhere between 2 and 12 feet by the year 2100. Just a three-foot rise—likely to occur by around 2030—would bring significant flooding to river-delta cities such as New Orleans and Cairo. Water could inundate huge tracts of arable land, especially in the Third World but also in places like the Netherlands and California's Sacramento Valley. Saltwater intrusion, moreover, would poison irrigation sources and bleed into the drinking-water supplies of many cities worldwide. Much valuable beach front would vanish forever, eroding two to five times faster than they do today.

6   Industry, however, continues to downplay the threat, and while the extent of the damage to the ozone layer may be disputable, the chemistry behind it is not. CFC's are not broken down in the lower atmosphere, so once released they rise slowly into the stratosphere. (Some 90 percent of the CFC's released between 1955 and 1975 are still on their way up.) The UV-light radiation in the stratosphere then breaks up the CFC's, freeing chlorine atoms. But chlorine has a chemical attraction for ozone and starts a chain reaction in which a single atom of chlorine can destroy up to 100,000 molecules of ozone, according to Rowland's estimates. NASA calculates that if CFC emissions continue at the present rate, 5 to 9 percent of the ozone layer will disappear over the next 50 years.

7   There is some evidence that ozone is vanishing even faster. The Nimbus 7 satellite has documented a 2.5 percent decrease over only five years. And British meteorologists last year reported that an ozone "hole"—a 40 percent depletion—opens up every October over the South Pole. The British scientists had been observing the ozone hole since 1977, in fact, but they waited eight years to alert the world to their findings because they couldn't believe their own data. The mind-set of other researchers predisposed them against believing in such a dramatic ozone decrease. NASA, for instance, had programmed the computers analyzing data from the Nimbus 7 to ignore abnormally low ozone readings, in the belief that they reflected measurement errors. Once the computers were reprogrammed, Nimbus 7 confirmed the existence of Antarctica's ozone

hole. Although the effect of CFC's in creating the hole each year is unclear, to Rowland the completely unexpected tear in the atmosphere is an early warning.   80

8   **Aquatic systems:** The resulting environmental damage is somewhat harder to assess. This week, for example, at a conference on ozone sponsored by EPA and the United Nations, Robert Worrest of Oregon State University will present studies showing that while the overall number of microorganisms in the ocean would not decline   85 much under the barrage of UV light, the relative numbers of different species would shift, because some are more sensitive to the rays than others. And this could mean wrenching ecological change. UV-light-resistant organisms like blue-green algae, for example, could come to dominate aquatic systems, driving out many UV-   90 light-sensitive plankton that commercially harvested fish feed on. And fish whose larvae float at the ocean's surface might be especially vulnerable: a 20 percent increase in UV light could kill 5 percent of the larvae of anchovies, which account for the bulk of the animal feeds used around the world. Even sublethal doses of UV   95 light can decrease the reproductive capacity of plankton that anchor the aquatic food chain, finds Worrest, "with rapidly occurring long-term effects as [the damage] propagates up the chain."

9   As the interaction of CFC's with ozone is better understood, researchers are turning their attention to the climatic effects. CFC's   100 are among the "greenhouse gases" that keep ground heat from escaping the earth's atmosphere. The best-known greenhouse gas is carbon dioxide, which is produced when fossil fuels are burned and forests (whose trees incorporate carbon dioxide) are razed. For years scientists have been warning that the ever-increasing emissions of   105 carbon dioxide would warm the globe, with dire consequences. Now they are seeing that other gases, especially including CFC's, contribute to the effect. Indeed, a gallon of CFC's traps more than 10,000 times more thermal radiation than the same amount of carbon dioxide. All together, the greenhouse gases are predicted to increase   110 earth's temperature an average of 3 to 8 degrees Fahrenheit by the 2030s—a change the size of which has never been experienced by the human species.

10   The most dramatic consequence of the greenhouse effect, of course, is the global flooding that would follow the melting of   115 glaciers. But the effect could drastically alter prevailing weather patterns, too. For one thing, meteorologists now believe that warmer oceans will spawn more powerful and more frequent tropical storms. An increase of only 2 degrees in average annual temperature, according to one calculation, will double the frequency of   120 hurricanes and extend the area over which they form. Even more disturbing is the projected impact on agriculture. Although higher temperatures can increase plants' productivity, the benefits would be short-lived. Because temperatures near the poles would rise three times as much as the worldwide average, global circulation   125 patterns that drive the weather will change. Species that evolved to fit particular niches would find themselves on new and hostile ground, in environments to which they were not adapted. With a

temperature increase of 7 degrees, for example, midlatitude bread- 130
baskets are expected to become arid, while marginal soils in the
north would get rain they could not utilize. One study predicts a 50
percent loss of precipitation in the American grain belt; another
foresees decreased yields of corn, wheat and soybeans of up to 10
percent. Nor will the seas take up the slack in food production.
Temperature differences between the poles and the equator make 135
ocean currents sink and rise, carrying nutrients scooped up from the
briny depths. As this temperature differential decreases, vertical
circulation and hence the amount of nutrients available to food fish
will also fall off, say Carl Wunsch of the Massachusetts Institute of
Technology. . . . 140

11   **In the bank:** As long as the chemistry of the upper atmosphere is
imperfectly understood, there can be no definitive answer to questions about when and how much CFC's and other gases will warm
the planet and deplete the ozone layer. But beneath the squabbles
over the exact amount of the warming, over how much the farm belt 145
will slip and how much farther the tides will encroach on the shores,
lie two facts. First, the ozone-depletion forecast Rowland and
Molina made a dozen years ago is remarkably close to current estimates. And second, the climate changes and ozone depletion that
CFC's are causing are "already in the bank," as Michael 150
Oppenheimer of the Environmental Defense Fund says; gases
released years ago have yet to make it to the stratosphere. Some
opponents of CFC regulation, like S. Robert Orfeo of Allied-Signal
Inc., argue for a wait-and-see approach, since "continued release of
CFC's will not pose a significant threat to the environment during 155
the time required to gain a better understanding of the science." But
that presumes CFC's innocent until proven guilty. . . . More and
more scientists worry that the longer regulatory action is
postponed, the worse the environmental problems will be for our
children. 160

REVIEW | THE SILENT SUMMER

Comprehension

1. What are CFCs used for?_____

_____

2. What effect do CFCs have on ozone?_____

_____

3. At what speed do the CFCs move up through the atmosphere? What
information does the reading give in support of your answer?

_____

_____

4. Why are some industries hesitant to stop producing CFCs?

_____

_____

_____

5. What are "greenhouse gases," and what effects do they have on the atmosphere?

_____

_____

6. What is the "ozone hole" and where does it occur?_____

_____

_____

7. How does too much ultraviolet light affect microorganisms in the ocean?

_____

_____

8. Why will flooding be a consequence of the greenhouse effect?

_____

_____

9. What does the author mean when he says the changes caused by CFCs are already "in the bank"?

_____

_____

Skill Review: Main Ideas in Paragraphs

Review paragraphs 1, 6, and 10; then, circle the statement below that most appropriately gives the main idea of the paragraph indicated.

1. Paragraph 1
   a. Chemicals don't have constitutional rights.
   b. There is still a great controversy over the effects of CFCs on the ozone.
   c. Industries do not want to stop manufacturing CFCs.
   d. CFCs have many uses in products we use such as plastics and aerosols.

2. Paragraph 6
   a. It is estimated that 5–9% of the ozone will be destroyed in the next 50 years.

  b. Industry disagrees with the idea that CFCs are destroying the atmosphere.
  c. It can be chemically proven that CFCs destroy the ozone.
  d. CFCs take a long time to work their way out of the atmosphere.

3. Paragraph 10
  a. The greenhouse effect will drastically affect weather conditions of the world.
  b. Hurricanes and tropical storms will be occurring more frequently in the future.
  c. Ocean currents and aquatic life will be altered because of the greenhouse effect.
  d. Global flooding will be the most noticeable effect of the greenhouse effect.

Textual Pattern: Cause/Effect Emphasis

1. Does this reading emphasize "causes" or "effects"?_____

_____

2. The diagram below depicts what happens as CFCs are released into the atmosphere as it is explained in paragraph 6. Fill in the missing steps.

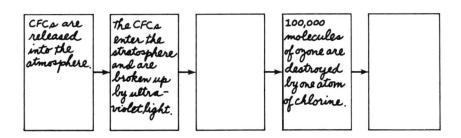

3. Reread paragraphs 4, 5, 8, and 10. As you read the paragraphs label the causes "C" and effects "E." Remember, in a chain reaction an effect can become a cause and a cause can also be an effect.

4. On a separate piece of paper, draw cause/effect diagrams of your own for paragraphs 4, 5, 8, and 10.

5. On a separate piece of paper, draw a diagram of your own which shows the causes and effect of the greenhouse effect as they are discussed in the supplementary reading "A Warmer Globe Just Around Corner" on page 196.

Questions for Further Discussion/Composition

1. Under the United States Constitution, a person is innocent of a crime until he or she has been proven guilty. The author says chemicals do not have that constitutional right. What does he mean? Do you agree? Why?

2. In previous readings, you have read about the destruction and in some cases the extinction of certain plants and animals. Is the destruction of the ozone a more serious kind of problem? Be as detailed in your answer as possible.

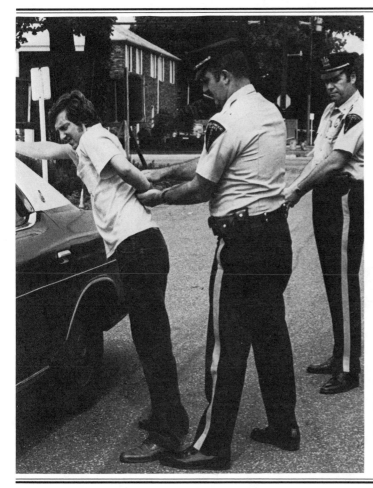

CHAPTER 5

*Lay not up for yourselves
treasures upon earth, where
moth and rust doth corrupt,
and where thieves break
through and steal.*

—New Testament
(Matthew 6:19)

CRIME

Crime is a word that brings out strong emotional responses in everyone. Many of us have been the victim of a crime, large or small. Perhaps you remember when the neighbor's son stole your favorite toy when you were small, or maybe the crime was more recent—and more serious. Whatever the case may be, you no doubt have ideas about what should be done to the offender, or what should be done so that the same thing doesn't happen to others. Some victims begin to feel guilty for not having done enough to prevent what happened.

We could fill hundreds of pages in talking about what victims can do, what they should have done, why people commit crimes, who commits the most crimes, what areas of the world experience higher crime rates, and so forth. But here in this chapter we are interested only in the possible solutions to crime. With so many types of crime, obviously we will not be able to talk about all of the problems that ought to be covered.

PROBLEM—SOLUTION

In the everyday world of business, science, and the humanities, problems constantly arise that require the attention of businessmen, scientists, and researchers. These people are paid to find solutions to various challenges, mysteries, or problems. The answers, once found, must be presented in a manner that will be clearly understood. Over the years several patterns have developed for the presentation of problems and their solutions. We will look for these patterns of organization in each of the reading selections in this chapter.

CONCLUSIONS AND INFERENCES

In addition to studying problems and their solutions, we will learn to draw conclusions and inferences from the writings of the authors. Conclusions are ideas that you develop on the basis of what you read and understand. Drawing a conclusion requires that you think *beyond* the words and ideas that are written. Inferences are ideas that are not expressed by the author directly but are understood by the reader. As a reader, you are, in effect, reading *between* the lines.

PREVIEW | CRIME: AN EVER-GROWING PROBLEM

Things to Think About

1. How would you describe the crime situation in your own country?

   Not too bad. But worst than 10 years ago,

2. What aspects or types of crime represent the most serious problem at the moment in your country?

   The stealing in the street. Steeling from people, bags, neclaces, watches.

3. What, if anything, is your country doing to solve these problems?

   I don't know. I think that nothing is being done.

4. What else should it be doing? _____

Vocabulary in Context

1. "Citizen groups have taken the law into their own hands by forming their own **vigilante groups** to administer 'judgment' when they feel that their criminal justice system has not performed its duty."

   vigilante group __a group of people to look after criminals, taking law in their hands__

2. "Experts argue whether the number of crimes committed is actually on the rise or whether there is simply a rise in the number of crimes reported. This issue is particularly true in cases of **conjugal** violence, the abuse of spouse or children."

   conjugal __husband and wife. / marriage__

Preview

1. Look at the title of this reading. What do you think the content of the reading is going to be?

    The crime is increasing

2. From the title, what is the author's emphasis: the problem or the solution? (Circle one.) As you read, indicate in the passage where the writer shifts from a discussion of the problem to a proposal of solutions.

3. Look at the following line from the article you are about to read. What do you think the author means by this?

    Whatever you do, wherever you live, you are a victim of crime whether you like it or not, whether you know it or not.

    *You have to suffer the consequences
    of crime in different ways and at any time
    even you don't like nor know it.*

READING ONE

CRIME: AN EVER-GROWING PROBLEM

1   Of the many problems in the world today, none is as wide-spread, or as old, as crime. Crime has many forms, including crimes against property, person, and government. There is even a class of crimes called "crimes without victims" (e.g., prostitution). Crime, in all its forms, penetrates every layer of society and touches every   5
human being. You may never have been robbed, but you suffer the increased cost of store-bought items because of others' shoplifting, and you pay higher taxes because of others' tax evasion. Perhaps your house is not worth as much today as it was a few years ago because of the increased crime rate in your neighborhood, or maybe   10
your business is not doing as well as it used to because tourism is down due to increased terrorism in your part of the world. What-ever you do, wherever you live, you are a victim of crime whether you like it or not, whether you know it or not.

2   Crime, especially violent crime, has risen to a point where many   15
people are afraid to walk alone in their own neighorhoods, afraid to open their door after dark, afraid to speak out and voice their own opinions. Some citizens have reacted by arming themselves with various weapons, legal and illegal, to defend themselves. Citizen groups have taken the law into their own hands by forming their   20
own *vigilante* groups to administer "judgment" when they feel that their criminal justice system has not performed its duty.

3   Experts argue whether the number of crimes committed is actu-

ally on the rise or whether there is simply a rise in the number of crimes reported. This issue is particularly true in cases of *conjugal* 25 violence, the abuse of spouse or children. Throughout much of history, cases of family violence and neglect often went unreported because of the attitude of society, which considered family matters to be private.

4   Other experts argue about who is really to blame for criminal 30 behavior: the individual or society. Researchers in the United States and Canada have identified several factors in society that contribute to the crime rate: massive urbanization, unemployment and poverty, and a large immigrant population. Other countries are more affected by factors such as politics, government corruption, and 35 religion.

5   The most important question that still remains unanswered, however, is how to stop crime from happening. In this chapter, we will look at a number of specific crimes and see what types of solutions are being proposed to combat them. In doing this, we shall see 40 how problems are presented and how solutions are offered.

REVIEW | CRIME: AN EVER-GROWING PROBLEM

Comprehension

1. Are you a victim of crime? Explain. *Yes. I pay higher taxes because of others' evasion. More expensive items because of others' shoplifting.*

2. True or false? Experts agree that the crime rate is rising. Explain.
    False. They argue wether the crime rate rises or wether the number of crime reported is increased.

3. What factors mentioned in the reading tend to increase the crime rate in your country?
    unemployment and poverty.

4. What are some of the methods or "solutions" that have been used over the years to prevent crime or at least to inhibit its growth?
    putting people in jail / capital punishment. physchiatic treatment. armed themselves against criminals.

Vocabulary Enrichment

In the following exercise, read each definition and fill in the word from those given below that fits the description. Once you have identified all the terms, then locate and circle them in the anagram. (You may work alone or in small groups as your teacher directs.) The first one has been done for you.

pickpocketing	criminal	terrorist
murder	juvenile	crack
rape	robber	counterfeiting
vigilante	handgun	theft
prostitute	burglary	Mafia
abuse	mugger	shoplifting
piracy		

assault and battery

___shoplifting___ taking merchandise out of the store without paying for it.

murderer / ___murder___ killing someone

thief – ___theft___ stealing another's property

burglar – ___burglary___ breaking and entering another's house to steal

___robber___ a person who illegally takes money from a *person or a* bank is usually called a . . .

terrorism ___terrorist___ a person who destroys property or kills innocent people for religious or political reasons is a . . .

___piracy___ illegally producing or copying the products of another company

counterfeiter ___counterfeiting___ making illegal money or currency

hooker (slang) ___prostitute___ a person who provides sexual services for money

___criminal___ a person who commits crime

___vigilante___ a person who takes the law into his or her *–guardian angels (New York)* own hands

___rape___ to forcibly have sexual relations with another

___Mafia___ one example of organized crime

___abuse___ severe harm to children, emotional or physical

pickpocket ___pickpocketing___ taking money from people's pockets

juvenile delinquent A young person who commits crimes is called a "___juvenile___ delinquent."

___crack___ a form of cocaine

manslaughter – cause death by being drunk, because you don't care.

_____*handgun*_____ a weapon used in many crimes

_____*mugger*_____ a person who attacks people in the street – *mugging*
with the intent to take their possessions

ANAGRAM: The words may be found vertically, horizontally, or on a diagonal.

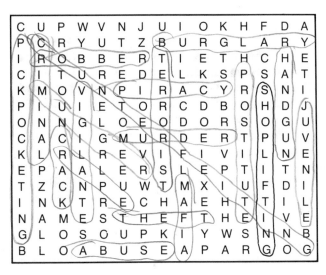

diagonally

Questions for Further Discussion/Composition

1. With regard to your personal life and your present neighborhood, what do you think is the number one precaution you should take to avoid being a victim of a crime?

2. What could your neighborhood council or representatives do to make your neighborhood a safer place in which to live and work?

3. What aspects of crime are most common in your school or workplace?

Conclusions and Inferences: An Introduction

Read the following dialogue:

T: "Honey? Let's go out to a movie tonight. Just the two of us."
F: "Oh, darling, that sounds like a great idea. We haven't been to a movie together in over twenty years. But what about the kids?"

T: "Oh, don't worry about the kids. I'll call Nancy next door. I'm sure she would agree to take care of them for a couple of hours."

From the conversation above, how old would you say these two people are?

last thirties or early forties.

How do these people get along with their neighbor Nancy?

very well

You answered the above questions by either: (1) filling in information based on assumption, common logic, or cultural norms, or (2) going beyond the information, adding to what was actually written. The first is called *making inferences;* the second, *drawing conclusions.* By analyzing the author's or character's choice of words and actions, and by using your knowledge of the world in general, you "understand" certain things that are not directly stated by the writer. The word "understand" is in quotation marks because the inferences and conclusions you are making may be right or wrong. Perhaps as you read your own cultural norms into this passage you might not come up with the same assumptions as the writer originally intended. It must be said that a reader's background knowledge may hurt or help the comprehension process, depending on whether or not that knowledge is compatible with the author's intent.

The distinction between inferring and drawing conclusions may seem difficult at the moment. Indeed the two processes are similar, so much so that they are often treated alike in many texts.

If you were asked whether or not the couple in the passage was married, you would take the information given, fill in **between** the lines, and say that they probably were, because of the terms they used when addressing each other—references to "the kids," the couple's having known each other for at least twenty years, and so on. This is making an inference.

If you were asked to guess whether or not the couple in the story really went to the movies that night, you would literally form the conclusion, by going **beyond** the actual content of the passage. You might say that you think they went, based on the fact that there seem to be no obstacles mentioned in the passage, the babysitting problem seems solved, and so on.

You may say you have never had experience with this kind of thinking before. But the fact is, you do it every day. Whether you are looking at a picture or watching other people as you walk down the street, you draw conclusions based on the information you receive from your senses (sight, smell, hearing).

We are often told, "Don't judge a book by its cover." And yet we do it unconsciously every day, by inferring or drawing conclusions—for example, about someone's socioeconomic status from his or her behavior, language, or clothes.

In reading, the process is just as common. Reading is an interactive process between the writer and the reader. Since every detail of a character's description, for example, cannot be related, much of how a character appears in the reader's mind is inferred by the reader.

Making inferences or drawing conclusions is the ability to develop, through general knowledge and logic, certain ideas from the information given. From the example dialogue above, you most likely guessed that the two people are married and are probably middle-aged. You infer their relationship because of the way they address each other and because of the reference to "kids." The information that they hadn't seen a movie together for over twenty years suggests an approximate age. You may also feel that they have a good relationship with their neighbor because the couple is relatively sure that Nancy will agree to watch the children while they are at the movies.

Part of developing this skill is knowing which conclusions can be made and which cannot. For example, do we know that Nancy is a teenager? No, we have no information that suggests her age. Can we infer that because this couple has been married for some time at least some of their children are teenagers? Again, we cannot. We have no way of knowing when this couple began having children. As you progress through this chapter, you will work through a variety of exercises to increase your ability to make appropriate inferences and conclusions as you read.

Problem–Solution: The Everyday World

Day in and day out, people are proposing new substitutes for fossil fuels, more efficient engines, better ways of treating industrial wastes, preserving nature, budgeting your money; the list is endless. Whether you are in business, the military, education, the medical profession, or government, there are problems that need to be solved.

Much of the material that you read in your chosen profession will contain proposals that claim to solve a problem. Accountants are hired to keep companies out of financial trouble. Diplomats are called in to find a solution that will bring peace to some war-torn part of the world. Advertising agencies are hired to help a product sell better. In all of these examples, it is important that the writers express their ideas clearly and uniformly and that the readers be able to follow the organization of the ideas as presented.

Let's assume that you work for the local government as the committee member in charge of transportation and that your city is faced with traffic jams in the early mornings and late afternoons. The mayor has asked for your recommendations to solve the problem. What are you going to do? How will you organize your letter or proposal? More to the point, how do English-speaking people organize their proposals?

As a reader, you should be aware of how these proposals are structured. In this chapter we will see how various people have used the problem/solution approach to write about crime.

PREVIEW | How to Keep Your Wallet Safe

Things to Think About

1. Have you ever had your wallet or purse stolen while you were working or shopping (or known someone who has)? Explain.

   Yes. My money was stolen from my purse.
   while I was out of my classroom with my students

2. Have you any idea how pickpockets operate? (What are their methods?)

   They Bumps you seemen accidentally but actually, the
   are robbing you at that moment.

3. Many pickpockets work in areas like airports, hotels, and tourist areas. Why is this? (Think of at least two reasons.)

   Too many people and nobody can realise the movement
   People is too busy with luggage, friends, new things to thing.
   in robbery).

4. In a moment, you will read what advice the author of this second reading has for us. Before you start reading, write down your own ideas about this problem. What advice would you give a friend who was planning a trip?

   Put this money in a safe place. Always Keep his eyes on his
   staff. And not take too much things on their
   hands.

Vocabulary in Context

1. "The telephone rang. 'This is Capt. Jack Davis from the 19th **precinct**,' the caller said. 'We've got your wallet, and the **perpetrator**.

Do you want to press charges?' He asked for the secret identification number that authorized the use of her automated-teller machine card. . . . When she **demurred**, he sighed and said, 'Look lady, we're just trying to do our job.' Reluctantly, she gave him the number.

"Later she realized that there was something **fishy** about 'Captain Jack Davis.' She called the real police, who confirmed that the caller was an **imposter**."

precinct _____

perpetrator _____

to demure _____

fishy _____

imposter _____

2. "A woman should never **dangle** a pocketbook from the shoulder or elbow. It's better to **clench** it under the arm."

dangle _____

clench _____

Preview

1. Read the first sentence of each paragraph. Then draw a line where the author's discussion of the problem ends and the presentation of the solutions begins.

    The line is drawn between paragraphs _____ and _____

2. Read the conclusion (paragraph 17). What is the main idea?_____

    _____

READING TWO

HOW TO KEEP YOUR WALLET SAFE

One evening after work, Jane Myers boarded a crowded Manhattan bus, her purse slung over her shoulder by its strap. When she transferred to another bus, she found her pocketbook open and the wallet gone.

2   At home, the telephone rang. "This is Captain Jack Davis from   5
the Nineteenth Precinct," the caller said. "We've got your wallet, and the perpetrator. Do you want to press charges?" He asked for

Reprinted with permission from Richard Wolkomir, "How to Keep Your Wallet Safe," *Reader's Digest*, December 1984, pp. 51–54.

the secret identification number that authorized use of Myers' auto-mated-teller machine (ATM) card. "This character's carrying a lot of money," he said, "and we need the number to see if he took it from 10 your account." When she demurred, he sighed and said, "Look, lady, we're just trying to do our job." Reluctantly, she gave him the number.

3   Later she realized that something was fishy about "Captain Jack Davis." She called the real police, who confirmed that the caller was 15 an imposter. They told her to call her bank. But the thief already had cleaned $200 out of her account. Nevertheless, because she had reported the card's disappearance promptly, the bank agreed to cover her loss.

4   According to the U.S. Bureau of Justice Statistics, Jane Myers is 20 just one of the more than 500,000 people estimated to fall victim to pickpockets and purse snatchers each year. The contents of the aver-age pocketbook—glasses, calculator and the like, but excluding cash—can easily exceed a hundred dollars in value. Stolen credit cards and debit cards, such as the ATM kind, can cost you even more 25 if you fail to report in time. Furthermore, your address and identi-fication are in someone else's hands.

5   "In Bogota, Colombia, there is said to be what amounts to a college for pickpockets," says Det. Kenneth Kleinlein, a pickpocket-prevention specialist with the New York City police special-fraud 30 squad. The course of study reportedly lasts some six to eight weeks at the "School of the Ten Bells," named for its final exam. A manne-quin, dressed in a man's vested suit, is said to hang by a wire from the ceiling. Stuffed in each of the suit's ten pockets are valuables, and attached to each pocket is a bell. The "students" must extract 35 all the contents without jingling a bell. "If they can do it, they

'graduate' and fan out to Boston, New York and other big U.S. cities," says Kleinlein.

6   Crime experts say that pickpockets focus on department stores, bus and railroad stations, sports stadiums, parades—wherever there are crowds. Most work in teams, watching you to see where you put your wallet after a transaction. Or in a crowd they may "fan" you, running feather-like fingers over your clothes until they locate your wallet.

7   The following suggestions will help you protect yourself:

8   • Pickpockets prefer to extract men's wallets from behind, where you can't see them. Thus, your most vulnerable pockets are the rear-trouser ones, followed by those on the sides. Least vulnerable is a jacket's inside pocket.

9   • If you carry a wallet in a trouser pocket, you can foil thieves by sealing the pocket with a safety pin. Nappy-surfaced wallets are harder to slide out than smooth leather ones. A thick rubber band around a wallet makes it stick on the pocket.

10   • A woman should never dangle a pocketbook from shoulder or elbow. It's better to clench it under the arm. Choose a pocketbook with as many impediments to pickpockets as possible—a flap over the top that clasps on the side, for instance, and zippers and snap pockets inside. Keep your wallet at the bottom of your purse, with everything else piled on top.

11   • Instead of carrying all your money, identification and credit cards in your wallet, spread them to various pockets. Never carry anything in your wallet that you don't need that day. Adds Det. Lucille Burrascano of the New York City police crime-prevention section, "Carry nothing worth fighting for, because you could get seriously hurt trying to resist a robber."

12   • Beware of scams. "A favorite trick is to get your name from your wallet, telephone you and say they're police and that you should come to the station to pick up your wallet," says Kleinlein. "When they see you leave the house, they burglarize it. Another ploy is to call up and demand a reward for returning your wallet. If you meet them and argue, the result is apt to be armed robbery. In either case, telephone the police at once."

13   • Don't carry your house keys in your wallet, because a thief then has easy access to your home. A pocket is a better place for keys. However, if thieves do get your keys, change locks immediately.

14   • When traveling, carry your passport, credit cards and other valuables in a money belt. Or sew in self-sticking fabric to seal your pockets. Once you reach your destination, lock valuables and important documents in your hotel's safe.

15   • If your wallet is lost or stolen despite these precautions, your first call should be to the police. Ask them to put the information into the FBI's National Crime Information Center computer, so it's available nationwide. The police report also puts on record the date you discovered your wallet was missing, a help in verifying that you reported credit-card loss promptly.

16   "Usually, if you report the loss of a credit card to the issuer before the thief uses it, you have no liability; otherwise your maximum liability is fifty dollars per card," says Richard Alderman, professor of law at the University of Houston Law Center and the   90 "People's Lawyer" for KPRC-TV News in Houston. "With a debit card, your liability increases the longer you wait. Generally, if you report within two business days of discovering the theft, your maximum liability is fifty dollars; if you wait more than two business days, you may be liable for up to five hundred dollars; and, if you   95 delay reporting for sixty days, you could lose all the money in your account, plus the amount of your overdraft protection." To facilitate reporting, keep a list of all your card numbers and documents, together with telephone numbers to call if they are stolen.

17   Alderman warns that you should also beware of carrying checks   100 in your wallet. You are not responsible for stolen unsigned checks, but should tell the bank the lost checks' numbers. However, you may be liable for losses from stolen signed checks—checks made out to cash or ones you have endorsed.

18   The more citizens who are alert to the possibility of stolen wal-   105 lets and pocketbooks, the fewer thefts there will be. And the FBI does provide an encouraging note. According to the most recent statistics, during 1983 the overall larceny-theft rate decreased by 7 percent, from 31 to 29 larcenies for every 1,000 Americans, the lowest rate recorded for this type of crime since 1978. FBI Director   110 William Webster attributes this decline, in part, to increased citizen awareness of crime-prevention precautions.

REVIEW | How to Keep Your Wallet Safe

Comprehension

1. True or false? Jane Myers luckily did not lose her wallet because she notified the bank quickly. ____F____

2. True or false? Over half a million people are victims to pickpockets each year in the United States. ____T____ *paragraph 4*

3. True or false? Pickpocket-prevention specialists must graduate from the "School of the Ten Bells." ____F____

4. True or false? According to the reading, the best place for a woman to carry a pocketbook is under the arm. ____T____

5. True or false? If you lost your wallet, your first call should be to the police, not the bank, even if your wallet contained credit cards. ____T____ *15 paragraph.*

6. True or false? If you report to the bank quickly that you have lost your credit card, you will not have any liability. ____T____

7. Which of the following protective techniques were mentioned? (Circle the letters of those that were mentioned.)

    (a.) A thick rubber band
    b. Secret pockets in the lining of your jacket
    (c.) Money belt *paragraphs*
    d. Mouse traps
    e. Scams *(tricks.)*
    f. Fans
    (g.) Keeping wallet at the bottom of your purse
    h. Small bells on your pockets
    (i.) Safety pins
    j. Dangling your purse from the shoulder
    (k.) Self-sticking materials

8. Does this article have a main idea? If so, what is it? _How To be_
    aware from   pickpockets.

Skill Review: Conclusions and Inferences

1. Assuming you were Chief of Police, what conclusions could you draw from this article in terms of how your department could combat pickpocketing. (If you were given the budget to hire two more policemen to aid in this matter, what type of assignment would you give them?)
    educate people / aware people from
    the ways they use to rob. / More patrol
    in crowded areas.

2. As a male, if you are not wearing a jacket, where's the next best place to put your wallet?
    In the front pockets

Textual Pattern: Problem/Solution

1. First, how did your advice in the preview compare with the advice given in the reading? Any similarities?
    Money in a safe place. Eyes always on the staff
    not too many things on the errands.

2. The solutions are divided into two types. What are they?
    Prevention (before)   Report (after)

3. In presenting the solutions, what assistance does the writer give to help you follow and remember his ideas?

_____

Questions for Further Discussion/Composition

1. Of all the protective methods that were discussed in this reading, which one do you think *you* will most likely use?

2. Do you have any other ideas that have come to mind since you read this article about protecting your wallet, purse, money, etc.?

3. Where do you think pickpockets work in your area? (If you were a pickpocket, in what areas of your neighborhood or city would you choose to work?)

Conclusions and Inferences: From What?

There are two main sources from which conclusions or inferences can be made: (1) the logic and experience of the reader, and (2) the content of the text itself. In this section we will talk about the sources from the text: conversation, action, facts and details, and the author's choice of words.

CONVERSATION

The words of the characters in a passage or article can lead the reader to infer certain things about that character. Look at the following lines:

"Did you do it, Bill?"
"Nope, not me, sheriff. I ain't never done nothin' like that."

Why do you suppose the sheriff is talking to Bill?

_____

What can you infer from Bill's language about his educational background?

_____

Authors use conversation to help their readers infer certain things about the characters. Sometimes characters talk about other characters. In an academic situation, however, conversation is not likely to present itself very often except in the study of historical or literary situations.

ACTION

The actions of the characters can lead you to draw conclusions about their background, intent, personality, and so forth. Read the following lines:

> The beauty queen jumped down off of the parade float with a sigh of relief. Noticing that no one was looking, she quickly turned aside, held one finger to the side of her nose, and blew. She sniffed quickly and ran to join the other beauty queens for the evening's banquet.

From her actions, what do you infer about this "queen"?

_____

Besides the way she blows her nose, what other actions tell you she does not seem to have much "royal blood"?

_____

FACTS AND DETAILS

A reader may use details or facts to draw conclusions about the subject of discussion. Read the following passage:

> Since the beginning, people and governments have tried a variety of solutions to crime. Governments have funded community-help programs against poverty and unemployment, created stiffer penalties, waged public education campaigns, boosted security and police forces, made punishment a public spectacle: all with varying results.

From the information given above, can we conclude the following? (Write "Yes," "No," or "Maybe.")

_____ The government doesn't seem to care about the crime rate.

_____ The final solution to crime has not yet been found.

_____ The government is still trying.

_____ Solving the problem of crime is not easy.

_____ Crime is a fairly recent social problem.

_____ Creating stiffer penalties doesn't help solve the problem.

AUTHOR'S CHOICE OF WORDS

Looking carefully at the author's choice of words can reveal information not directly stated in the text. It may allow you to draw conclusions concerning the point of view of the author. Look at the following passage as an example:

> The government has spent millions of dollars each year to control our coast lines, airports, and borders. In addition, military units have been flown to foreign countries to assist in tracking down drug manufacturing plants and in capturing the ring leaders. In the long run, however, the only way we're going to be able to stop the rising tide of illegal drug use is to educate the people. And we all know how successful we've been with that!

What is the author's opinion concerning her nation's ability to solve the problem of illegal drug use?

_____

What words or phrases in the text allow you to make this inference?

_____

In conclusion, there is much in a text that allows you to fill in where information or details are missing. Further examples and exercises in this chapter will help you be more aware of this skill. Of course, the text is not all you have to rely on. You contribute from personal logic and previous experience or knowledge, which we will cover in the next section on making inferences.

Problem–Solution: The Problem

After reading the article on pickpocketing, you should have some idea about how writers approach a problem and discuss their proposed solutions. The article was clearly organized for easy reading. This is not always the case, however, and the organization can be much more difficult to perceive. In this lesson we shall discuss in detail the first half of this type of reading: the presentation of the problem.

The problem can be presented in one of several ways, or, more likely by some combination. In the reading on pickpocketing, the problem was introduced by an **anecdote**. (Resist the urge to look up this word in your dictionary and read on!) An anecdote is a narrative example or story. In that reading, we read the story of how Jane Myers was fooled by the pickpockets who called her posing as police.

There are other ways to introduce the problem as well. Related to anecdotes are **examples**. Examples are like anecdotes, only much shorter. They are not narrative necessarily and usually do not exceed one paragraph in length. A writer may begin with several examples instead of one anecdote in order to gain the interest of the reader.

Some writers begin with **statistics** intended to catch the reader's attention, such as: "Every three seconds, some innocent person is beaten and robbed in the United States each day," or "Look around your classroom. One out of every three of your classmates will die of a heart attack before they reach the age of 65." Statistics can be simple tables and percentages or personalized in examples like the one on heart attacks just mentioned. Personalized statistics can have a strong impact on the reader. This is also the strength of examples and anecdotes. In narratives we as readers see ourselves in the victim's role.

Either before or after these examples or statistics, there is usually a formal **statement** or **definition** of the problem. Following the statement and examples, the writer may continue with a further discussion of the problem by relating its history, giving further examples, or outlining the causes of the problem. If the article is to be rather short, however, the author may turn directly to the solutions.

EXAMPLE

Go back now for a closer look at how the author presented and developed the problem in the article you read on pickpocketing. The first few paragraphs contain the story of Jane Myers. Then we have the formal statement or definition of the problem, followed by two paragraphs giving further background information into the problem.

In summary, the presentation of the problem consisted of three parts:

Anecdote ⟶ Statement ⟶ Further background information

PREVIEW | Auto Theft Turns Pro

Things to Think About

1. Have you or someone you have known ever had a car stolen? Do you have any idea how the thief got in and stole the car? Explain.

_____

_____

2. If you were a thief, what would you do with the cars you stole?

_____

_____

3. What suggestions do you have for car owners to prevent their cars from being stolen?

_____

_____

_____

_____

4. Is there anything the government can do to solve this problem?

_____

_____

_____

_____

Auto Theft Vocabulary

Match the word with its definition. (Work with a partner.)

1. underworld *e*
2. fence *h*
3. hit men *g*
4. racket *c*
5. crook *a*
6. hoodlum
7. ring *b*
8. gangland execution

5 – **a.** a criminal

7 **b.** a criminal organization

4 – **c.** illegal business

8 – **d.** murder by members of underworld, especially organized crime

1 – **e.** a noun referring to the organization, businesses, and way of life of those involved in illegal professions

6 – **f.** a juvenile delinquent; a minor who commits crimes or other antisocial behavior

3 – **g.** people hired to "mug," attack, or kill people

2 – **h.** a business that provides an outlet for the resale of stolen or counterfeit items and material

Vocabulary in Context

1. "A car owner shouldn't depend on the VIN (Vehicle Identification Number) marks already in place. A good idea is to **etch** the VIN . . . in several hard-to-find spots, using an engraving pencil . . ."

    etch _____

2. "In one common **gambit**, a thief will buy a wreck from a junkyard to get its title and VIN. The crook then steals an identical car . . ."

gambit _____

3. ". . . the FBI, state and local police agree that auto thefts can be **curbed**. Here's what the government, and you as an individual, can do . . ."

curbed _____

Preview

1. Look at the title of this reading. What does the expression "turns pro" mean? (Ask a classmate if necessary.)

_____

2. What do you think this title is trying to say about the crime of auto theft?

_____

3. Read the first paragraph now. What two methods does the author use in this paragraph to introduce the problem of auto theft?

_____

_____

4. Scan the reading quickly by reading the first sentence of each paragraph until you find where the author shifts from problem to solution. Draw a line there with a pencil or pen.

READING THREE

Auto Theft Turns Professional

*Stealing cars to order has become a billion-dollar racket, with its own underworld infrastructure of thieves, "chop shops," fences—even hit men. But it **can** be stopped.*

1   Every 28 seconds, somewhere in the United States a car is stolen. That's 1.1 million vehicles a year. If your turn is next, chances are you will never get your car back. If you do, it possibly will have been stripped for parts. When Connecticut police showed a West Hartford owner his new Buick Riviera—minus fenders, hood, doors and wheels—he wept.   5

2   Back in the 1960's, when joy riders did most of the stealing, nearly 90 percent of the cars were quickly recovered. Today, with professionals running this $1.7-billion-a-year racket, roughly 496,000, or close to 45 percent, "disappear" for good. Most are gob-   10
bled up in "chop shops," where cars are cut into spare parts for resale.

3   The market in hot parts is bigger than ever, because the demand—for spare doors, fenders, front hoods and so on—far outstrips the supply. Ever since the 55-mile-an-hour speed limit went   15
into effect, damage in accidents has diminished, with the result that fewer cars end up in the junk heap to become a legal source of spare parts. The current depressed state of the economy has also increased the demand for parts, since people are keeping their cars longer.

4   The professional car thief works on order. Say the front end of a   20
salesman's Chevrolet is damaged in an auto accident. He takes the car to a nearby body shop where a "nose job," a replacement front-end assembly, is recommended. He is told that it's "cheaper and quicker than banging it all out."

5   The body man calls his local parts dealer, who is linked to one of   25
two hundred salvage "hot lines." There is nothing dishonest in this; it happens every day. But on that line, according to Russell McKinnon, executive vice president of the Automotive Dismantlers and Recyclers Association, there may be a crook fencing for an auto-theft ring. For the crook, that phone call is "one on the wall"—an   30
order to steal.

6   That night, for an easy few hundred dollars, a young hoodlum hunts down residential streets and through parking lots for the right color and model Chevrolet. Two-thirds of all auto thefts take place at night and over half occur in residential areas.   35

Thomas R. Brooks, "Auto Theft Turns Pro." Reprinted with permission from the September 1982 *Reader's Digest.* Copyright © 1982 by The Reader's Digest Assn., Inc.

7   In his jacket, the thief carries a "slim-jim"—a long, flexible metal strip with a hooked end. He slips it between the closed window and door frame to unlock the car. Once inside, he slides a long, thin saw into the steering column to break the ignition lock, or uses a "dent puller"—a tool used in repair shops to straighten dents—to pop the lock. A good car thief can get a car moving in a minute. 40

8   Later, at the chop shop, a crew armed with acetylene torches, crowbars and screwdrivers cuts the car up within an hour for a quick high-yield profit. The front end brings $1500 to $2500 for economy cars, $5000 to $7000 for new luxury models. Doors are worth $50 to $500 each. 45

9   Often crooks simply throw the rest of the car away. Or they may leave it with a complacent junkyard dealer who destroys traceable parts and then sells the rest of the body and frame for scrap.

10   Sometimes the crooks do not move fast enough, and police raid a cutting plant. When the Boston police raided a Roxbury taxi and auto-body service, they recovered vehicles and stripped parts—36 Chevrolet doors, a dozen transmissions, engines, radiators and seats—worth $500,000. 50

11   Despite the lucrative and growing demand for stolen parts, many rings prefer to keep cars intact. In New York City, one racketeer stole 21 cars and started a rent-a-car business. Detroit poachers stole 23 cars, including three police cars, and used them to expand a taxicab company. 55

12   A Los Angeles operation, dealing mainly in Mercedes-Benzes, racked up $1.2 million in resales before the police broke it up. 60

13   Some 100,000 hot cars are shipped overseas each year. The best customers are Caribbean, Latin American and oil-rich nations. A new Ford LTD, retailing here for about $10,000, brings $20,000 in Mexico. A $26,000 Mercedes sells for over $100,000 in Algeria. 65

14   But if stealing cars is no sweat, providing them with "paper" is a test of ingenuity. Every vehicle manufactured must have a vehicle identification number (VIN)—it will look something like "IH57H5Z401067"—stamped on the engine or transmission. In addition, since 1969 a tag is usually affixed to the top left corner of the instrument panel cover. The VIN is the single most important clue in tracing a stolen car. 70

15   In one common gambit, a thief will buy a wreck from a junkyard to get its title and VIN. The crook then steals an identical car. Armed with the title and VIN, he replaces the stolen car's number with the one from the wreck. Then the stolen car can be registered or sold to an unsuspecting buyer. 75

16   In all, car theft cost us $4 billion in 1980, including the value of the cars stolen and the cost of trying to recover them. According to Denis M. Cavanagh, the FBI's specialist in auto thievery, "The number of auto-theft rings is definitely on the increase." To make matters worse, the mob has moved in. Over the past ten years, 24 gangland executions in the Chicago area alone have been linked to auto-racket takeovers. 80

17   Yet the authorities—the FBI, state and local police—agree that 85

auto thefts can be curbed. Here's what the government, and you as an individual, can do:

18   • Says Russell McKinnon, "We must create an audit trail that will allow police to trace the movement of a vehicle or major part from the time it leaves the original owner until it runs through a scrap processor." For instance, salvage dealers should be required to maintain scrap-vehicle manifests. Then a purchaser of parts would get a receipt bearing the VIN of the vehicle from which each part came. This would enable police to spot-check a dealer's inventory for illegal stock.

19   • The government should automatically revoke titles on all junkyard vehicles and provide a salvage certificate (valid only for junkyard use) instead.

20   • A car owner shouldn't depend on the VIN marks already in place. A good idea is to etch the VIN, or your own special "brand," in several hard-to-find spots, using an engraving pencil, or scratch it under the hood or trunk. Even dropping business cards into door interiors can help. One half-stripped auto was identified when the owner recalled that he had used a piece of shoe box as a washer under the transmission plate.

21   • When leaving your car, always remove your key from the ignition, close all windows and lock all doors. Unbelievably, nearly one in five autos stolen has been left either unlocked or with the keys in the ignition.

22   • Do not leave your license or registration in the car. Always leave the auto's title at home. Thieves can use these documents to sell a car fraudulently.

23   • Keep packages and valuables out of sight. CB radios, tape decks, and other expensive items left in full view invite theft.

24   • Always park your car in a well-lighted area and avoid parking in the same place. Park with front wheels cut sharply to left or right, so the car is difficult to tow away.

25   • Use special locks and alarms. Many auto-insurance companies give discounts on theft coverage if you install such anti-theft devices.

26   • Finally, curb your greed. The market for stolen goods now rivals legitimate business only because thousands of ordinary citizens are hungry for a bargain. Yet a terrific deal may mean it's crooked. If instinct tells you a car door is "hot," don't buy it.

27   The FBI and the police can bust individual car-theft rings. But without significant citizen involvement, these authorities will make only a small dent in this ever-increasing racket. "We can stop auto theft only if we eliminate the market," says Paul W. Gilliland, president of the National Auto Theft Bureau.

28   Auto theft is a billion-dollar industry because we let it be—by leaving cars unlocked, by patronizing unscrupulous dealers, by providing a market for fences. If we make theft difficult, resale impossible and detection certain, this criminal industry will collapse.

REVIEW | AUTO THEFT TURNS PRO

Comprehension

1. What is a "chop shop"? *A chop for cutting a car into peaces for resale*

2. How long does it take a good car thief to start a car? *1 minute*

3. Where do most car thefts take place? *residential areas. b*
   a. at shopping malls
   b. in residential areas
   c. in downtown business areas
   d. near train stations and airports

4. What is a VIN and how does it help to prevent auto theft? *The idatification number.*

5. Name one thing the government should do to prevent auto theft.
   Give a salvage certificate.

6. List three things you can do to protect your car.
   a. *Not park in dark places.*
   b. *Lock the Rockers.*
   c. *etch the VIN on different parts on the car.*

7. What does the author mean by the title "Auto Theft Turns Pro"?
   (How has the nature of auto theft changed in the last twenty years?)
   It became more organized, less individual.

8. Some stolen cars are shipped to foreign countries. Why? *To get better prices.*

Skill Review: Conclusions and Inferences

1. "The government should automatically revoke titles on all junkyard vehicles and provide a salvage certificate (valid only for junkyard use) instead."

   From the sentence above, we may infer that (circle all that apply):
   a. Titles are not presently valid at junkyards.

b. Titles usually remain with the cars at the junkyard.

c. Owners do not normally give the junkyard dealer the title to their cars when they take them to a junkyard.

d. Revoking the titles would help prevent cars from being stolen.

2. "When leaving your car, always remove your key from the ignition, close all windows and lock all doors."

Which of the following statements can we infer from the sentence above? (Circle all that apply.)

a. Not everyone takes their keys with them when they leave the car.

b. Some people do not lock up when they leave their cars.

c. Most people never leave their keys in the ignition when they leave.

d. A majority of the people lock their cars most of the time.

e. Your car will not be stolen if you lock the car and take your keys with you.

3. What can we conclude about car theft? Is it increasing or decreasing? Explain.

It is increasing (2⁷ paragraph)

4. According to the article, which is more important or more effective in eliminating auto theft: the police or the public? Explain.

The public. Being aware of the problem, Locking the lockers and windows. Avoiding to buy from unscroupulous dealers.

Textual Pattern: Problem/Solution

In our lesson before this reading we discussed several approaches or methods for presenting the problem. There are five sections to this author's presentation. Two have been identified for you. Fill in the other three.

1. _____

2. Explanation on causes for the development of the problem.

3. _____

4. More examples.

5. _____

Questions for Further Discussion/Composition

1. Before you read this article on car theft, you were asked what suggestions you had for car owners to prevent the theft of their car.

Now that you have finished the article, what suggestions would you offer to a friend who was about to buy a car?

2. According to the advice in the reading, where would be the best place in your neighborhood to park your car at night?

3. If you were given the assignment to speak at a student forum about car theft, what advice would you give concerning places to park while at school. (Are there any areas around your school or place of work that might be dangerous places to leave a car? Be specific.)

Conclusions and Inferences: The Reader

In addition to using the information in the text (such as conversation, actions, etc.) to draw conclusions, readers can use their own experience, knowledge of the world, and logic. Most writers assume that their readers will approach a reading or article with a certain amount of common knowledge of the topic—a certain amount of shared background. Remember, writers always write with a particular audience in mind. The problem, then, for you as a second language speaker is that you may not always have the necessary background information or experience to fill in the information the writer has not written about.

Because of differences in cultural background, the logic that the writer assumes you will apply may or may not be obvious to you. The following example will illustrate the point:

"What should I do?" he asked himself over and over again. The boss had been wrong to fire him. Nobody knew yet, but tomorrow his boss would announce the firing. His family name and honor that he had worked so hard to establish would soon be ruined. True, the company store he was in charge of had been losing many of its customers lately. But it was not his fault that one of the employees had been selling company secrets to competing businesses. How could he make the boss understand or change his mind? What was he going to do? How would he tell his wife when she came home from shopping? And then an idea came to him. He slowly went to the kitchen and took out a large knife. "Yes," he said, "I have to."

What is the man going to do?_____

_____

What details in the text suggest that he will do what you say?

_____

_____

_____

In small groups or as a class (as your teacher directs) discuss your answers and reasons for each.

The conclusion you should make here is that reading comprehension is not just knowing what all the words mean and simply adding them together like math. Figuring out the outcome of the short story above is not as easy as adding up the details. The author may think the ending is clear, but then the story was not intended for you. It was obvious to the author that the man was going to commit suicide to restore honor to his family name. Other people, of course, would not think of this. Their immediate conclusion would be that the man is obviously going to murder the boss before he can announce the firing tomorrow.

There are other possible endings to this story as well, as we are sure you found out in your class discussion. To a great degree, making inferences (the appropriate ones, that is) is dependent on the reader and writer sharing the same logic and background. Unfortunately, for the second language reader, logic is based on cultural values and personal experience.

In conclusion, you must realize that the more you know about the topic you are studying, the language, and its people and culture, the more successful you will become in making inferences and interpreting what you read.

Problem–Solution: The Solution(s)

The second half of the Problem–Solution approach is, of course, the presentation of the possible solutions. Perhaps by now you are already familiar with at least some of the methods that will be discussed.

If more than one solution exists for a certain problem, as is frequently the case, writers often discuss each one, beginning with the earliest and ending with the most recent. Similarly, writers may begin with the least effective and end with the most effective. Authors may also seem to use no apparent order, saving their favorite solution for the end. In any case, the most important solution is usually found near the end. This knowledge should help you know where to concentrate your energy.

If the problem is complex, an author may divide the problem into several aspects and talk about specific solutions to each aspect. For example, in an article on house burglaries, an author might talk about simple things like good lighting and carelessness. Then the author might discuss security devices and finish by discussing what homeowners can do to help each other by forming neighborhood watch groups, and so forth. In a related approach, writers take each of the examples cited in the presentation of the problem and discuss specific solutions.

In some cases, solutions are not rated against each other but are simply given in table or list form. For example, an article about controlling insects and other pests might include a table. For each type of pest, a corresponding pesticide might be recommended. In list form, solutions are often identified by number, by letter, or by other symbols such as asterisks (*), dashes (—), or bullets (•).

Finally, in addition to discussing the solutions, authors usually give advice on what to do if the solutions do not work or preventative measures fail to prevent the problem from occurring.

Let's go back to the previous two readings. These two articles are very similar in how they present the solutions. Both authors give the solutions in list form. (That is to say, the authors are not proposing one particular solution as being better than the others).

What symbol did they both use to indicate each solution? _____
How many solutions are offered in the article on pickpocketing?
_____

How many solutions are offered in the article on auto theft? _____

In the article on auto theft, the solutions are divided into two groups:

What are they? _____ _____

In the following reading on commercial piracy, see whether you can identify the methods and organization used in the presentation of the solutions.

PREVIEW | COMMERCIAL PIRACY

Things to Think About

1. Do you know what a "cheap imitation" is? Can you think of any cheap imitations that you have seen (or perhaps bought)?

2. What kinds of items or merchandise are most often illegally copied or imitated?

_____

_____

_____

3. Is there a difference between taking a company's money and taking its business products? Explain.

_____

Preview

1. Define the following words:

   commerce _____

   to pirate _____

   lackadaisical _____

   counterfeit, phony, fake, bogus _____

2. Scan the quote at the beginning of the reading. What do commercial pirates do?

   _____

3. Read the last paragraph. What seem to be the focus and intended audience of this article?

   _____

4. In paragraph 5, you will see the formal definition of the problem: Read it and rewrite it in your own words below (with the help of a classmate or dictionary if necessary).

   _____

   _____

5. a. As you read, draw a line with your pencil or pen when you discover where the problem ends and the presentation of the solutions begins.
   b. Be aware of how the solutions are presented. Be prepared to answer questions on the organization of the presentation of the authors' solution(s).

READING FOUR

COMMERCIAL PIRACY

*"Every day, American companies see their valuable
patents, copyrights, and trademarks ignored, misused,
and blatantly ripped off by commercial pirates."*

1   The Food and Drug Administration recalled 357 heart pumps used in hospitals across the country because these $200 intra-aortic balloon pumps, which help maintain heartbeat during open-heart surgery, were believed to contain potentially dangerous, cheap counterfeit parts.   5

2   The American Medical Association has become concerned over phony "look-alike" narcotics—so-called because they are the color, size, and shape of legitimate tranquilizers and amphetamines and even display forged trademarks. "Look-alikes" are believed responsible for at least 12 deaths, including a 17-year-old New Mexico boy   10 who fell into a coma after swallowing two phony biphetamines.

3   Some counterfeit parts were discovered in the space shuttle, in NATO aircraft, and were reportedly installed in personal helicopters of Queen Elizabeth II and the late Egyptian Pres. Anwar Sadat.

4   In a counterfeit Chevron fungicide sold to Kenya for use on   15 coffee crops, pirates substituted chalk. The phony material destroyed a large percentage of one of Kenya's leading crops. Unbeknownst to Chevron, this counterfeit was brewed in Taiwan.

5   The list goes on. Commercial piracy is the trafficking in counterfeit products or services which incorporate characteristics of   20 authenticity in order to deceive.

6   One type—trademark counterfeiting—involves the attachment of seemingly real trademarks or brand names to bogus products or services, thereby fooling consumers into thinking they have bought the legitimate item. Fake designer jeans and cosmetics of poor   25 quality, but carrying the well-known label, are examples. . . .

7   Every day, American companies see their valuable patents, copyrights, and trademarks ignored, misused, and blatantly ripped off by commercial pirates. While $35,000,000,000 may sound like a payment on our national debt, it is what Americans will probably   30 pay for licensed products this year (licensed products are those that carry a familiar name lent to them for a royalty by the owner of that name). Licenses can be as ritzy as Yves St. Laurent jewelry, or as cuddly as Strawberry Shortcake on a sheet.

8   Japanese prosecutors are considering indicting 11 people sus-   35 pected of importing at least 6,000 Taiwanese-made counterfeits of Cabbage Patch dolls. News reports quoted Japanese police as saying that as many as 17,000 copycat dolls were the hit of Christmas 1983

Judith Miller and Mark Miller, "Commercial Piracy." Reprinted from *USA Today Magazine*, November 1985. Copyright 1985 by the Society for the Advancement of Education.

and 1984 in the U.S. and are available in limited quantities in Japan
at a higher price than these cheap imitations.   40

9   The rapidly growing problem of commercial piracy also threat-
ens the health and safety of consumers, costs American jobs, and
sabotages the ability of U.S. businesses to compete. Explained Sen.
Matthias: "Commercial counterfeiting . . . has the potential for killing people. Commercial counterfeiting used to be limited to high   45
fashion luxury items, but today . . . such things as prescription
drugs and automobile parts have become targets for counterfeiting." For example, bogus brake drums have caused fatal car accidents.

10   Rip-offs of American intellectual property rights take different   50
shapes, but the harm to American industry always is enormous. The
variety of counterfeit goods is limited only by the fertile imagination of the commercial pirate. The auto parts industry alone estimates that it suffers $3,000,000 worth of damage yearly. One study
estimated that trade in pirated goods accounts for two per cent of   55
total world trade!

11   Piracy in video games increased from 10% of the market in the
1970's to 30% today. In what can only be described as Freudian, one
Taiwanese pirate firm adopted as its slogan, "Your Game, My
Game," which is printed on its company stationery.   60

COUNTERFEIT APPLES

12   The flood of pirated computers into world markets graphically
shows what commercial pirates can do to a company's copyrights
and patents. Apple II has the dubious honor of being the pirates'
favorite because it is so popular and has a vast number of software   65
programs. According to Albert Eisenstat, vice president and general
counsel of Apple, "look-alike" Apple II's began showing up in the
Far East in early 1982, mostly assembled in tiny, household-sized
shops. Counterfeit Apples, virtually identical to the real thing,
reached the U.S. market within a few months. Despite the Apple   70
Company's registering trademarks and copyrights with Customs,
filing lawsuits, and bringing an action before the International
Trade Commission, the volume of phony Apples has grown. Large
piratical firms invaded the U.S. market, ready, willing, and able to
make and distribute "look-alike" Apples by the thousands.   75

13   Apple pirates can be as clever as they are greedy. They have
contrived sly schemes to trick Customs. Duplicators change the
physical design and name. Moreover, disassembled or partially
assembled bogus computers have been imported—legally—
because, if they are not accompanied by semiconductor chips con-   80
taining copyrighted Apple software, they are allowed to enter the
U.S. Once past Customs, it is smooth sailing to add the infringing
chips. One pirate included a separate mini-program that scrambled
the pirated Apple program so the theft couldn't be spotted by
Customs!   85

14   This mess was created by a Customs decision not to detain computers unless they also contained patented chips. According to a

1984 report by the House Subcommittee on Oversight and Investigations, *Unfair Foreign Trade Practice: Stealing American Intellectual Property: Imitation Is Not Flattery:*   90

15   This decision has created a hole in the regulations large enough to drive a truck full of counterfeit computers through. Piratical computer importers also vary their ports of entry. After one company had 10 to 15 computers seized in San Francisco, it tried elsewhere. . . . It is not known if shipment to other, less vigilant ports went undetected.   95

Osborne, IBM, and Radio Shack computers are being copied as well. . . .

16   Furthermore, according to the Subcommittee Report, this "contributes to our balance of payments deficit."

17   Taiwan, Mexico, Indonesia, the Philippines, Hong Kong, 100 Thailand, Brazil, Singapore, Nigeria, and Colombia are major sources of fakes. In some countries, commercial piracy has become the de facto national industrial strategy!

18   Pirates can prevent a company from recouping its research and development investment, thus killing a small firm. For example, in 105 1970, Stanford Ovshinsky, head of a small high-tech company, obtained patents on a process that showed promise in upping computer memory storage. His firm's R&D created the process.

19   Then, in 1983, a giant Japanese firm boldy announced at a New York press conference that it had discovered the same process. 110 Ovshinsky, enraged, testified that his patented process was well-publicized in *Scientific American*, a National Academy of Sciences report, and his own lectures. Ovshinsky claimed he had made trips to Japan and held technical discussions with that Japanese company in the mid-1970's regarding a licensing arrangement for his 115 process. Thus, when the Japanese company made its announcement 13 years later, Ovshinsky, flabbergasted, remarked, "It was just incredible, in fact, unbelievable to me . . . because of the arrogance."

20   Ovshinsky and his company had no choice. "We had to sue," he 120 said. "The appropriation of property is theft." Ovshinsky believed the Japanese company's plan was to tie him up in litigation until his patents expired, then to flood the market with their pirated product. Because his firm was relatively small, the litigation cost would siphon funds needed for R&D of new technologies—the essence of 125 his enterprise's survival. Without punishment, Ovshinsky explained, this practice would continue against small American high-tech concerns.

MORE DETERRENCE IS NEEDED

21   U.S. laws protecting intellectual property rights are weak and 130 don't threaten the ballooning avalanche of pirated goods. For example, there are virtually no criminal penalties for trademark or patent rip-offs. Massive changes are necessary in civil and criminal statutes relating to copyrights, trademarks, and patents. Penalties

must be made more severe, and the coverage of protection under 135
these laws should be expanded and updated.

22   Despite the best-laid plans of U.S. Customs personnel, there
aren't enough of them or sufficient funds to stop the flow of pirated
goods into the U.S. Moreover, laws to protect intellectual property
rights of goods marketed by American companies in Third World 140
nations are notoriously weak, and enforcement is lackadaisical or
absent, especially against local companies who violate an American
firm's trademark. . . .

23   If little is done to combat the problem, it will undoubtedly
spread. For example, organized crime is now taking its chunk out of 145
commercial piracy, particularly in the sale and distribution of elec-
tronics and clothing. According to the subcommittee Report,
"Given the high profit in such activity, the role of organized crime is
expected to increase."

24   James Bikoff, president of the International Anticounterfeiting 150
Coalition, testifying before Congress, cited a news report that law
enforcement agencies implicated the Genovese crime family in a
conspiracy to market fraudulent designer jeans. Bikoff further
charged he was aware of a case involving mob ties with counterfeit
watches and, possibly, medications.   155

25   Progress has been made in bilateral and multilateral efforts to
increase protection afforded intellectual property rights and to
encourage foreign governments to crack down on pirates. Unfortunately, existing international agreements, such as the Universal
Copyright Convention or the 1883 Paris Convention for the Protec- 160
tion of Industrial Property, are outdated and impotent to combat
the problem. . . .

26   Hundreds of Customs agents are routinely dispatched at American ports to cut the avalanche of pirated merchandise. In addition,
Special Customs Service Teams, containing about six auditors and 165
investigators each, are stationed at 40 U.S. ports as part of "Operation Tripwire."

27   "Tripwire" agents on the prowl for such illicit goods as fraudulent computers, medical services, designer jeans, airplane and auto
parts, and electronic, textile, and steel items with deceptive labels 170
have received special training from companies so they will better be
able to spot counterfeits.

28   A coalition of American businesses urged Congress to impose
sanctions on foreign nations where pirated products are produced.
As Bikoff told the *Los Angeles Times,* "The United States is the single 175
most lucrative market for counterfeit goods." According to Bikoff, a
study by the International Trade Commission showed that bogus
products invading the U.S. are concocted in 43 countries, 30 of
which are in the Far East. For their own good, Bikoff warned American consumers to buy only from reputable merchants.   180

29   Alas, the Consumer's Golden Rule must be that, if a bargain
seems too good to be true, it is. Frequently, however, consumers
know they are buying fakes, but don't care. If you do care, here is
some advice from the International Coalition: Examine merchandise for workmanship and read labels. If a jar of petroleum jelly, for 185

instance, has its chief ingredient misspelled on the label, it's forged. Know what legitimate retail prices are—too utopian a price cut should be suspect.

30   Some things are being done by legislators about business buc- caneers. A 1982 amendment to a Federal law provides for a five-year 190 term in jail and/or a $250,000 fine for individuals or a $1,000,000 fine for corporations.

31   Bikoff hopes a California law that went into effect Jan. 1, 1984, will be used as a model by other states. According to this law, any company guilty of trafficking in phony trademarks is liable for tri- 195 ple the damages incurred by the real trademark holder and triple the profits earned from selling the phony, plus lawyers' fees and court costs.

32   The companies themselves are not taking commercial pirating of their products lying down. For example, the Apple Company has 200 filed 40 lawsuits in 16 countries to block the sale of fake Apples.

33   In Philadelphia, in April, 1984, Joel M. Isadore, a student, received the dubious distinction of being the first U.S. citizen to go to prison on a guilty plea of breaking American copyright laws. Isadore and three others pleaded guilty of smuggling counterfeit 205 Apple II computers into the U.S. from Taiwan. Guilty pleas also came from two brothers who run three Philadelphia importing firms.

34   As Sen. John Danforth (R-Mo.), chairman of the Senate Subcom- mittee on International Trade, told a press conference: "The United 210 States will not tolerate the wholesale piracy and counterfeiting of American merchandise."

REVIEW | COMMERCIAL PIRACY

Comprehension

1. True or false? Thanks to increased awareness by the governments, the problem of piracy is growing smaller. _____

2. True or false? The United States is the main market for pirated items. _____

3. True or false? Organized crime figures have been involved in com- mercial piracy for many years. _____

4. Which of the following industries were mentioned as victims of piracy?

Apple computers	Cabbage Patch dolls
jewelry	clothing
cosmetics	sports equipment
automobile manufacturers	shoes
medicine	military
furniture	art

5. a. In what part of the world are most of the counterfeiting or pirate businesses located?

_____

b. Why is this so? _____

_____

_____

6. Two types of piracy are discussed in this article. What are they?

_____   _____

Skill Review: Conclusions and Inferences

1. From the last line of this article, do you think the author feels the problem will be solved or not?

_____

2. From the information and testimony given in this article, what conclusions may the reader make about Far Eastern governments?
   a. Many government officials are corrupt.
   b. Many government officials seem unconcerned about piracy.
   c. Some governments actively support piratical industry.
   d. Many of the officials do not understand the concept of "piracy."

3. Choice of words often reveals an author's opinion or position concerning a certain subject. For each pair of words below, circle the word that shows a stronger emotional bias.

different	strange
clever	sneaky
macho	manly
waste	extra
proud	cocky
overweight	fat

4. In the following quote from the article, which word clearly reveals the author's opinion on customs laws? (Underline it.)

This mess was created by a Customs decision not to detain computers unless they also contained patented chips.

Textual Pattern: Problem/Solution

1. Which paragraph supplies the formal statement of the problem?

_____

2. Give one example from the article for each of the following categories:

    a. statistic: _____

    b. example: _____

    c. anecdote: _____

3. Current solutions are ineffective according to the author. How does the author propose to improve this situation?

    _____

    _____

    _____

4. What are businesses doing to combat piracy? _____

    _____

    _____

    _____

5. According to the author, what should individuals do to help?

    _____

    _____

    _____

    _____

6. Can you think of other possible solutions the author did not mention? List your solutions below.

    _____

    _____

    _____

    _____

7. To review the organization of this article, detail the four stages in the author's development of the situation concerning commercial piracy.

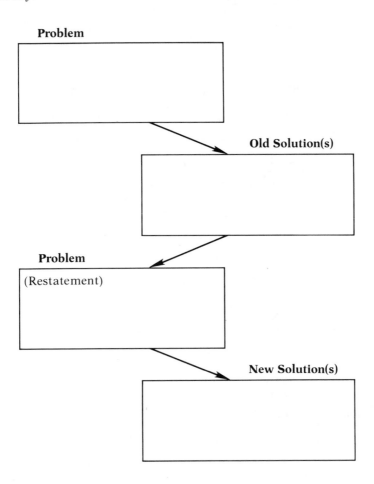

Problem

Old Solution(s)

Problem

(Restatement)

New Solution(s)

Questions for Further Discussion/Composition

1. This article is obviously written from an American point of view. What might other countries' points of view be on this issue?

2. What should our responsibility as a consumer be in this issue? If we know that the products in a particular store are pirated, should we buy them? Is this the same or different from buying a car that we know was stolen?

3. Pirated items come in many sizes, big and small. How many of your own copies of cassette tapes or computer software are pirated or copied? Is this still the same crime?

Problem–Solution: Purpose and Balance

Just to review for a moment, below are the basic steps or sections used in the development of problems and their solutions:

PROBLEM

1. Anecdotes, examples, or statistics (to gain the reader's interest and establish the existence of the problem)
2. Formal statement, definition, or description of the problem
3. Further development through other examples, history, etc.

SOLUTION(S)

1. Description of the solution(s) already in use
2. Proposal of other possible solutions
3. Discussion of the solution(s), including advantages, limitations, etc.
4. Possible repetition of some examples of the problem for the purpose of seeing specific application of solutions
5. Concluding remarks on the present and future relationships between the problem and the solution(s). (Authors may reemphasize their preferred solution if that was the intended purpose of the article.)

The selections you have read so far in this chapter obviously are not as complicated as what you see above. Authors would not use all these steps unless they were writing a fairly long paper or article, nor are authors obligated to follow the order exactly as printed above.

Authors pick and choose according to the intended length of the writing as well as their purpose in writing. A sales manager, for example, might detail a problem by describing instances in which deals have fallen through. The manager would then state the nature or source of the problem, followed by proposals for its elimination.

The balance of the discussion concerning problems and solutions depends on the writer's purpose. If the purpose is to talk about solutions, as in a brochure on car theft, then very little space will be taken up by examples or history of the problem. On the other hand, a witness testifying for a government investigation on police corruption may spend most of the time talking about the problem, with few solutions to offer.

In the "Commercial Piracy" selection that you read, there was an imbalance in the discussion of the problem and solution. The writer was more concerned about discussing the size and seriousness of the problem. Be thinking about emphasis in the following article on burglary.

PREVIEW | THERE'S A BURGLARY EVERY 10 SECONDS—MY TURN

Things to Think About

1. What does the word *burglary* mean? _____

    _____

2. What is the difference between a burglar and a thief? _____

    _____

3. What special measures of precaution should you take if you are going away on a vacation or business trip?

    _____

    _____

    _____

    _____

    _____

Vocabulary in Context

1. "Officer Coleman did suggest that I install a metal guard plate over the lock, to **thwart** lock pulling **devices**, similar to those used by car thieves."

    thwart _____

    devices _____

2. "All of these systems can be installed as local or central-office alarms. Local alarms simply **create a racket** on the **premises**, whereas central-office alarms alert the local alarm company, which calls the police. . . . Central-office alarms can either sound on the **premises** or be silent. Police everywhere prefer the noisy alarms."

    create a racket _____

    premises _____

3. "The police can help here . . . they will lend you an engraving kit so you can mark cameras, videotape recorders, computers and the like. You can then put **decals** on doors and windows to notify would-be burglars that your goods can easily be **traced**."

    decals _____

    traced _____

4. "They will each do a security survey and estimate what I need and how much it will cost **to deter** future thieves."

   to deter _____

Preview

1. Read the first two paragraphs. Do you notice anything different about the style or approach of this author compared with the style in the previous readings in this chapter? Explain.

   _____

   _____

2. Read the last paragraph. Does the author think it is worthwhile to use the solutions that are available nowadays?

   _____

   _____

3. Look back once more at the list of steps or strategies that writers use when presenting problems and solutions. Be aware of these as you read this article. (Though the style is different in this reading, the writer uses basically the same strategies as other writers.)

4. As you read, draw a line where you find the division between the problem and the solution.

READING FIVE

THERE'S A BURGLARY EVERY 10 SECONDS—MY TURN

1   A company that sells burglar alarms is sending a rep to my apartment. Next week a locksmith will come. They will each do a security survey and estimate what I need and how much it will cost to deter future thieves.

2   It's been nearly three months since the burglary. The rational explanation for my procrastination is simple. I have nothing left for anyone to steal. But I know there is another, emotional reason. I still

Jean A. Briggs, "There's a Burglary Every 10 Seconds—My Turn." Reprinted by permission of *Forbes* magazine, January 2, 1984. © Forbes Inc., 1984.

don't like thinking about the burglary. Not that it was violent. I was away at the time, traveling in the Middle East. When I returned the apartment was neat and orderly. It wasn't until the following day, reaching for a watch, that I discovered I had been robbed.

3   The watch wasn't in its little blue velvet case. Funny, I thought. I reached for another watch. Its red satin case was empty, too. My pearl ring, my jade ring, my little emerald ring from Peru and a ring with a diamond and ruby chips—all were gone. So were some jade teardrop earrings I had just received for my birthday. Only a silver and turquoise Hopi Indian ring remained. My heart seemed to drop straight to my knees, where it pounded wildly.

4   Perhaps my friend who has a key had stopped by and had taken these things for safekeeping. I clung to that thin hope even after I discovered that the locks on one of the windows opening onto the fire escape were open, and that there were also grimy fingerprints on the window frame.

5   I called my friend. No such luck. He came over to comfort me and I called the police. They arrived within minutes, but what could they do? The jewelry was gone, the burglar was gone. The police listened; they made a report. They suggested I get better locks for my windows.

6   My reactions were guilt and remorse. Somehow I felt it was my fault that I had lost those beautiful things—treasured gifts, remembrances of my travels, family keepsakes, even my grand-mother's wedding ring. Why hadn't I been more careful?

7   I had felt so secure in my apartment, believing as I did that the courtyard and fire escape were simply inaccessible. Why had I had this blind spot? After all, I had once found a large kitchen knife on the fire escape, a knife that I now recognize was wonderfully suited to opening window locks. At the time I thought someone in an apart-ment above me had carelessly dropped it. Dumb!

8   Eventually I called my insurance agent. Unfortunately he couldn't offer much consolation. My policy, like most policies, has a limit on jewelry, and I didn't have any floaters—special riders to cover specific items. Still, I did get a check right away for the $500 limit of my coverage.

9   I can, of course, also deduct some of the loss when I file my tax returns in April. But that's about all I can expect. Return of the jewelry is unlikely, particularly since the case was closed the day I reported it (as I discovered the night the policewoman came over to take fingerprints). In Manhattan a detective is not assigned to the case unless the loss exceeds $10,000.

10   To anyone in a police department anywhere, my tale is all too familiar though the total number of household burglaries in the U.S. declined 10% in 1982 from 1981, one burglary still takes place every 10 seconds in this country. The vast majority occur during broad daylight—between 9 A.M. and 2 P.M.—when residents are away from home. Usually, the burglar gets in fairly easily through a door or a window. "In this area," says Sergeant Pete Toomey of the Charlotte, N.C. police department, "they usually pry open the back door."

11   There are some exotic entries: the thief in Minneapolis who 60
pushed in a wall air-conditioning unit and crawled through the
shell, the one in Philadelphia who gained access by pushing in a
clothes dryer vent, the pair in Charlotte who crawled under a house
and cut an opening in the floor (only to have a china cabinet fall on
them), the "plumber" in Oklahoma City who made unsolicited vis-
its to houses labeled FOR SALE, etc. 65

12   But burglars seldom need to be so industrious. An empty dwelling advertises itself—newspapers and flyers piling up on doorsteps,
unshoveled walks, uncut grass, dark windows night after night,
even the absence of garbage for a few days.

13   Gaining entry is usually a breeze. Windows and doors are the 70
most vulnerable points. Many locks—ordinary clamshell window
locks, for example, or doorknob locks with throws less than an inch
long—are easy to defeat. If he has to, a determined burglar will
make his own opening in a door, floor, ceiling or wall.

14   The name of the game is to make getting into your place more 75
trouble for the burglar than getting into somewhere else. The police
themselves stand ready to help. Most departments around the country now have crime prevention units (a legacy of the short-lived and
controversial Law Enforcement Assistance Administration). They
will visit your home and do a security survey, suggesting ways to 80
better secure doors, windows and other entryways. This service is
absolutely free.

15   Detective Jack Meeks of the New York Police Department's
crime prevention unit explains, "We like to have a one-two punch.
We like to see good hardware and good software." He means good 85
locks and good alarm systems.

16   But what really galls police is the carelessness that makes so
many burglaries child's play. For example, people who live in high-
rise buildings wrongly assume their apartments are safe because of
the presence of a doorman. Or they foolishly give out their keys to 90
tradespeople, cleaning persons, even building personnel. Veteran
New York police warn tenants to change locks when they move into
an apartment, and to give spare keys to no one. One cop wearily
recounted a typical series of thefts in a building: The thief enters the
building either through a ruse (such as making a delivery) or when 95
the doorman is occupied. Working from the top floor down (less
traffic) he simply tries door after door, and opens the ones offering
least resistance.

17   Police officer Stephan Coleman of the 13th precinct, on Manhattan's East Side, visited my apartment last week. He thought my 100
front door and the two locks on it were adequate. The door is solid
wood covered with metal, and there's no gap between it and the
frame. Hollow core doors can be kicked in, and gaps invite prying.
The mortise lock, buried in the door itself, has a healthy throw that
fits snugly into the groove in the plate opposite. The other, a dead- 105
bolt lock that I had installed when I moved in, while not the most
pick-resistant on the market, has a sufficiently long vertical drop
bolt. Officer Coleman did suggest that I install a metal guard plate
over the lock, to thwart lockpulling devices, similar to those used by

car thieves, and he suggested that I replace the peephole with one 110
with a wider angle of vision. As for my windows, he recommended
the relatively inexpensive technique of "pinning" them. That means
drilling a hole through each corner of the top sash of the bottom
window and halfway through the bottom sash of the top window
and inserting two easily removable nails. Pinning makes the win- 115
dow impossible to open from the outside without breaking the glass.

18   The same technique can be used on sliding glass doors. Police
also recommend installing screws in the space above sliding doors
so they can't easily be lifted out.

19   For my apartment Officer Coleman thought a hardwire alarm 120
would be appropriate. That's the kind that goes off when the contact
between points is broken. There are also alarm systems that can
sense movement in a given space. These are based on three different
technologies—infra red, ultrasonic and microwave—each with
advantages and disadvantages.   125

20   All of these can be installed as local or central-office alarms.
Local alarms simply create a racket on the premises, whereas central-office alarms alert the local alarm company, which calls the
police or carries out your other instructions. Central-office alarms
can either sound on the premises or be silent. Police everywhere 130
prefer the noisy alarms. "We want all hell to break loose," says
Meeks. "We want to annoy the neighbors so they'll call the police.
We want to scare the burglar away. Remember, he is probably
armed and is potentially dangerous. Time, noise and light are the
burglar's worst enemies."   135

21   All alarm systems require some common sense. False alarms are
everyone's enemy. In some areas, including New York City, if the
police respond to three false alarms in 90 days, they won't respond .
anymore.

22   Okay. You have taken care of the hardware and the software. 140
What more can you do? The answer is to know exactly what you
own and what it's worth, and to make sure you have adequate insurance coverage. It's also a good idea to mark your valuables in some
way. The police can help here, too. As part of Operation Identification (another legacy of the LEAA) they will lend you an engraving 145
kit so you can mark cameras, videotape recorders, computers and
the like. You can then put decals on doors and windows to notify
would-be burglars that your goods can easily be traced. Marked
goods, obviously, are harder to sell.

23   Jewelry, antique furniture, and fine art are, of course, more diffi- 150
cult to protect. But you can photograph and "fingerprint" even delicate works of art without damaging them. (An appraiser will tell
you how. If you need one, contact the Appraisers Association of
America, 60 East 42nd Street, New York, N.Y. 10165, for names of
local appraisers in your area.   155

24   A final defense the police recommend is a Neighborhood Watch
program. You and your neighbors agree to look out for one another.
The local crime prevention officer will be happy to give your group a
few tips.

25   Such preventive medicine does work, although there is seldom 160
evidence of its effectiveness. But if there is a wave of burglaries in
your neighborhood, chances are, the homes hit will not be those
with the best—but those with the easiest—pickings.

REVIEW | THERE'S A BURGLARY EVERY 10 SECONDS—MY TURN

Comprehension

1. True or false? Police prefer the noisy type of alarms, instead of the silent ones. _____

2. True or false? All alarm systems require a certain amount of common sense. _____

3. True or false? A relatively inexpensive way to secure front doors is called "pinning." _____

4. True or false? It is normally safer if you live in high-rise apartment buildings. _____

5. True or false? According to statistics, most burglaries occur in the daytime. _____

6. According to Briggs, besides having the appropriate "hardware" and "software," what else should you do?

_____

_____

7. Define "Neighborhood Watch." _____

_____

8. What are a few of the signs that careless homeowners give to let burglars know that no one is home?

_____

_____

9. What were the reactions and feelings of the author when she realized that her precious jewelry had been stolen?

_____

_____

10. What do you feel is the main idea of this article (in your own words)?

_____

_____

11. Time, light, and _____ are the burglar's worst enemies.

Skill Review: Making Inferences

1. What inferences are we to make from the author's following statements?

> I had once found a large kitchen knife on the fire escape, a knife that I now recognize was wonderfully suited to opening window locks. At the time I thought someone in an apartment above me had carelessly dropped it. Dumb!

_____

_____

2. From the information given in the article, tell how you think the burglar got into the author's apartment.

_____

3. All the author's valuable jewelry was gone. "Only a silver and turquoise Hopi Indian ring remained," according to the author. What possible inferences or conclusions can we draw from this? (Write down at least two.)

a. _____

b. _____

c. _____

d. _____

Textual Pattern: Problem/Solution

1. In which paragraph does the author formally end her discussion of the problem and define her solutions? Write the key sentence below.

_____

_____

2. This key idea is restated once more elsewhere in the article. Write the sentence below.

_____

_____

3. Through the discussion of the security of her own apartment, Briggs offers a number of suggestions or solutions. Consult the article again and fill out Officer Coleman's evaluation.

Security Evaluation

Name of owner: _Jean A. Briggs_

Type of dwelling: _Apartment_

Item:	Adequate	Not Adequate
Front door		
Back door		
Garage door		
Sliding doors		
Peephole		
Door locks (reg.)		
Door locks (dead bolt)		
Lighting		
Alarm systems		
Recommendations:		

4. Briefly, what **additional** areas of security did the author talk about?

_____

_____

_____

_____

_____

5. The following is a graphic representation of the organization Jean Briggs uses to discuss the problem of burglary and its solutions. From the random list below, identify and write in each stage.

Problem:

Statistics   Details   Examples   Anecdote

Solution:

Solutions for anecdote   Definition   Other suggestions

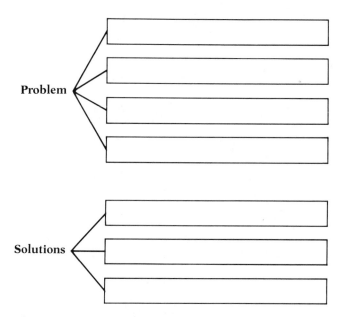

Questions for Further Discussion/Composition

1. When you think of your dormitory, apartment, or house, what particular advice do you feel you should follow immediately to prevent a burglary?

2. Where do you think is a good place to hide your valuables if you are going to be gone for a day or two?

3. There is a lot of debate currently on whether homeowners should own handguns for protection of person and property. What is your opinion?

CHAPTER 6

*There can never be a
moment of true standstill
in language, just as little as
in the ceaselessly flaming
thought of men.*

—Wilhelm von Humboldt
(1767-1835)

LANGUAGE

L anguage is a fascinating field of study to which many people have devoted themselves. Some seek to define and describe the many languages that exist (literally hundreds; thousands if we include the many dialects). Others seek to teach these many languages to others. The search to understand humanity's unique possession has gone on for thousands of years. Much has been learned, and much still awaits discovery.

CLASSIFICATION

Classification is one of the most common activities of the human mind. It is something we do every day to make sense of the world around us. We categorize everything we see, smell, and hear in order to help us understand and remember. If we did not do this, our memories would be overcome with millions upon millions of seemingly unrelated objects, people, and phenomena. Though all humans classify what they experience, not all people or cultures classify in the same way. In this chapter we will discuss the nature and principles of classification and their purposes for the English-speaking people of the world.

REMEMBERING WHAT YOU READ

By this time you may be saying to yourself, "Okay, I've learned lots of skills, but I still can't remember much of what I've read." Perhaps you have wondered from time to time why some people seem to be able to remember more of the material they read without seeming to spend any more effort than you do. Retaining information and recalling it later are skills that are very important if all your other skills are to make a difference. In this chapter we will discuss ways in which you can improve your ability to remember and use the information you obtain through reading.

Classification: The Everyday World

Classification is a tool for survival. We divide the people we know, the objects we see, and the events we are involved in so that the world around us will make sense. We put our clothes into separate drawers so we won't be late for work. We separate our tools so we can fix a leak before the entire kitchen is flooded. We separate people into groups according to social class, professional relationships, and so forth, so we will react appropriately.

When we see the words *banana, apple, orange,* and *grapes* we think immediately of the fact that all of these are fruits. This is their class or category. Or perhaps we think more generally of the category of food. When you see the following list of names, what do you think of?

John Wayne
Marilyn Monroe
Robert Redford
Meryl Streep   _____
Sylvester Stallone
Bette Davis

How about this list of names?

Placido Domingo
Elvis Presley
Diana Ross   _____
Boy George
Tina Turner
Luciano Pavarotti

You see? You have been classifying all your life! Your brain does it unconsciously to help it remember and keep track of things. The following demonstration should help you to see this. Look at the list of items below for ten seconds and then cover it up.

bath towel, fork, chair, toothbrush, envelope, knife, pen,
soap, desk, plate, shampoo, cup, stamp, bread, razor

Now how many of the items can you remember? Write down as many as you can.

_____

_____

Now look at the following lists of items for ten seconds and cover them back up.

soap	desk	cup
bath towel	chair	bread
shampoo	pen	plate
razor	envelope	fork
toothbrush	stamp	knife

Now how many of the items can you remember this time?

_____

_____

If you are like most people, you remembered more of the items the second time. In fact, it was the ability to logically group language units that allowed you as a baby to learn your first language. You succeeded in learning the rules of grammar and remembering which words were verbs, which were nouns, and so forth. In reading and writing, you are simply asked to use this thought process consciously.

STATEMENT OF CLASSIFICATION

In writing, when only one topic is discussed, it is usually a **description** or **definition**. A discussion of two things is usually for the purpose of **comparison**. When discussing several or more objects and their relationships, we are dealing with division or **classification**.

When classifying, authors will usually state what the classification is and what its underlying principle is. As you might expect, this statement can usually be found in the introductory portion of the reading. If it's not there, quickly check the concluding remarks for a summary statement of the classification.

PREVIEW | WHAT KIND OF LANGUAGE ARE YOU USING?

Things to Think About

1. From the title we can guess that the author of this next reading is probably going to discuss some of the "kinds" of language or languages that are used today. What do you think the author means by "kind"? There are several possibilities. List several ways in which language can be classified.

    a. _____

    b. _____

    c. _____

2. Have you thought much about language or what it is used for? List below some of the specific communicative functions or purposes of language.

a. _____   b. _____

c. _____   d. _____

e. _____   f. _____

Preview

1. Read the introduction and underline the statement of classification. What is the topic of this article?

   Topic: _____

2. How many "kinds" of language is the author going to discuss?

   List them: _____

   _____

3. According to the introduction, are we going to be reading about kinds of language or kinds of languages? Explain.

   _____

   _____

READING ONE

WHAT KIND OF LANGUAGE ARE YOU USING?

1   Language has more than one purpose. We might say that language operates on different levels, except that the word "levels" suggests higher and lower planes in a scale of value, and this is not intended here. We shall deal with three functions: the informative, the expressive, and the directive. To say that language has these three functions is to say that there are three different reasons for speaking. One reason, or purpose, is to communicate factual information. This is the informative function. We speak also in order to express our feelings, to "blow off steam," or to stir the feelings and attitudes of the person we are talking to. We shall call this the expressive or "emotive" function. And, finally, we speak in order to get people to act. This is the directive function.

2   Some illustrations are in order. A book on astronomy describes the solar system and the stars. We learn that the diameter of the earth is about 8,000 miles; that of the sun, about 800,000 miles; a ratio of 100 to 1. We learn that the star Betelgeuse has a diameter three hundred times that of the sun. This means that if the earth is represented by a baseball, about three inches in diameter, then Betelgeuse would have a diameter of almost a mile and a half. We may learn that there are as many stars in the heavens as there are grains of sand on all the seashores of the world. I have just been using language to communicate information.

3   Expressive language is a second type. When I talk about the United States Senator I like least, I may let off some steam, and relieve my pent-up feelings. I may even infect you with my feelings, making you feel as I feel. The poet, of course, is a specialist in expressive language, as in the lines:

> Comes the blind Fury with th' abhorred shears
> And slits the thin-spun life.

These lines give expression to John Milton's feelings and perhaps make us feel as he felt. When we tell our friends a funny story, to get a laugh, we express our feelings, too, and affect theirs.

4   The third type, directive or action-provoking speech, is illustrated by examples like: "Do unto others as you would have others do unto you," or "Praise the Lord, and pass the ammunition!" We say these things to get action. Ceremonial language, such as "I am happy to meet you," "What a beautiful baby!" and conversation about the weather, also have a directive purpose: to establish social rapport, and to get a friendly response.

5   There are, then, at least three different purposes of discourse. We may also make a somewhat similar classification for words, that is, for words taken by themselves. A basic distinction here is between what we shall call neutral words and emotive words. Neutral words merely convey ideas to us, as when I say, "The sun rose at six this morning." The words in this sentence do not arouse our emotions. But words like "God," "love," "freedom," and "communism" are so closely connected with our total attitudes to life that they are likely to arouse emotional reactions. This division of words into neutral and emotive, however, is relative to our personal experiences, for there is nothing in the word itself which makes it neutral or emotive. If a word conveys nothing but an idea to you, then it is neutral to you; if it arouses your emotions, then it is emotive to you. The word "bread" is a neutral word to me, but to a "fat boy" or a starving man, it may be fraught with emotion. Nevertheless there are some words which can be counted on to make almost everyone "see red," so to speak, like the word "traitor."

6   This classification of words is independent of our classification of the functions of language, for those who wish to inform may use either type, as may those who want to express their feelings, or to get action. In general, however, neutral words will be used when we wish merely to inform, emotive words when we wish to be expressive.

REVIEW | WHAT KIND OF LANGUAGE ARE YOU USING?

Comprehension

1. True or false? Neutral words are not used in expressive situations.
   _____

2. True or false? Informative language does not contain emotive words. _____

3. True or false? Whether a word is neutral or not depends on the individual. _____

4. True or false? "Stop!" is an example of expressive language.
   _____

5. True or false? A joke would usually be an example of expressive language. _____

6. If the earth was represented by a baseball, which is about 3 inches in diameter, how big would our sun be? (Give your answer in feet.)

   _____

7. How are the classification of words and the functions of language related?

   _____

Skill Review: Drawing Conclusions

1. Would it be possible for a linguist to classify all the words in a particular language as either neutral or emotive? Why or why not?

   _____

   _____

2. Analyze the following phone conversation and define its parts according to three functions of language. (There may be more than one right answer.)

		Function
Peter:	Hello?	_____
John:	Hi, this is John.	_____
	What are you doing right now?	_____
Peter:	Just watching TV.	_____
	Why do you ask?	_____

                                        Function

John: Well, I was wondering if you'd
        like to play football.   _____

Peter: Sure!   _____
John: Good. I'll see you at Rick's house
        in 10 minutes.   _____

Textual Pattern: Classification

1. In classifying something or a group of things, an author chooses a
    principle (in this case, language functions), introduces the first cate-
    gory, defines it, and provides examples. Each of the following cate-
    gories is then defined by comparison to the previous one(s) and
    illustrated by examples as well.
        Use the information in the reading to fill in the outline below.

    The Three Functions of Speech

    a. _____ Definition:

                        Examples:

    b. _____ Definition:

                        Examples:

    c. _____ Definition:

                        Examples:

2. Provide an example of your own for each of the three categories:

    a. _____

       _____

    b. _____

       _____

    c. _____

       _____

Remembering What You Read: Association

In the introduction, we raised the issue of remembering what you read.
You may say to yourself that you are just one of those unlucky people
who do not have a good memory. Psychologists, however, say that this
is not true. Besides, there are several different types of memories.

One of the keys to improving your ability to remember what you read is understanding how your memory works in processing and storing information. (Other areas of memory include experience and manual skills, but we will not discuss them here.)

The key word here is *works*. Your memory must *work* at remembering what you read. Memory is not a passive skill. Your eyes do not simply burn words or ideas onto your brain cells. Very few people have memories that act like a camera—taking pictures of everything they glance at. For most of us, remembering requires a conscious effort to arrange and store information in a way that makes it easier to recall later. One important principle that increases your ability to remember is—**association**.

Look at the following list of items:

bath towel, fork, chair, toothbrush, envelope, knife, pen, soap, desk, plate, shampoo, cup, stamp, bread, razor.

"Wait!" you say, "I've seen this list before!" That's right. In our introductory lesson on classification, we talked about how your mind classifies information and experiences in order to remember them and make sense of the world. Classification is a form of association. Classification is the process by which we form groups on the basis of shared or common characteristics. We think of the fork, knife, bread, and plate as items associated with eating.

When you were asked to view the same collection of words already classified into three groups, it became easier to remember more of the items. The principle is similar in reading. If the ideas do not seem related to each other, then you will have a hard time remembering them. The key is to understand the relationships between the ideas or paragraphs. You must try to understand the overall pattern or organization that governs the ideas you are reading about. This is the main purpose for teaching you the textual patterns in the first seven chapters of this textbook. Having a pattern in mind allows you to make the appropriate associations between ideas as you read.

We have all had the experience of reading something that we couldn't seem to understand (even in our own language) because it was on something we knew nothing about. As human beings, we learn and remember by associating new information (experiences, etc.) with what we already know. In this way we expand and update our understanding of the world. If we have no previous knowledge or concept about a particular topic, however, it becomes extremely difficult to remember, or understand, much of that topic. So, our prior knowledge is a foundation for the process of association.

Much of the initial difficulty of reading in a foreign language is simply the vocabulary. Beyond vocabulary, however, is the reader's knowledge of the content or topic.

This is why we have asked you to think about the topic before each of the readings. The preview questions are intended to help you realize how much or how little you may already understand about the topic. These questions also give you an opportunity to obtain more information through discussion with your classmates. Naturally, the more you know, the more you can associate. And the more you associate, the more you will comprehend and remember.

One of the keys to remembering, then, is to *associate* ideas in a meaningful way, and then to *associate* these ideas with what you already know and with what you are doing in your personal life.

Classification: The Principle

When people categorize objects or events, they do it on the basis of only one principle or criterion. This does not mean that objects cannot be divided on the basis of other criteria, but that only one is used at a time. In this manner, the categories do not overlap. The qualities or characteristics which form each subgroup are exclusive of the qualities of the other groups. For example, we might divide the students at your school by race, religion, height, grade point average, etc. There are numerous ways to classify students, but only one principle is used. Look at each of the following two sets of items. Identify the principle of classification that was used in each.

Set 1

A	B	
blond	carrot	
baker	criterion	_____?
broken	clip	
bottle	computer	

Set 2

A	B	
cat	monkey	
lion	ape	_____?
tiger	chimpanzee	
leopard	baboon	

It is a faulty classification that divides a group into the good, the bad, and the ugly. The third category is not related to the first two by the same principle. Ugly people can be members of either of the first two groups.

Nor could we divide the men we know into the following groups: (a) tall, (b) short, (c) blond, (d) overweight. The first two categories are related to the principle of height, but the latter two are unrelated.

It is the reader's primary responsibility to identify the ruling principle for the classification. This principle is strongly linked with the author's main idea and purpose. Look at these introductory sentences and identify the topic and the principle.

1. Students at my university can be divided into three groups: Orientals, Polynesians, and Europeans.

    Topic: _____

    Principle: _____

2. There are basically three types of writing systems in use today: pictographic, syllabic, and alphabetic.

    Topic: _____

    Principle: _____

3. When authors write, they do so for the purpose of entertaining, informing, arguing, summarizing, or giving directions.

    Topic: _____

    Principle: _____

4. Theories concerning the origin of language can essentially be divided into three categories. The earliest group can be labeled "divine origin" theories. After these, we have the "socio-evolutionary" theories. And the most recent attempts to explain the origins of language fall under the category of "psycho-evolutionary" theories.

    Topic: _____

    Principle: _____

As you approach each of the remaining readings, try to establish the author's principle of classification as early as you can, preferably in the previewing stage. Then, as you read, try to confirm your intitial expectation.

PREVIEW | THE VARIETY OF CONVERSATIONS

Things to Think About

1. Why do people talk? In other words, what are the purposes of conversation? Record your ideas below.

    _____

    _____

    _____

_____

_____

_____

_____

2. When was the last time you had a serious "heart-to-heart" conversation with a member of your family?

_____

Can you remember what you talked about? _____

_____

_____

Vocabulary in Context

1. "There are many other types of direct interchanges between speakers and listeners confronting one another, remarkably **diverse** in motivation and character, ranging from cocktail party **chitchat** and dinner table **chatter** to the most serious of political debates."

diverse _____

chitchat _____

chatter _____

2. "In addition, like play itself . . . conversation that is playful in **intent** rather than seriously motivated is conversation that is enjoyable for its own sake, and not pursued for any **ulterior** purpose."

intent _____

ulterior _____

3. "If, in rare instances, the persons involved in such talk have an emotional intimacy that affects their dealing with one another, this **unduly** complicates matters for them by introducing constraints and **impediments** which **skew** this type of conversation from its normal course."

unduly _____

skew _____

Using the word-attack skills you learned in chapter 1, break the word **impediments** into its prefix, stem, and suffix, and define it.

_____

4. Of course, many words are not definable from context. Look at the word in the context below. If it is unfamiliar, look it up in your dictionary.

"A good social conversation can never be planned in advance. It just happens if the circumstances **fortuitously** favor its occurring."

fortuitous(ly) _____

Preview

1. Read the introductory paragraphs (1–3) and underline the statement of classification. How many types of conversations will the author discuss? _____

2. From what you have read, what other aspect of speech has the author previously talked about?

_____

_____

3. Read the conclusion and list the four main types of conversations.

_____   _____

_____   _____

READING TWO

THE VARIETY OF CONVERSATIONS

1   Forums following instructive lectures or persuasive speeches are just one kind of conversation and discussion. It is a very special kind because such question and answer sessions draw their substance from a speech made and listened to and they take direction from the purpose that motivated the speech. There are many other types of direct interchanges between speakers and listeners confronting one another, remarkably diverse in motivation and character, ranging from cocktail party chitchat and dinner table chatter to the most serious of political debates and business conferences and the most exalted university seminars and scholarly symposia.

2   In order to set forth the rules for making different types of conversation more pleasurable and profitable, it is necessary to classify them, noting the characteristics that distinguish them from one

another. We must do so for the same reason that we found it neces-   15
sary earlier to distinguish the two main types of uninterrupted
speech—the persuasive and the instructive—and to consider the differences in the role of the listener with respect to each.

3   I propose the following fourfold classification of the types of
two-way talk—the kinds of conversation. It is convenient for our   20
purposes even if it is probably not exhaustive.

4   The first division is between playful and serious conversations.
By playful conversation, I mean all forms of talk that have no set
purpose, no objective to achieve, no controlling direction. In addition, like play itself, which is that form of human activity in which   25
we engage purely for the pleasure inherent in the activity itself,
conversation that is playful in intent rather than seriously motivated is conversation that is enjoyable for its own sake, and not
pursued for any ulterior purpose.

5   Another name for this kind of talk is "social conversation." It is   30
the easy, informal talk that takes place in pleasant companionship
with one's friends or associates. It may be informative, but it need
not be, nor need it be enlightening though it may also be that. It
simply gives pleasure and, by doing so, it brings persons together in
friendship or helps to make them better acquainted with one   35
another.

6   A good social conversation can never be planned in advance. It
just happens if the circumstances fortuitously favor its occurring.
To set in advance what is to be discussed is to plan something akin
to a business meeting. Social conversation should be permitted to   40
wander. There is no goal to reach, nothing to decide.

7   The remaining three types of conversation, according to this
scheme of classification, are all serious rather than playful. They are
purposeful and directed. Here the major division is between conversations that are essentially and intimately personal and those   45
that are impersonal.

8   What I have in mind when I use the phrase "personal conversation" is often called a "heart-to-heart talk." All of us can recall

one or another occasion in our lives when we have said to someone
near and dear to us, "Let's have a heart-to-heart talk about that." 50

9 The phrase "heart-to-heart talk" can be misleading if it is misin-
terpreted to mean that we engage in such talk using our hearts
rather than our minds. All talk, playful or serious, personal or
impersonal, involves the exercise of the mind. But the so-called
heart-to-heart talk is one in which we use our minds to talk to one 55
another about things that affect our hearts—our emotions and feelings, our affections and disaffections.

10 Such talk is concerned with emotional problems of deep concern to the persons involved. It is deeply serious, probably more
serious than any other kind of talk, for it aims to remove emotional 60
misunderstandings or to alleviate, if not eliminate, emotional ten-
sions.

11 The two remaining types of talk, both serious, are impersonal
rather than personal. One can be called theoretical because it aims
to effect a change of mind. It is instructive if the persons involved 65
acquire knowledge they did not have. It is enlightening if they come
to understand what they did not understand before, or come to a
better understanding of the matters considered.

12 The talk is practical if it aims at the adoption of a course of
action, the making of a decision that affects action, or the alteration 70
of emotional attitudes and impulses that may have consequences
for subsequent action. When it deals with emotions and impulses
for the practical purpose of selling merchandise, of winning political support, of getting a business plan or policy adopted, the talk is
still impersonal rather than personal. 75

13 The persuader of others with some practical purpose in view
usually plays upon the emotions of those whom he is trying to persuade. His own emotions may not be involved except for the purpose at hand. But in the personal or heart-to-heart talk, the
emotions of all the parties come into play in direct confrontation. It 80
is the kind of talk that occurs between husband and wife, parents
and children, members of a family, lovers and friends—never persons who do not have intimate relationships with one another that
bind them together emotionally.

14 The seller and buyer are not thus related, nor are the business 85
executive and his associates, nor those who talk with one another to
achieve some political goal. They are usually strangers or mere
acquaintances. Even if they happen to be friends, the ties of friendship and love do not enter into the picture. If, in rare instances, the
persons involved in such talk have an emotional intimacy that 90
affects their dealing with one another, this unduly complicates matters for them by introducing constraints and impediments which
skew this type of conversation from its normal course.

15 The personal or heart-to-heart talk usually involves two persons
or at most only a few. It usually takes place under circumstances 95
that are private rather than public. It is never the kind of talk that
the persons involved would wish to have recorded in the minutes of
the meeting, nor is it conducted by having a prepared agenda for the
occasion. It may happen spontaneously without preparation, or it

may be planned by one person and proposed to the other with a   100
time and place appointed or set for its occurrence. However it happens, it is always a significant event in their lives, affecting them
and no one else.

16   Impersonal talk, either instructive or persuasive, may involve
two persons, a few, or a larger group. If the persons involved have   105
been associated with one another for some time, that association
will affect the ease with which they can communicate with one
another. They will have some acquaintance with one another's
vocabularies, one another's intellectual commitments, one
another's assumptions or prejudices. If they come together for the   110
first time and converse as strangers, they face obstacles to effective
communication that must be surmounted and are often difficult to
overcome.

17   In personal or heart-to-heart talks, the persons involved face
each other as equals. Even when the inequality of age or maturity is   115
present, as in heart-to-heart talks between parents and children,
friendship or love tends to level the participants and is usually facil-
itated by ignoring any inequality that exists.

18   Not so with any form of impersonal talk. Here it makes a great
difference whether or not the persons engaged confront each other   120
as equals. The usual business conference is a case in point. So, too, is
the seminar in which a teacher conducts a discussion with students,
or in which the moderator or chairman of discussion plays a role
that is different from that played by the other participants.

19   The first kind of talk, the playful kind that I have called "social   125
conversation," can take place most effectively in relatively small
groups. The best is often just between two persons, but the group
can be slightly larger. It is a matter of common observation that
when the group exceeds five or six persons, it usually breaks up into
two quite separate conversations. . . .   130

20   This gives us four main types, as follows: 1) social conversation;
2) the personal, heart-to-heart talk; 3) the impersonal, theoretical
talk that is instructive or enlightening; and 4) the impersonal, practical talk that is persuasive with respect to action.

REVIEW | THE VARIETY OF CONVERSATIONS

Comprehension

1. True or false? "Heart-to-heart" talks usually involve only two peo-
    ple. _____

2. True or false? "Impersonal" talk may involve only two people.
    _____

3. True or false? Another name for "heart-to-heart" talk is "social con-
    versation." _____

4. What is the purpose of "playful" talk? _____

_____

5. Under which category would the author put:

   A classroom lecture? _____

   Talking about a lecture? _____

6. Give a personal example of "impersonal, theoretical talk."

   _____

   _____

7. Give a personal example of "impersonal, practical talk."

   _____

   _____

Textual Pattern: Classification

1. The author actually has several layers of classification in this reading.

   What is the first principle of classification: _____ vs. _____

   What is the second principle of classification: _____ vs. _____

   What is the third principle of classification: _____ vs. _____

2. In defining the categories or divisions, authors use phrases of comparison and contrast. Highlight several of these in the reading and list them below.

   _____   _____

   _____   _____

   _____   _____

   _____   _____

   _____   _____

   _____   _____

3. Like much of "real-life" material, this article does not end cleanly with a conclusion after discussing the four categories of two-way talk. The writer goes on to give more information. Below, label each of the paragraphs according to its topic (one of the four categories of conversations).

Paragraph

1. _____
2. *Introduction* ⎫
3. _____ ⎬
⎭

4. *Playful* _____

5. _____

6. _____

7. _____

8. _____

9. _____

10. _____

11. _____

12. _____

13. _____

14. *Impersonal (both types)*

15. _____

16. _____

17. _____

18. _____

19. _____

20. *Conclusion* _____

Remembering What You Read: Visualization

In the previous lesson on memory we discussed the role of association. Association is the mind's ability to link ideas in a meaningful way and the ability to relate these ideas to what you already know. Completing these two steps successfully leads to comprehension.

Visualization is an aid to the process of association. There is a saying that goes like this: "A picture is worth a thousand words." Why is this so? Apparently the mind remembers visual images well, and they have a great impact on our actions and thoughts. This is why television is such a powerful influence in our lives (both for good and for bad). It is one thing to read about how terrible war can be. It is quite another thing to actually see photos of the dead and the dying.

In addition to its powerful emotional impact, a picture can reveal as many details and ideas as could be expressed by a thousand words. In the business world, pictures, graphs, and photos are used to convince, persuade, and explain. A graph like the one at the top of page 271 can easily tell you whether you should invest in stocks right now.

This simple graph can save a thousand words of explanation. It is clear that now is not the time to buy stocks. If you have to read the thousands of words explaining market trends, you should try to translate that information into graphic form. You should try to create a simple graph in your mind: Is the price of stocks going up or down? Once you have answered that basic question you can add further detail to the image if necessary.

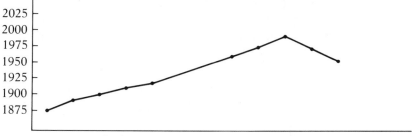

Mon. Tue. Wed. Thu. Fri. Sat. Sun. Mon. Tue. Wed. Thu. Fri. Sat. Sun.

The key here is that it is easier to remember a simple graph than hundreds, maybe thousands of words. As readers, we have associated the individual ideas (price average each day of the week) with each other. We understand the overall relationship between the prices over the past two weeks (the price average is going down). And we relate this trend to what we already know about stocks from our past experience (or past reading). Therefore, we "understand" that now is not a good time to buy.

Visualization has made all this work easier. A week from now if you were asked to remember how the stocks were doing a couple of weeks ago, there is a fairly good chance that you would still be able to recall this graph, but it is not likely that you would remember the words of the article in the *Wall Street Journal* that would have accompanied the graph.

In the first five chapters of this text, we have asked you many times to sketch out the relationships of the ideas in the article you were reading. Or you have been asked to fill in boxes in flow charts and diagrams to indicate the relative position of the ideas as the authors presented them. These assignments allow you to work with a graphic or visual representation of the words in the text.

Fluent readers often make these types of images or sketches when they must remember the material they are reading. However, you would not want to do this when reading novels. A different kind of visualization is used in this situation. We visualize what we are reading as if we were one of the characters. We "see" the action as if we were there. If the mind did not have this ability, reading would not be nearly as enjoyable or nearly as *memorable!*

As we read a mystery tale or an exciting adventure story, our minds visualize automatically. One of the keys to reading academic or professional material is to learn to visualize the relationships between ideas consciously. Some readers make notes in the margins of the material they are reading. It also helps to make flow charts or sketches.

In conclusion, visualization is sometimes an automatic and sometimes a conscious process that the mind uses to increase its ability to remember what has been read.

EXERCISE Look at the accompanying diagram, which represents the information contained in the first reading of this chapter. In the second box draw a diagram that will help you remember the main ideas of the second reading.

What Kind of Language Are You Using?

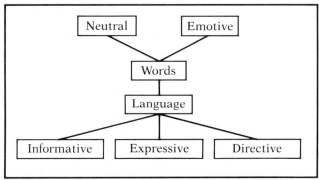

The Variety of Conversations

Classification: Organization and Purpose

Writers may take several approaches when classifying information or objects. In this lesson we will look at different types of organization as they relate to the author's purpose.

SORTING UP

In this approach, the author attempts to tell the readers how the objects being discussed are related, starting with the bottom of the hierarchy. An author might classify the French language as follows:

The French language belongs to a group of languages known as the Latin languages. Other Latin languages include Italian, Spanish, Portuguese, and Rumanian. These languages are all descendents of Latin, which, under Roman influence, spread throughout much of Europe.

In turn, the Latin group of languages belongs to a family called Indo-European. Indo-Europeans are believed to have originated in Northern Europe thousands of years ago. Indo-European is comprised of several other groups in addition to the Latin group. It also includes Celtic, Germanic, Hellenic, Balto-Slavic, Albanian, Armenian, and Indo-Iranian.

In this example the material broadens in scope. If we were to continue this model, the next paragraph would discuss the larger group that the Indo-European languages belonged to. This is the method that we call *sorting up*.

SORTING DOWN

In this method, the opposite of sorting up, the author begins with a topic and shows how it is made up of smaller units. For example, the discussion of the French language above would begin with the Indo-European language family and proceed in reverse order.

CHRONOLOGICAL ORDER

Dividing up a topic on the basis of time is sometimes called *process analysis*. This does not necessarily mean a step-by-step approach (as in "How to Make Bread"), but each category marks a "development" in the evolution of the topic. For example, a writer might divide the topic of dinosaurs into several categories according to the time periods during which they lived on the earth. A writer discussing English might use the common classification of Old English, Middle English, and Modern English. In the final passage of this chapter, the author, Fred West, discusses theories about the origins of language. He divides his discussion into "Early Theories," "Later Theories," and "Recent Theories."

ORDER OF IMPORTANCE

A writer may also order the categories so that the most important (for the author's purpose) is discussed last. In the discussion of the Indo-European language family, if the intended audience is English-speaking, a writer may wish to emphasize the Germanic group in order to discuss the origins of English in greater detail (see the diagram on page 274).

A writer may sort up or down. In either case, the intention is often to end with a discussion or further classification of one particular group. A good example of this is the last article in this chapter concerning the origins of language. In this case chronological order also parallels the order of importance.

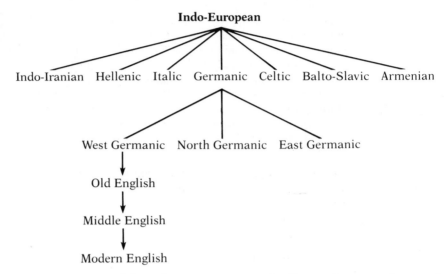

Indo-European

Indo-Iranian   Hellenic   Italic   Germanic   Celtic   Balto-Slavic   Armenian

West Germanic   North Germanic   East Germanic

Old English

Middle English

Modern English

In any event, although it is important for the reader to understand classification as a method of analysis and explanation, it is equally important for the reader to be able to determine what type of organization the writer has chosen. Determining the organizational type will help you as a reader understand the purpose and emphasis of the analysis.

PREVIEW | THE INTERNATIONAL LANGUAGE OF GESTURES

Things to Think About

1. What do the following gestures mean to you? (Write "nothing" if the gesture has no meaning to you.)

a.

o'kay

b.

two, victory or peace

World war II   1960's

c. worry ?

d. nothing

e.  by, by.

f. look

g.  nothing. I'm thinking

2. Have you ever had an embarrassing or amusing experience involving gestures while traveling? Explain.

_____

_____

_____

_____

_____

_____

3. Draw and define a gesture from your culture in the space provided.

Vocabulary in Context

1. "Because of the **pervasiveness** of travel and television, however, an emblem is often known in the countryside even if it is not used there."

pervasiveness _widespread_

2. "Many people are so eager to please that they will invent a gesture **on the spot**."

on the spot _at once / at the moment_

Preview

1. Read the introductory paragraph. What technique have the authors used to introduce their topic? (Refer to the lesson on page 222.)

with an anecdote

2. Paragraph 7 introduces the statement of classification. What is it?

Division Sorting up

3. One of the three categories mentioned in the statement is developed further. Quickly scan the second half of the article to discover which one it is.

emblems

READING THREE

THE INTERNATIONAL LANGUAGE OF GESTURES

1   On his first trip to Naples, a well-meaning American tourist thanks his waiter for a good meal well-served by making the "A-Okay" gesture with his thumb and forefinger. The waiter pales and heads for the manager. They seriously discuss calling the police and having the hapless tourist arrested for obscene and offensive public   5
behavior.

2   What happened?

3   Most travelers wouldn't think of leaving home without a phrase book of some kind, enough of a guide to help them say and understand "Ja," "Nein," "Grazie" and "Ou se trouvent les toilettes?"   10
And yet, while most people are aware that gestures are the most common form of cross-cultural communication, they don't realize that the language of gestures can be just as different, just as regional and just as likely to cause misunderstanding as the spoken word.

4   Consider our puzzled tourist. The thumb-and-forefinger-in-a-   15
circle gesture, a friendly one in America, has an insulting meaning in France and Belgium: "You're worth zero," while in Greece and Turkey it is an insulting or vulgar sexual invitation.

5   There are, in fact, dozens of gestures that take on totally different meanings as you move from one country or region to another.   20
Is "thumbs up" always a positive gesture? Absolutely not. Does nodding the head up and down always mean "Yes"? No!

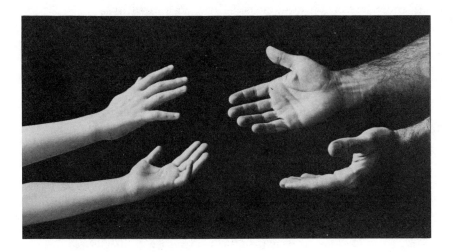

Paul Ekman, Wallace V. Friesen, and John Bear, "The International Language of Gestures," *Psychology Today*, May 1984, pp. 64–69. Reprinted with permission.

6   To make matters even more confusing, many hand movements have no meaning at all, in any country. If you watch television with the sound turned off, or observe a conversation at a distance, you become aware of almost constant motion, especially with the hands and arms. People wave their arms, they shrug, they waggle their fingers, they point, they scratch their chests, they pick their noses.

7   These various activities can be divided into three major categories: manipulators, emblems, and illustrators.

8   In a manipulator, one part of the body, usually the hands, rubs, picks, squeezes, cleans or otherwise grooms some other part. These movements have no specific meaning. Manipulators generally increase when people become uncomfortable or occasionally when they are totally relaxed.

9   An emblem is a physical act that can fully take the place of words. Nodding the head up and down in many cultures is a substitute for saying, "Yes." Raising the shoulders and turning the palms upward clearly means "I don't know," or "I'm not sure."

10   Illustrators are physical acts that help explain what is being said but have no meaning on their own. Waving the arms, raising or lowering the eyebrows, snapping the fingers and pounding the table may enhance or explain the words that accompany them, but they cannot stand alone. People sometimes use illustrators as a pantomime or charade, especially when they can't think of the right words, or when it's simply easier to illustrate, as in defining "zigzag" or explaining how to tie a shoe.

11   Thus the same illustrator might accompany a positive statement one moment and a negative one the next. This is not the case with emblems, which have the same precise meaning on all occasions for all members of a group, class, culture or subculture.

12   Emblems are used consciously. The user knows what they mean, unless, of course, he uses them inadvertently. When Nelson Rockefeller raised his middle finger to a heckler, he knew exactly what the gesture meant, and he believed that the person he was communicating with knew as well.

13   The three of us are working on a dictionary of emblems. . . . In looking for emblems, we found that it isn't productive simply to observe people communicating with each other, because emblems are used only occasionally. And asking people to describe or identify emblems that are important in their culture is even less productive. Even when we explain the concept clearly, most people find it difficult to recognize and analyze their own communication behavior this way.

14   Instead, we developed a research procedure that has enabled us to identify emblems in cultures as diverse as those of urban Japanese, white, middle-class Americans, the preliterate South Fore people of Papua, natives of New Guinea, Iranians, Israelis and the inhabitants of London, Madrid, Paris, Frankfurt and Rome. The procedure involves three steps.

15   Give a group of people from the same cultural background a series of phrases and ask if they have a gesture or facial expression

for each phrase: "What time is it?" "He's a homosexual." "That's good." "Yes." And so on. We find that normally, after 10 to 15 people have provided responses, we have catalogued the great majority of   75
the emblems of their culture.

16   Analyze the results. If most of the people cannot supply a "performance" for a verbal message, we discard it.

17   Study the remaining performances further to eliminate inventions and illustrators. Many people are so eager to please that they   80
will invent a gesture on the spot. Americans asked for a gesture for "sawing wood" could certainly oblige, even if they had never considered the request before, but the arm motion they would provide would not be an emblem.

18   To weed out these "false emblems," we show other people from   85
the same culture videotapes of the performances by the first group. We ask which are inventions, which are pantomimes and which are symbolic gestures that they have seen before or used themselves. We also ask the people to give us their own meanings for each performance.   90

19   The gestures remaining after this second round of interpretations are likely to be the emblems of that particular culture. Using this procedure, we have found three types of emblems:

20   First, popular emblems have the same or similar meanings in several cultures. The side-to-side head motion meaning "No" is a   95
good example.

21   Next, unique emblems have a specific meaning in one culture but none elsewhere. Surprisingly, there seem to be no uniquely American emblems, although other countries provide many examples. For instance, the French gesture of putting one's fist around the   100
tip of the nose and twisting it to signify, "He's drunk," is not used elsewhere. The German "good luck" emblem, making two fists with the thumbs inside and pounding an imaginary table, is unique to that culture.

22   Finally, multi-meaning emblems have one meaning in one   105
culture and a totally different meaning in another. The thumb inserted between the index and third fingers is an invitation to have sex in Germany, Holland and Denmark, but in Portugal and Brazil it is a wish for good luck or protection.

23   The number of emblems in use varies considerably among   110
cultures, from fewer than 60 in the United States to more than 250 in Israel. The difference is understandable, since Israel is composed of recent immigrants from many countries, most of which have their own large emblem vocabularies. In addition, since emblems are helpful in military operations where silence is essential, and all   115
Israelis serve in the armed forces, military service provides both the opportunity and the need to learn new emblems.

24   The kind of emblems used, as well as the number, varies considerably from culture to culture. Some are especially heavy on insults, for instance, while others have a large number of emblems for hun-   120
ger or sex.

25   Finally, as Desmond Morris documented in his book, *Gestures,*

there are significant regional variations in modern cultures. The findings we describe in this article apply to people in the major urban areas of each country: London, not England as a whole; Paris, 125 not France. Because of the pervasiveness of travel and television, however, an emblem is often known in the countryside even if it is not used there.

REVIEW | THE INTERNATIONAL LANGUAGE OF GESTURES

Comprehension

1. True or false? No matter what languages people speak, gestures are always understood. __F__   ③

2. True or false? Manipulators have meaning independent of the spoken word. __F__   ⑧

3. True or false? In most cases, emblems are used consciously. __T__   ⑫

4. True or false? The best way to gather research about gestures is to observe people communicating with each other in natural settings. __F__   ⑬

5. True or false? Emblems do not generally pantomime the action they represent. __T__   ⑱

6. Of the three categories of gestures discussed, the authors seemed most interested in ___emblems___

7. Illustrators help explain what is being said but have no ___meaning___ on their own.   ⑥

8. ___illustrators___ are sometimes used when the speaker can't think of the right word(s).   ⑩

9. Rockefeller's gesture was an example of a(n) ___emblem___ ⑫

10. What is a "unique emblem"? ___specific meaning in one culture but none elsewhere.___ ㉑

11. Why does Israel have so many emblems (two reasons)? ___too many immigrants with their own culture everybody go to the military service where emble are helpful to keep the essential silence.___

12. If one can speak the language fluently, what reason is there for the need to study gestures as well?

To reinforce their expressions with out words. For emphasis.

13. The authors' research shows that there are ___*3*___ types of emblems.

14. Give an example of a manipulator. *the hands rubs, squeezes*

15. When asked for a gesture that meant "sawing wood" Americans sometimes just invented one by making a sawing motion with their arm. This, however, is not an example of an emblem. It is an example of a(n) ___*pantomime (false emblem.*
illustrator

Skill Review: Main Idea

Restate or summarize the main idea(s) of this article in two or three sentences:

_____

_____

_____

_____

Textual Pattern: Classification

Draw a simple diagram of your understanding of gestures.

gestures

Gestures { manipulators / illustrators / emblems { popular / unique / multi-meaning

manipulate illustrators emblems

popular unique multi ti-mea ning

Questions for Further Discussion/Composition

1. If you have not had the opportunity, share with your classmates the gesture you drew before the reading and its meaning.

2. Discuss gestures you've seen recently (perhaps even in a movie or on television) that you do not understand the meaning of.

Division: A Close Cousin

Earlier we mentioned that classification and division are basically the same process. To a certain degree this is true. In classification a writer is arranging a large collection of objects into a number of meaningful chunks or units. Division, on the other hand, takes what is already a perceived whole and breaks it down into smaller units. This distinction is not always clear, and many texts and teachers choose not to attempt an explanation of the difference since the analysis in either case is quite similar.

A marine biologist might take a collection of shells and classify them according to species. The important thing to remember is that one principle is being used to categorize the members of the collection. In this case, the shells are being classified according to species. A child might place the shells into piles according to color. Each principle would be equally valid for the purposes of the person making the classification.

An example of division would involve a person taking an orange (a perceived whole) and proceeding to divide it into its component parts— peel, seeds, juice, pulp, etc. An auto mechanics instructor might divide internal combustion into several stages (intake, compression, ignition, explosion, exhaust) for the purpose of helping students to better understand the system. This particular type of division is often called *process analysis*.

In the article you are about to read, the author describes the various types of language teaching institutions that people may choose from and what their characteristics are. There is no single principle for the author's categorization. That is, the various language learning opportunities are not divided on the basis of size. Nor are they classified on the basis of cost. The author simply introduces each type of teaching system that is available and gives a description of each. The unifying principle is the fact that they are all types of language teaching institutions. For this reason, the rhetorical processes of division and classification have also been called *collective description*. This article is a collection of comparative descriptions of each category.

PREVIEW | Take Your Pick of Language Lessons

Things to Think About

1. Why have you chosen to study English where you are now?

_____

_____

2. What sort of advantages and disadvantages are there in:

Studying abroad? _____

_____

_____

Studying at home?_____

_____

_____

Studying at a private language school?_____

_____

_____

3. Do you have any specific questions in mind about language schools that you hope this article will answer?

_____

_____

Vocabulary in Context

1. "To assure quality, choose a program that is **affiliated** with an institution you trust."

*affiliated*_____

2. "The price for the ten-day course includes **refreshers,** meaning you can return to the center as often as you wish, on an individual basis, for a '**tune-up.**' "

*refreshers*_____

*tune-up*_____

Preview

1. According to the subtopic headings, how many different types of language lessons is the author going to talk about?

_____

_____

2. According to the introduction, who is the author's intended audience?

_____

_____

3. After reading the first two paragraphs, answer the following question: What two factors should you remember in choosing the type of language lesson that is the best for you?

_____

_____

Assignment

Underline words you cannot understand from the context. In the review exercises, you will be asked to write down five of these and provide the appropriate definitions from a dictionary.

READING FOUR

TAKE YOUR PICK OF LANGUAGE LESSONS

1   For Americans seeking to learn or brush up on a foreign language, the options available can be as confusing as an irregular French verb. Group lessons or private? Gradual learning or so-called total immersion? Traditional classroom instruction or some experimental method? And how much should it cost?   5

2   As you investigate the possibilities, don't let price be the most important consideration. Although the best programs are often expensive, the quality of language instruction doesn't automatically

improve as the price rises. The important thing is to find a style of
learning that suits your needs.   10

LEARN IT AT HOME

3   Learning at home via a home study course is often the most
convenient, though not necessarily the most efficient. You can go at
your own pace and needn't adjust your schedule to accommodate a
regular class. Sets of recorded lessons are available at book and   15
record stores or by mail order. They usually cover only the more
common languages, and most do not go beyond the needs of the
casual tourist. The tapes and records consist of groups of phrases
and conversations you learn by repetition. A set of four to six tapes
and accompanying workbook might cost about $125.   20
4   Taped lessons used by the Foreign Service Institute's School of
Language Studies to train diplomats are more complete and cover a
wider range of languages. The State Department does not market
these tapes directly, but they are available by writing to Order Section, National Audio-Visual Center, General Services Administra-   25
tion, Washington, D.C. 20409. Ask for the FSI catalog. The price for a
basic course of about 20 cassette tapes and a text is $100 or so; the
more cassettes, the higher the price. Delivery generally takes four to
six weeks after receipt of your order.
5   Some of the FSI tapes are available more quickly but at a sub- 30
stantially higher price from the commercial distributor Audio-
Forum, Suite 33, On the Green, Guilford, Conn. 06437.
6   If you want to earn credits toward a degree or prepare yourself
to read foreign literature, consider a university correspondence
course. A one semester course generally costs about $125 for begin- 35
ners, postage not included. Any audio materials used may involve
extra cost. Course quality is comparable to on-campus offerings. All
assignments are reviewed by a professor or instructor and then
returned, usually within a week.
7   Language courses are included among the 12,000 courses listed 40
in Guide to Independent Study Through Correspondence Instruction, prepared by the National University Continuing Education
Association. It is available in libraries or from Peterson's Guides,
P.O. Box 2123, Princeton, N.J. 08540, for $4.50 plus $1.25 for postage
and handling. A new edition was scheduled for January 1983.   45
8   One caveat about university correspondence courses: "If your
object is to achieve minimal conversational skills, either for business or pleasure, you may not be willing to expend the effort
required for these courses, according to Dr. Robert Batchellor, associated with the NUCEA guide. Self-instruction requires a commit-   50
ment of at least ten hours per week.
9   The National Association of Self-Instructional Language Programs (NASILP) assists schools in designing and operating self-
instruction programs based on tape learning supplemented by text
and tutorials and eligible for college credit. NASILP keeps up with 55
all of the options, including commercial programs, and will help
you find a course to fit your specifications, whether or not it is an
NASILP product. For information, write to John B. Means,

Executive Director, NASILP, Box 38, Humanities Building, Temple University, Philadelphia, Pa. 19122.   60

LOCAL CLASSROOMS

10   If home study doesn't appeal to you, adult education courses at local schools or community organizations such as the YMCA might fit the bill. Courses usually meet once a week in the evenings for two to three hours for several months. Prices generally range from $40 to   65 $100.

11   Many language teachers moonlight at adult education programs, and some of the courses are first-rate. However, even the good ones usually have more than ten students—not the best teacher student ratio for a language class. Try to meet the teacher   70 before you sign up and discuss your reasons for studying the language. Even if the course is not for you, the teacher may be able to help you find a private tutor at prices ranging from $10 to $30 an hour.

TOTAL IMMERSION   75

12   More practically oriented than courses with an academic slant are the "total immersion" or "quick fix" programs that are offered by some colleges and universities.

13   To assure quality, choose a program that is affiliated with an institution you trust. Among the best known sponsors are the   80 Language Outreach Education program headed by Prof. John Rassias at Dartmouth; Georgetown University in Washington, D.C.; Middlebury College in Vermont; and Monterey Institute of International Studies in California.

14   These programs are effective, quick and expensive. Most involve   85 some traditional classroom instruction. Innovative techniques, such as role-playing, may also be employed in a restrained way. The Rassias noncredit program, for example, relies to some extent on the inhibition shattering, acting-out methods he uses in credit courses for undergraduates. The cost of the Rassias program this   90 year, including room and board was a maximum of $600 for ten days or $1,200 for one month.

15   At Georgetown, Spanish and Portuguese are usually offered during the summer. The term is approximately six weeks, and the cost this year, not including room and board, ranged from $450 to $1,710   95 depending on the number of credits.

16   Middlebury offers courses during the summer. Arabic, Chinese, French, German, Italian, Japanese, Russian and Spanish were offered this past summer; the costs ranged from $1,710 to $2,322, including room and board.   100

17   Eight languages, including Arabic, Chinese, Japanese and Russian, were offered in a nine-week credit program at the Monterey Institute this summer. The cost was $1,060 plus $590 for housing excluding meals.

CULTURAL INSTITUTES   105

18   Cultural institutes located in large cities often offer courses designed for American travelers. The Alliance Francaise and the Japan American Society each has courses in about 18 cities across the U.S. In Atlanta, Boston, Chicago and San Francisco, you learn basic German at the Goethe Institute.   110

COMMERCIAL SCHOOLS

19   Commercial language schools generally charge more than universities for comparable courses because they sell "custom-tailored" instruction. This necessitates keeping many instructors on call so that the school can design courses to fit almost any need.   115

20   Berlitz, best known in this field, has 67 outlets in this country. It routinely refuses to discuss prices until you go in person to design your program. The recommended program for a beginner may cost well over $1,000. Lessons are generally private and, depending on your needs, may be of the total-immersion type. There are no lec-   120 tures, and grammar is taught by example. Students learn initially by imitation and can expect to go on to conversation in a few days.

21   Inlingua is a Berlitz competitor based in Switzerland, with 18 schools in the U.S. Inlingua offers small and large group sessions as well as private instruction. Seven weeks of lessons twice a week in a   125 group of five to ten students costs $115, plus $12 for the textbooks.

SMALLER SCHOOLS

22   Besides the giants of the language business, there are also many small commercial schools, some with excellent track records. Michel Thomas Language Centers, for instance, based in New York   130 City, does not advertise but relies on word-of-mouth recommendations. Thomas uses no rote learning, no homework, no tests. Languages are usually taught on an individual basis but sometimes in small groups of no more than five or in organizational groups of about ten.   135

23   Spending about eight hours per day, most Thomas students complete the two-phase program in ten days. Fees for Western languages start at $850 per person in a group of ten for the ten-day program or for an individual 30-hour mini course and go as high as $3,500. An organization in a city that doesn't have a Thomas center   140 can have instructors brought to it by paying their transportation, room and board.

24   The price for the ten-day course includes refreshers, meaning you can return to the center as often as you wish, on an individual basis, for a "tune-up." Michel Thomas Language Centers offers a   145 money-back guarantee after the first day if you're not satisfied. Write to Michel Thomas at 110 E. 59th St., New York, N.Y. 10022.

25   There are several newcomers—innovative programs often ignored by traditional teachers. Some students find that they can

learn with these methods even when others have failed. A few of the 150
better-known methods include Counseling Learning, the Lozanov
Method and the Silent Way. With these, drill and memorization are
largely replaced by highly different methods. For example, Sug-
gestopaedia (another name for the Lozanov Method) has students
listening to their teacher against a background of carefully selected 155
classical music.

26   You can learn more about these methods in *Teaching Languages,
A Way and Ways,* by Dr. Earl W. Stevick of the Foreign Service
Institute (published by Newbury House, Rowley, Mass. 01969,
$12.95 paperback).   160

GETTING YOUR MONEY'S WORTH

27   No matter what method you choose, you want to get your
money's worth. How can you be a savvy consumer in an industry in
which the results depend in part on the student?

28   —First, don't make your decision based on volume of advertis- 165
ing. A familiar name is not necessarily a sign of an effective program. Seek out former students for referrals, and preview a class or
at least meet a teacher before you enroll.

29   —Ask how often you will speak in class. In general, the more you
speak, the more you will learn. Look for experienced instructors. 170
Your teacher should have a good command of English as well as
fluency in the language you want to learn. It is helpful in learning
correct pronunciation to hear an authentic accent, but clear expla-
nations are important in mastering the structure of the language.

30   —If you consider going to a commercial school don't be swayed 175
by lists of their "big name" clients. Many language programs have
their proponents, but you want what is right for you, not what is
right for celebrities or corporations.

31   —Don't accept a course in which you simply parrot rote exercises. A program that sustains motivation and teaches you to speak 180
your own thoughts is a far better deal, even if it costs more. Look for
an attentive, energetic instructor and a set of milestones to show
you that you are making progress.

32   All of this does not mean you should be taking lots of tests.
Learning a language as an adult is not the same thing as going back 185
to school. It should not give you that "Sunday night, homework not
done" feeling. And a program that advertises goals in terms of how
many words you will know is better avoided. What good are 3,000
words if you don't know how to put them together?

33   Sometimes you cannot know what a program is like until you 190
are in the thick of it. Cut your losses if you think you made a poor
choice. Even if you're not entitled to any refund, it is better to leave
a bad class than to stick it out and get discouraged.

REVIEW | Take Your Pick of Language Lessons

Comprehension

1. True or False? Some language learning institutions charge more than $2,000. _____

2. True or False? The better schools advertise heavily because they can afford it. _____

3. True or False? Berlitz is a famous commercial school for language learning. _____

4. True or False? Total immersion programs usually meet about twice a week. _____

5. True or False? Adult Education classes are usually the cheapest of all classes. _____

6. True or False? A simple test of the quality of an institution is the number of words they can teach you in a given period of time. _____

7. True or False? Another simple test is to ask how often you will be able to speak in class. _____

8. According to this article, what should the maximum number of students in a language learning class be if the class is to be effective?

   _____

9. If you're just interested in picking up conversational ability in a language, which of the choices discussed should you avoid?

   _____

   _____

10. Name one of the new language learning methods that were mentioned near the end of the article.

    _____

Skill Review: Inferences/Main Idea

1. As you shop around for the best way for you to learn a foreign language, you should remember four important points. Name them.

   a. _____

   b. _____

c. _____

d. _____

2. If you were a poor college professor who wanted to learn another language in your spare time or during the summer, which method(s) would you choose (or could you afford)?

_____

_____

_____

3. If you were very rich, which method of learning would you choose?

_____

4. With the purposes that you have for learning English, are you in the right program now? Why? Why not?

_____

_____

_____

_____

_____

_____

5. What should you do if you find yourself in the wrong class, or a poorly organized, ineffective institution?

_____

_____

Remembering What You Read

On a separate sheet of paper, organize in a table the various types of language learning situation in terms of cost.

Textual Pattern: Classification

1. What devices did the author use to help you see the organization of the article clearly and immediately?

_____

_____

_____

2. Finish the outline that has been started for you. (Do this on a separate sheet of paper.)

    I. Introduction (with questions and caution)
    II. Home study programs
        A. Taped lessons (Foreign Service Institute)
            1. National Audio Visual Center
            2. Audio-Forum
        B. University correspondence course
        C. Nat'l Assoc. of Self-Instructional Language Programs
    III. Local classrooms

Vocabulary Exercise

Write down the five words you underlined in the article and provide a proper definition for each (according to their use in the article).

1. _____ : _____

_____

2. _____ : _____

_____

3. _____ : _____

_____

4. _____ : _____

_____

5. _____ : _____

_____

Questions for Further Discussion/Composition

1. If you were very rich and had the opportunity to set up an "ideal" language school, what facilities and activities would you plan for? What sort of curriculum, materials, and methods would you use?

2. Assume that you had the opportunity to talk with the director of the language learning institution or business where you are now studying. What suggestion would you offer to improve the program and achievement of the learners?

PREVIEW | THE ORIGIN OF LANGUAGE

Things to Think About

1. What specific questions come to your mind when you think of the "origins of language"?

   How was the first way of communication
   How many words they had.
   Had every body the same initial sounds.
   in the beginning.

Vocabulary in Context

1. "Certainly if we accept the **premise** that language did not suddenly emerge fully developed one bright day, then it follows that language evolved out of some proto-communication system."

   premise _first statement_

2. "By recalling the past and planning for the future, man advanced to **time-binding.** His mind broke through the sense-limiting medium of time and he was now able to hold the continuum of time—past, present, and future—simultaneously in his mind through word-symbols."

   time-binding _____

3. "People have always **speculated** upon how language began; consequently, we have with us today an extensive collection of theories and guesses. . . . In 1866 the French Société de Linguistique **forbade** any discussion at its meetings of the origins of language, on the grounds that such **speculation** was absolutely **fruitless.** Nevertheless, **speculation** continues."

   to speculate _questioned_
   forbade _prohibited._
   fruitless _unsuccessful, utiless._

Preview

1. Scan the reading and indicate below how the material on the origin of language is classified.

   Ancient Theories   Later theories
   Modern Theories

2. What principle of classification is the author using?____ *Time*

3. Which of the three categories do you think is the most important? Why?

    Modern because it has more possibilities to be successful because of the avances of technique.

4. This material is from a freshman-level college textbook. What course do you think this textbook is used in?

    In a linguistic coursese,

READING FIVE

THE ORIGIN OF LANGUAGE

1   People have always speculated upon how language began; consequently, we have with us today an extensive collection of theories and guesses, some rather ridiculous, others with more than a trace of credibility to them. In 1866 the French Société de Linguistique forbade any discussion at its meetings of the origins of language, on 5 the grounds that such speculation was absolutely fruitless. Nevertheless, speculation continues. We are still curious about how it all began.

2   Most recently certain feminists have pointed out that language is a powerful brainwasher (which it is) and a prehistoric device 10 invented by men to perpetuate the myth of masculine superiority. Just look at such vocabulary items as "man," "mankind," "humanity." And according to ancient, man recorded scriptures, the first human creation of God was a man named "Adam," which in Hebrew means "man." 15

ANCIENT THEORIES

3   Before the middle of the eighteenth century, theories of the beginning of language generally fell into the category of Divine Origin. According to these early theories, man was created almost instantaneously, and at the moment of his creation, speech was 20 provided him as a divine gift. So goes the biblical story of the Garden of Eden. God created Adam and speech simultaneously, for

God spoke with Adam and Adam answered him. The language they used was Hebrew.

4   However, there have been exceptions in the Judeo-Christian world to the believers in Hebrew as the original tongue. In the seventeenth century, Andreas Kemke, a Swedish philologist, patriotically asserted that in the Garden of Eden God spoke Swedish, Adam spoke Danish, and the serpent spoke French. One wonders what the French had done to offend the good Swede. Another patriot theorist was the sixteenth century Dutchman Goropius Becanus, who asserted that the language of the Garden was Dutch. It was probably from his statement that Elizabethan dramatist Ben Jonson borrowed the words: "I'll show you a treatise penned by Adam—and in High Dutch. Which proves it was the primitive tongue."

5   Of course, other cultures had divinely inspired original languages, too. The Egyptians considered themselves the oldest civilization; therefore, the original language was Egyptian, passed on to the humans of ancient Egypt through their god-ancestors. This assumption was checked out at least once, according to the historian Herodotus. A seventeenth-century B.C. Egyptian ruler named Psammetichus had enough curiosity to try an experiment. On the premise that babies, if left alone, will grow up speaking "the" original language, Psammetichus had two babies taken at random from an ordinary family and given to a shepherd to raise. He ordered the shepherd to speak not a word to the babies, only tend to their needs. When they were two years old, the little ones one day abruptly greeted the shepherd with *"Becos."* The shepherd immediately reported this to Psammetichus, who checked it with his counselors. The counselors informed the king that *becos* meant "bread" in Phrygian, so in true scientific spirit Psammetichus announced that Phrygian was the original language.

6   Just as the first divinely descended Egyptian pharaoh brought speech to man, so did the Chinese emperor T'ien-tzu, the Son of Heaven. In Japan, the divine creator of man, complete with language, was Amaterasu, the sun goddess. In the Middle East it was Enlil, "the spirit of the word which stilleth the heaven above." The Greco-Roman chief god was Zeus-pater, of Jupiter, the "father of light." When we find practically the same myths about the creation of man and language occurring in American Indian folklore, we are irresistibly attracted by the psychologist Carl Jung's belief in a collective unconscious, a vast common reservoir collecting all of mankind's unconscious memories; from this reservoir rise similar patterns of experience and behavior among different peoples. These archetypal, or basic, forms reveal themselves in religion, art, and myth. Myth has been defined as the story preserved in popular memory of a past event, the original history of mankind. One recurring characteristic of the creation myths of the American Indians is the function of the light god. The creator-teacher of the Mayas was Itzamma, also know as Kin-ich-ahau, which translates into "Lord of the sun's face," or the dawn. The culture god of the Iroquois was

Ioskeha, "about-to-grow-white," or, again, the dawn. The Algonquian deity was Michabo, god of light.

7   So we see that generally the creator-god was also a light god. We can interpret the myths, then, as saying that language came with the dawn of reason. And since **Linguistics,** the scientific study of language, cannot be studied in a vacuum any more than can any other discipline, we must consider the findings and theories of such kindred subjects as psychology, anthropology, sociology, and poetry. If we accommodate our thinking to primitive expression as revealed through mythology, then we may suppose that at least subconsciously these so-called primitive peoples were not actually stating an instantaneous, or mechanistic, creation of language, but were more likely personifying the evolution of developing man to a point where language became a necessity. . . .

LATER THEORIES

8   Speculation on the origin of language moved from the realm of fancy and entered what is called the "organic phase" in the latter part of the eighteenth century with the publication of Johann Gottfried von Herder's *Uber den Ursprung der Sprache (On the Origin of Language)* in 1772. This was the period when Immanuel Kant and others set the stage for the theory of the evolution of man, so well stated about a century later by Charles Darwin. Herder argued that language was too imperfect to have been a divine gift; it came about through man's own groping efforts toward reasoning. Language, he said, was the result of an "instinctive impulse similar to that of an embryo pressing to be born."

9   Darwin argued against any distinctly "human" quality of language. In *Descent of Man* (1871), he maintained that there is only a difference of degree between the language of man and the cries of animals. He reasoned that man's language, like man himself, came from a more primitive form, probably expressions of emotion. For example, the feeling of contempt or disgust is accompanied by a tendency to puff out air through the nose or mouth, and this makes such sounds as "Pooh!" or "Pish!" Max Muller, a contemporary who disagreed with Darwin on this point, nicknamed it scornfully the **Pooh-Pooh** theory.

10   Darwin's argument was pretty well discredited by later scholars such as Edward Sapir, who pointed out that language is directed toward someone to achieve a result. An involuntary cry of pain can come with no intent to communicate. This counterargument works well enough as far as separating speech from animal cries, but who can say what actually went on at the dawn of reason? At some time in his development, primitive man learned to classify and manipulate sounds for a purpose, but the sounds had to come first.

11   "In the twentieth century Edgar Sturtevant humorously proposed that language developed from emotive expressions for the purpose of lying. That is, originally the cries and other expressions of fear, pain, and anger were involuntary utterances. Then, when a

man—a very perceptive primitive man—noticed the submissiveness of his mate when he roared with anger, he deliberately developed the involuntary sound-symbol as a tool to keep his domestic affairs under control. He faked anger when he actually felt none, thus becoming the proto-liar.   125

12   Muller, the greatest popularizer of linguistics in the nineteenth century, proposed what he called the **Ding-Dong** theory of the origin of language. Somewhat similar to Socrates' argument that language came about naturally, Muller's theory claimed a mystic harmony or correlation between sound and meaning. In primitive man was an   130 instinct by which every impression from without received its vocal expression from within. Just as in nature every object, when struck by a solid body, gave off its own peculiar sound (like a bell when it is struck), so man's mind gave off a particular response to the various impacts which the world made upon it. There were four hundred or   135 so basic sounds which made up the roots of this original language. For example when primitive man was confronted by a wolf, the sight rang a bell, so to speak, and he instinctively said, "Wolf!" Muller later rejected his own theory.

13   Another theory which we can mention briefly is the **Yo-He-Ho** 140 theory. This theory suggests that language first began in a social setting (which is valid enough so far), that of men working together. Strong muscular action, such as a man swinging an axe or a sledgehammer, caused the breath to be expelled forcibly for relief. The vocal cords vibrated, a specific rate of vibration for a specific 145 action, thus producing a particular and distinct sound for each particular kind of work. The sound identified with that action became the name of the action: "Heave!" "Haul!" "Push!" Grunts do indeed result from muscular exertions, and some of these grunts may become incorporated in words or word formations. But to assume 150 an entire language built from grunts is rather ridiculous.

14   A more tenacious theory has been the **Bow-Wow** theory, so named by the energetic Max Muller. Also referred to as **Onoma-topoetic** or **Echoic**, the theory suggests that first words were imitative of natural sounds: the cry of birds, the call of animals, the 155 noise of storms, rivers, and so on. Muller rejected this theory, commenting sarcastically that it applied very well to cackling hens and quacking ducks, but the bulk of language operated outside the barnyard.

15   However, no matter how small the percentage, virtually every 160 known language has some echoic words in its vocabulary, mainly nouns and verbs. In English we have "babble," "rattle," "hiss," "ripple," "pee-wee," "cuckoo," "hiccup." The dictionary lists scores of others as imitative, and they keep coming in. "Burp" has now been extended to "burp gun"; "zip" developed into both verb and 165 noun, and extended to "zipper." Earlier forms of English may reveal this echoic quality more than their modern forms. For example, "laugh," which doesn't necessarily sound echoic today, derives from Old English *hlaehhan* or *hliehhan*. Keeping in mind that in Old English initial h's were strongly aspirated, or huffed, pronounce 170 these words and note the obvious imitation of a laugh. We also have

"slurp," which is quite similar to its Dutch original, *slurpen*, a sound-symbol recognizable to all enjoyers of soup. The English signal for silence "Sshh!" isn't too far from Latin *susurrus*, meaning "whisper."   175

16   An argument against the onomatopoetic theory of the origin of language is that we hear and imitate the sounds of nature within the limitations of our first language. (That means, of course, the language of the culture we are raised in, not the so-called original language.) Textbooks frequently cite as an example of cultural influ- 180 ence the fact that a rooster crowing in English says "Cock-a-doodle-doo"; in French, "*Coquerico*"; in Italian, "*Chiccirichi*"; in German, "*Kikeriki*." This example really proves nothing, however, because all these languages stem from the same **Proto-Language** (or "ancestor" language) and are daughter languages in the same linguistic family. 185 A case could possibly be made that in the proto-language these sounds were one. A better argument to support the "limitations of our first language" would be to bring in terms that are not from our own language family. For example, the echoic word for "thunder" is, in French, *tonnere;* in German, *Donner;* but in Keresan (an Amer- 190 ican Indian language group), *ko-o-muts.*

17   An interesting fact that has surfaced as a result of studies in languages of primitive cultures is that some of the most primitive cultures use the least number of echoic speech items, while a sophisticated language like English with its half-a-million word-hoard 195 uses perhaps the most. And apparently this characteristic of English existed even before the language was first recorded.

18   Even more hardy than the bow-wow theory is the **Gesture** theory, which states that words and language developed from meaningful gestures. According to Darwin, while the hands were 200 employed in gestural signals, they could not be used for other necessary work. Nor could hand signals be transmitted and received in the dark. Something else was needed: vocal signals were inevitable. Around the turn of the twentieth century, Wilhelm Wundt, an experimental psychologist, elaborated considerably on this theory, 205 and reputable linguists and psychologists continue to discuss it. Certainly if we accept the premise that language did not suddenly emerge fully developed one bright day, then it follows that language evolved out of some proto-communication system. Most likely that system was vocal gesture, such as anthropoid apes use. Then, at 210 some intermediate stage during the millennia of trial and error, progress—or even survival—depended more upon vocalization and less on gesture. Perhaps, as Darwin suggested, because it was dark, or he had his hands full, or his companion was not looking, primitive man had to communicate, so he gestured with his tongue, 215 simultaneously making a sound. . . .

MODERN THEORIES

19   The physical equipment was there for the production of speech. But speech is not simply a manipulation of physical limbs and organs. Psychological development was needed, too. Speech, as 220

language, is the result of man's ability to see phenomena sym-
bolically and of the necessity to express his symbols. For example, a
man looking at a natural phenomenon like a river sees not just a
flowing body of water; to him, the river may symbolize a destructive
agent which could drown him. To another man the river might   225
symbolize just the opposite; he might see a supply of life-giving
liquid for plants and animals. Another man might see the river as an
environment for fish. Still another might see it as a cool, comfortable place to swim on a hot day. To communicate these different
psychological impressions, man needed more word-symbols, such   230
as "cool," "wet," "dangerous," "good," and so on. In order for us to
come up with a credible theory of the origin of language, we will
have to know a great deal more about the psychological development of early man.

20   Most anthropologists today agree that man as we know him and   235
language developed together. This does not mean that the
appearance of either was instantaneous. According to the geological
time scale, man came into existence during the Pleistocene Epoch,
which means he has been on earth for a million years or more. The
factors which led to the development of *Homo sapiens* also led to the   240
development of language. Man's posture became upright, giving
him additional visual range; his eyes became stereoscopic, further
improving his vision by increasing his three-dimensional depth per-
ception. The cerebral cortex, virtually nonexistent in fish and other
lower creatures, developed tremendously in evolving man. With   245
this development of his brain, he passed from subhuman to human.
He graduated from a sort of trial-and-error learning to reasoning
powers; he began to invent and use tools; and he began to speak. . . .

21   By recalling the past and planning for the future, man advanced
to time-binding. His mind broke through the sense-limiting   250
medium of time and he was now able to hold the continuum of
time—present, past, and future—simultaneously in his mind
through word-symbols. To expand his new world of objects, events,
space, time, and qualities such as mass, velocity, form, color, texture, he created yet more word-symbols. With more ideas to think   255
about and discuss with his companions, he increased his inventory
of word-symbols, originally indicators of concrete phenomena that
he could see close at hand, to include more abstract symbols. With
these new words he communicated to others the unseen danger of
the distant river and of the great cave bear. Such words in turn   260
allowed even more abstractions of thought. Society became more
complex, and so did language. Thus cause became effect and effect
became cause.

22   But again, we have no definite historical evidence to actually
show the progression from a primitive language to a sophisticated   265
one. As far back as we can trace languages historically, or even
reconstruct them through the comparative method (which will be
discussed later), they have all included words for such abstract con-
cepts as bravery, nobility, deception, and freedom. This is equally
true of the so-called primitive cultures today: they all have highly   270
developed languages.

23   Is there really good reason, then, to continue the search for an original theory? Some scholars think so. They feel that some tentative yet probable theory or its genesis is necessary to the development of an adequate psychology of language. But perhaps it's the 275 other way around. According to psycholinguist Roger Brown, when we learn more about the psychology of language, we will be able to construct a satisfactory origin myth. At any rate, the study of languages has always intrigued mankind, as the history of linguistics will show.   280

REVIEW | THE ORIGIN OF LANGUAGE

Comprehension

speculated

1. True or False? Mankind has always theorized about the origins of language. _____T_____

2. True or False? According to Charles Darwin, the gift of language is not unique to human beings. _____T_____

3. True or False? Darwin had a great influence on the early development of theories concerning the divine origin of language. _____F_____

4. True or False? The physical equipment for speech has always been present. _____T_____

5. True or False? Even most primitive people's languages are highly developed. _____T_____

6. Which of the following languages have been considered to be the original? (Circle all that apply.)

Hebrew	French	Swedish
Egyptian	Phrygian	Japanese
Greek	Chinese	Latin
Dutch	Danish	English

7. Give two examples from your own language of "onomatopoeia."

    _____

    _____

8. How is the use of tools related to the development of language?

    _____

    _____

    _____

    _____

9. Max Muller labeled Darwin's theory the "_____ " Theory.

Skill Review: Conclusions and Main Ideas

1. Which theory(ies) do you think would be the most important to remember for an exam? Why?

_____

_____

_____

2. What are the author's conclusions about further study of the origins of language?

_____

_____

Textual Pattern: Classification

1. To confirm your guess in the pre-reading section: What principle was used to categorize the theories about the origins of language?

_____

Why did the author choose this method? Are there other possible ones?

_____

_____

2. On a separate sheet of paper, create a table that will organize the material you have read on the origins of language.

Questions for Further Discussion/Composition

1. Some say that language is the unique gift of human beings. It is what separates us from all other animals. Don't other animals talk to each other (especially intelligent animals like apes and dolphins)?

2. Are there any animals that have not been studied carefully that you think might have a "language" ability?

3. What are the origins of your native language?

4. So far we have talked about origins. What about the future? What do you see happening to your native language in the future (perhaps in light of what is happening to it right now)?

CHAPTER 7

Not like the brazen giant of Greek fame,
  With conquering limbs astride from land to land;
  Here at our sea-washed, sunset gates shall stand
A mighty woman with a torch, whose flame
Is the imprisoned lightning, and her name
  Mother of Exiles. From her beacon-hand
  Glows world-wide welcome; her mild eyes
    command
The air-bridged harbor that twin cities frame.
"Keep ancient lands, your storied pomp!" cries she
  With silent lips. "Give me your tired, your poor,
Your huddled masses yearning to breathe free,
  The wretched refuse of your teeming shore.
Send these, the homeless, tempest-tost to me,
  I lift my lamp beside the golden door!

—Emma Lazarus, "The New Colossus"
(a poem that was inscribed
on a plaque at the base of
the Statue of Liberty in 1903)

IMMIGRANTS IN AMERICA: A LAND OF PROMISE?

The history of the United States is a history of immigrants. People have come seeking a better life. Families and individuals have fled their homes in search of freedom from political oppression, economic hardship, or starvation. Many have come with dreams of streets paved with gold and land and jobs for the choosing. Many have come seeking adventure. But America has not always been "the promised land" that immigrants thought it would be. Some have been denied admission and sent home; others have had difficulties with a new language, new laws, and customs, and have become discouraged.

The readings in this chapter discuss many of the major issues surrounding immigration in the United States. The quota system, exclusionary laws, prejudice, slavery, and illegal aliens are some of the issues discussed.

These readings are not all written in one textual pattern. They are review readings that give you the opportunity to practice reading patterns from the first six chapters. Often several patterns are combined in one reading. Furthermore, there are no lessons in this chapter. The skill review and textual pattern review exercises all come from lessons in the first six chapters.

PREVIEW | AMERICA: A NATION OF NATIONS

Things to Think About

1. Do immigrants come to your country regularly?_____

2. Has there ever been a time when an unusually large number of immigrants came at once? What were their reasons for immigrating?

   _____

   _____

   _____

3. What countries do you think have the highest number of immigrants today? Why do these countries have such large immigrant populations?

   _____

   _____

   _____

4. Why do you think the United States has such a large population of immigrants?

   _____

   _____

5. Should a country like the United States limit the number of people who are allowed to immigrate? Why?

   _____

   _____

Preview

1. Skim through the first sentence of each paragraph to determine what textual pattern is being used by the author.

   _____

2. Scan the reading for dates. Write down the dates as you see them. What sequence does the author seem to be using: narrated or natural?

   _____

   _____

   What is the time frame for this reading?

   _____

3. Complete the following word form chart before reading "America: A Nation of Nations." If you are not sure of the difference in meaning among these words look them up in a dictionary. Place an *X* in the box if no form exists.

Verb	Noun	Adjective	Adverb
immigrate	*immigration*		X
migrate			
emigrate			

READING ONE

AMERICA: A NATION OF NATIONS

1   As Oscar Handlin said, "Once I thought to write a history of the immigrants in America. Then I discovered the immigrants were American history." No study of the United States would be complete without a discussion of immigrants because America is a nation of immigrants. Since 1607, when the first English settlers   5 reached the New World, over 45 million people have migrated to the United States. This represents the largest migration of people in all of recorded history. In slightly more than 350 years, a nation of over 200 million people has been built by persons who came from all

parts of the world and all walks of life. Every aspect of American life, from business to athletics, has been influenced in one way or another by immigrants. No one could ever completely understand this "teeming nation of nations," as the poet Walt Whitman called it, without first knowing something about the history of America's leading import—immigrants.

2   America first started to become a nation of many nationalities during the colonial period. Because America was undeveloped, demands for manpower were great. Consequently, immigration had to be stimulated. This was accomplished by the indenture of servants. Landowners promised to pay a person's way to this new country if the immigrant agreed to work for a certain amount of time (usually five years) after he got here. These indentured servants came from all parts of the world, but Europe was the primary source. The other means of getting manpower was to import slaves, usually from Africa. At one point it was estimated that two-thirds of all the immigrants in America were "colonists in bondage." By the time the first federal census was taken in 1790, the population was already extremely diverse in origin. As might be expected, the majority, 60 percent, were of English descent, 14 percent were Scottish or Scottish-Irish, 9 percent German, 4 percent Catholic Irish, and 13 percent were of various other origins.

3   Even though immigration started as early as the 1600s and continued through the colonial period, the massive influx of immigrants to America really began around 1815. Between 1607 and 1815, a period of slightly over 200 years, the population of America grew to nearly 8.4 million. In the subsequent 115 years, however, waves and waves of immigrants increased that total by nearly 35 million. Five million immigrants entered the United States legally between the years 1815 and 1860, 10 million between 1860 and 1890, and more than 20 million between 1890 and 1930. The peak year of the nineteenth century was 1882, when nearly 800,000 immigrants arrived. The highest annual total ever was in 1907, when 1,285,349 immigrants were processed into this country.

4   Most histories of U.S. immigration divide this era of massive immigrant influx into what is called the "old immigration" (before 1896) and the "new immigration" (after 1896). Although there were significant differences between the origins and languages of the old and new immigrants, their motives for coming were remarkably similar. Europe was overcrowded, and several severe famines forced millions of people to leave. Likewise, revolutionary changes in agriculture and technology forced many working-class people out of their familiar lifestyles. America was the place most people chose as their new home.

5   The early 1920s marked the beginning of what can be called a restrictive immigration era. Americans were becoming increasingly alarmed over the economic and social problems their newly industrialized nation was experiencing. Problems such as labor strikes and economic unrest were common. Although immigrants were hardly the cause of most of these difficulties, they were often blamed for many of them.

6   Congress reacted to this alarm by passing laws that excluded further immigration of certain races and by taking the responsibility of immigrant processing away from the seaboard states. The first of the exclusionary laws were passed against the Chinese. And the first federal port of entry, Ellis Island, was built in New York harbor. Further laws were passed that disallowed the entry of individuals with certain diseases, criminal records, or radical political opinions. When these measures didn't have the full effect that was expected, Congress adopted what has become known as the quota system. This system allowed each country an annual immigration quota that was in direct proportion to the number of each "national origin" in the existing U.S. population.

7   The quota system was used, with a few minor changes, until 1965. There were, however, several notable exceptions to the annual quotas. In 1950 some 400,000 Hungarians were permitted to enter following the Soviet Union's suppression of an uprising in their homeland. In the early part of the 1960s, 675,000 Cubans who fled Cuba after Castro seized power were permitted entry. In more recent times, hundreds of thousands of Southeast Asian refugees, primarily Vietnamese, Cambodian, and Laotian, were allowed to immigrate when their countries fell to communist rule.

8   In 1965, a law was passed that gradually abolished the quota system that had been used for nearly 45 years. Quotas were replaced with a system that was more favorable to all concerned. The 1965 act provided a ceiling of 170,000 immigrants annually from the Eastern Hemisphere, with a limit of 20,000 from any single country. An annual limit of 120,000 immigrants was established for immigrants from the Western Hemisphere.

9   The most recent page in U.S. immigration history is being written about the thousands of immigrants entering this country illegally. When the United States Immigration and Naturalization Services (INS) started enforcing strict limitations, the thousands and thousands of immigrants who did not qualify to enter legally started coming in illegally. These *illegals*, as they are called, have been entering in such great numbers that America is now facing some very serious problems. The most prominent problem, of course, is economics. The United States no longer has the capability to accommodate, or the demand for, the large numbers of immigrants that it once had. The problem of illegal immigrants has gotten so out of hand that America may have to completely shut its doors on the very people who built it—immigrants. America has always been a land of immigrants, but will it continue to be such?

REVIEW | AMERICA: A NATION OF NATIONS

Comprehension

1. Use the partially completed chart below to outline the major eras in United States immigration history. Include approximate dates for each era. You will have to turn back to the reading to complete this exercise.

United States Immigration

   I. *Colonial period (1607-1815)*

 II.

     A.   *(before 1896)*

     B.   (   )

 III.

 IV.

   V. *Illegal immigration* (   )

2. What did Oscar Handlin mean when he said that immigrants were American history?

3. What did Walt Whitman mean when he called America a "nation of nations"?

4. During what time period did America experience its greatest influx of immigrants?

5. What were some of the factors that caused the United States to become more restrictive of the number of immigrants that were allowed to enter?

6. What is the quota system? What purpose did it serve?

7. How does the Act of 1965 differ from the quota system?

_____

_____

_____

8. What is the most serious immigration problem facing the United
   States today?

_____

_____

Skill Review: Charts and Graphs

Convert the following statistics on U.S. immigration into a graph
representing the number of immigrants from Europe and all other
countries. You may use either a line graph or a bar graph. Draw your
graph on a separate sheet of paper.

U.S. IMMIGRATION STATISTICS

	All Countries	Europe
1860s	2,314,824	2,065,270
1870s	2,812,191	2,272,262
1880s	5,246,613	4,737,046
1890s	3,687,564	3,558,978
1900s	8,795,386	8,136,016
1910s	5,735,811	4,376,564
1920s	4,107,209	2,477,853
1930s	528,531	348,289

Statistics from *Encyclopedia Americana*

Questions for Further Discussion/Composition

1. The author notes that "America was the place most [immigrants]
   chose as their new home." Why do you think that was so?

2. America's immigration laws have gone from unrestricted immigration to a very strict quota system. In your own words, summarize
   why this has happened.

PREVIEW | WHY THEY CAME

Things to Think About

1. Has your family ever moved from one place to another, e.g., from one neighborhood to another, or one city to another? What were the reasons for moving?

   _____

   _____

2. What do you think would make a person leave his or her homeland and migrate to a strange land?

   _____

   _____

3. Do you know anyone who has migrated to another country? What were his or her reasons for doing so?

   _____

   _____

4. What are some reasons people would want to migrate to the United States and not another country?

   _____

   _____

   _____

Preview

1. To whom does the word "they" in the title refer?

    _____

    _____

2. Does the title give any indication of the type of textual pattern that will be used in the passage? Explain.

    _____

    _____

    _____

    _____

3. Skim the first line of each paragraph. Can you find any words or phrases that help you identify the textual pattern used? List any you find.

    _____

    _____

    _____

    _____

4. Skim the first sentence of each paragraph. How many reasons for people to migrate to the United States can you identify?

    _____

5. Who wrote this article? What is he famous for?

    _____

    _____

6. The following boldface words have been taken from "Why They Came." Read each sentence carefully; then use the context to determine the meaning of the boldface words. Write a definition or synonym in the space provided.
    a. Immigrants had to **abandon** old ties and familiar landmarks, and to sail across dark seas to a strange land.

        abandon _____

    b. Many immigrants came because they were forced to seek **refuge** from the cruelty of Hitler's Germany.

        refuge _____

    c. Not all religious sects have received the **tolerance** and understanding for which they came. The Puritans of the Massachusetts

Bay Colony showed as little tolerance for **dissenting** beliefs as the Anglicans of England had shown them. They quickly **expelled** other religious groups from their society.

*tolerance*_____

dissenting _____

expelled _____

d. Minority religious **sects**, from the Quakers and Shakers through the Catholics and Jews to the Mormons and Jehovah's witnesses, have at various times suffered persecution.

sects _____

e. Early immigrants came on ships. In 1620, for example, the May-flower carried a **cargo** of 102 passengers to the New World.

*cargo*_____

READING TWO

WHY THEY CAME

1   Not many decisions could have been more difficult for a family to make than to say farewell to a community where it had lived for centuries, to abandon old ties and familiar landmarks, and to sail across dark seas to a strange land. Today, when mass communica-tions tell one part of the world all about another, it is quite easy to   5
understand how poverty or tyranny might compel people to exchange an old nation for a new one. But centuries ago migration was a leap into the unknown. It was an enormous intellectual and emotional commitment. The forces that moved early immigrants to their great decision—the decision to leave their homes and begin an   10
adventure filled with uncertainty, risk and hardship—must have been of overpowering proportions. As Oscar Handlin states, the early immigrants of America "would collide with unaccustomed problems, learn to understand alien ways and alien languages, man-age to survive in a very foreign environment."   15
2   Despite the obstacles and uncertainties that lay ahead of them, millions did migrate to "the promised land"—America. But what was it that moved so many to migrate against such overwhelming odds? There were probably as many reasons for coming to America as there were people who came. It was a highly individual decision.   20

_____

Excerpts from *A Nation of Immigrants* by John F. Kennedy. Copyright © 1964 by Anti-Defamation League of B'nai B'rith. Reprinted by permission of Harper & Row.

Yet it can be said that three large forces—religious persecution, political oppression and economic hardship—provided the chief motives for the mass migrations to America. They were responding, in their own way to the pledge of the Declaration of Independence: the promise of "life, liberty and the pursuit of happiness."

3   The search for freedom of worship has brought people to America from the days of the Pilgrims to modern times. In 1620, for example, the Mayflower carried a cargo of 102 passengers who "welcomed the opportunity to advance the gospel of . . . Christ in these remote parts." A number of other groups such as the Jews and Quakers came to America after the Pilgrims, all seeking religious freedom. In more recent times, anti-Semitic and anti-Christian persecution in Hitler's Germany and the Communist empire have driven people from their homes to seek refuge in America. However, not all religious sects have received the tolerance and understanding for which they came. The Puritans of the Massachusetts Bay Colony showed as little tolerance for dissenting beliefs as the Anglicans of England had shown them. They quickly expelled other religious groups from their society. Minority religious sects, from the Quakers and Shakers through the Catholics and Jews to the Mormons and Jehovah's Witnesses, have at various times suffered both discrimination and hostility in the United States.

4   But the diversity of religious belief has made for religious toleration. In demanding freedom for itself, each sect had to permit freedom for others. The insistence of each successive wave of immigrants upon its right to practice its religion helped make freedom of worship a central part of the American Creed. People who gambled their lives on the right to believe in their own God would not easily surrender that right in a new society.

5   The second great force behind immigration has been political
oppression. America has always been a refuge from tyranny. As a
nation conceived in liberty, it has held out to the world the promise
of respect for the rights of man. Every time a revolution has failed in
Europe, every time a nation has succumbed to tyranny, men and
women who love freedom have assembled their families and their
belongings and set sail across the seas. This process has not come to
an end in our own day. The Russian Revolution, the terrors of
Hitler's Germany and Mussolini's Italy, the Communist suppression
of the Hungarian Revolution of 1956, the terrible wars of Southeast
Asia (Vietnam, Cambodia, etc.)—all have brought new thousands
seeking sanctuary in the United States.

6   The economic factor has been more complex than the religious
and political factors. From the very beginning, some have come to
America in search of riches, some in flight from poverty, and some
because they were bought and sold and had no choice.

7   And the various reasons are intertwined. Thus some early arriv-
als were lured to these shores by dreams of amassing great wealth,
like the Spanish conquistadors in Mexico and Peru. These adven-
turers, expecting quick profits in gold, soon found that real wealth
lay in such crops as tobacco and cotton. As they built up the planta-
tion economy in states like Virginia and the Carolinas, they needed
cheap labor. So they began to import indentured servants from
England (men and women who agreed to labor a term of years in
exchange for eventual freedom), and slaves from Africa.

8   The process of industrialization in America increased the
demand for cheap labor, and chaotic economic conditions in Europe
increased the supply. If some immigrants continued to believe that
the streets of New York were paved with gold, more were driven by
the hunger and hardship of their native lands. The Irish potato
famine of 1845 brought almost a million people to America in five
years. American manufacturers advertised in European newspapers, offering to pay the passage of any man willing to come to
America to work for them.

9   The immigrants who came for economic reasons contributed to
the strength of the new society in several ways. Those who came
from countries with advanced political and economic institutions
brought with them faith in those institutions and experience in
making them work. They also brought technical and managerial
skills which contributed greatly to economic growth in the new
land. Above all, they helped give America the extraordinary social
mobility which is the essence of an open society.

10   In the community he had left, the immigrant usually had a fixed
place. He would carry on his father's craft or trade; he would farm
his father's land, or that small portion of it that was left him after it
was divided with his brothers. Only with the most exceptional tal-
ent and enterprise could he break out of the circumstances in life
into which he had been born. There were no such circumstances for
him in the New World. Once having broken with the past, except for
sentimental ties and cultural inheritance, he had to rely on his own

abilities. It was the future and not the past which he had to face. 100
Except for the Negro slave, the immigrant could go anywhere and
do anything his talents permitted. A large, virgin continent lay
before him, and he had only to weld it together by canals, railroads
and roads. If he failed to achieve the dream of a better life for
himself, he could still retain it for his children.   105

11   This has been the foundation of American inventiveness and
ingenuity, of the variety of new enterprises, and of the success in
achieving the highest standard of living anywhere in the world.

12   These were the major forces that started this massive migration
to America. Every immigrant served to reinforce and strengthen 110
those elements in American society that had attracted him in the
first place. The motives of some immigrants were commonplace.
The motives of others were noble. Taken together they add up to the
strengths and weaknesses of America.

REVIEW | WHY THEY CAME

Comprehension

1. What are the major reasons people immigrated to America?

   _____

   _____

2. Which of the answers given in question 1 do you think brought the
   most immigrants? Why?

   _____

   _____

   _____

   _____

3. Does the author give any examples or say anything to support your
   opinion in question 2? If so, what are they?

   _____

   _____

   _____

4. In your opinion, are the motives for emigrating given in this passage
   the same motives people have today? Explain.

   _____

   _____

5. List any motives that you think the author might not have mentioned.

   _____

   _____

   _____

   _____

6. As time changes, so do circumstances. Can you think of any new reasons for people to emigrate—reasons that might not have existed a hundred years ago?

   _____

   _____

   _____

7. The author mentions that there has been more than one economic reason for immigrants to come to America. What are those reasons?

   _____, _____,

   _____.

8. In what way did immigrants seeking economic freedom strengthen the U.S. economy?

   _____

   _____

   _____

Skill Review: Main Ideas

The following sentences have been taken from "Why They Came." In the space provided write the main ideas in your own words.

1. Not many decisions could have been more difficult for a family to make than to say farewell to a community where it had lived for centuries, to abandon old ties and familiar landmarks, and to sail across dark seas to a strange land.

   _____

   _____

   _____

2. The forces that moved early immigrants to their great decision—the decision to leave their homes and begin an adventure filled with

uncertainty, risk and hardship—must have been of overpowering proportions.

_____

_____

3. Yet it can be said that three large forces—religious persecution, political oppression and economic hardship—provided the chief motives for the mass migrations to America.

_____

_____

4. The diversity of religious belief has made for religious toleration. In demanding freedom for itself, each sect had to permit freedom for others.

_____

_____

5. Every immigrant served to reinforce and strengthen those elements in American society that had attracted him in the first place.

_____

_____

Textual Pattern: Cause/Effect

Draw cause/effect diagrams for the following paragraphs. After you have drawn a diagram, summarize in your own words what you think the main idea of the paragraph is.

Paragraph 6:

Main idea: _____

_____

Paragraph 7:

Main idea: _____

_____

Paragraph 9:

Main idea: _____

_____

Paragraph 10:

Main idea: _____

_____

Complete the following cause/effect diagram of the reading "Why They Came."

Causes

| 1. Freedom of Worship
Examples:
_____
_____ |

Effect

| Millions immigrate
to the United States,
from the days of
the Pilgrims to
modern times. |

| 2. |

| 3. |

Questions for Further Discussion/Composition

1. In the reading "America: A Nation of Nations," the author mentioned several different groups of immigrants who came to the United States. List as many of those groups as you can; then indicate which of the three reasons for immigration mentioned in this reading brought the group here.

2. In your opinion, which of the three reasons given is the most important reason for migrating to another country? Why?

PREVIEW | ANGEL AND ELLIS: ISLANDS OF TEARS

Things to Think About

1. Approximately how many immigrants enter your country each year?

Ellis Island.

The immigrants' first view of Angel Island barracks.

2. What procedure must a person follow in order to legally immigrate to your country?

   _____

   _____

3. Is there some building or facility in which immigrants entering your country are processed? If so, where is it?

   _____

4. Have immigration policies and procedures in your country changed in recent years? In what ways?

   _____

   _____

Preview

1. Does the title of the reading give you any indication of the type of textual pattern that will be used in the passage? Explain your answer.

   _____

   _____

2. Skim the first line of each paragraph to confirm what pattern is being used. Indicate your conclusion below.

   _____

3. Where are these two islands located?

Angel Island: _____

Ellis Island: _____

4. What were they used for?

Angel Island: _____

Ellis Island: _____

5. Are they still being used today?

Angel Island: _____

Ellis Island: _____

READING THREE

ANGEL AND ELLIS: ISLANDS OF TEARS

1   For most of the nineteenth century, admission into the United States was simple. Immigration was encouraged and unrestricted; there were no federal barriers or tests for entry. However, as time passed and the number of immigrants increased, it became necessary to establish an orderly system for processing the thousands and   5
thousands of immigrants arriving daily. At first individual states set up their own systems, but after 1882 the federal government took over the responsibility and developed guidelines for extensive background checks on those entering the country. Because the immigrants continued to arrive in such large numbers, eventually it   10
became necessary for the government to build federal ports of entry or "reception centers" to process the immigrants.

2   Two of the most extensively used federal "reception centers" were Ellis Island on the East Coast of the United States and Angel Island on the West Coast. Though both centers were used for   15
basically the same purpose—processing, detaining, and in some cases rejecting immigrants—the ways in which they accomplished these tasks were as diverse as their geographical locations.

3   Until the early part of the 1800s, Ellis Island (so named for one of its original owners—Samuel Ellis) had been owned by the state of   20
New York. In 1808 the United States government purchased the island to use as a fort and arsenal. However, by the late 1800s, the government was faced with the problem of an overcrowded immigrant depot in New York City—Castle Garden. Castle Garden simply could not accommodate the many immigrants that were   25
arriving. Ellis Island was seen as an ideal location for a new and much bigger immigrant "reception center." The island's greatest

advantages were that it was located near a major U.S. city—New York—and that it was an island, which would facilitate the detention of immigrants until they could be effectively processed. 30

4   On January 1, 1892, Ellis Island was officially opened as a federal immigration station. The first immigrant to pass through the station was Annie Moore, a 15-year-old from County Cork, Ireland. On that day, 2,251 people entered their new country through the doors of Ellis Island. In the days, weeks, and years that 35 followed, thousands and thousands of immigrants were processed through Ellis Island, making it the most used immigration port of entry in U.S. history.

5   Even though it was the most used port, it was not necessarily the most popular place with the immigrants. Emotions of the newly 40 arriving immigrants ran high. Fear and uncertainty were common parts of the Ellis Island experience. The too frequent scenes of families being split and parting account for Ellis' nickname—Island of Tears.

6   A majority of the immigrants who passed through Ellis' doors 45 were men and women leaving industrialized nations of Southern and Eastern Europe. They came not so much to find streets paved with gold, as some newspapers had advertised, but to escape decaying economies, war, famine, or political oppression.

7   Almost daily between 1892 and 1954, U.S. officials inspected 50 thousands of immigrants on passenger ships anchored in New York harbor. Those who had traveled first class were assumed to be rich and healthy. They could go to the mainland with few questions asked. Passengers in third class or lower were sent to Ellis Island.

8   As the immigrants disembarked at Ellis they were herded up the 55 stairs of the giant red-brick building to the Great Hall, the bustling center of immigration processing. It was there that the immigrants were first subjected to a variety of medical tests and questioned on subjects such as name, nationality, marital status, and occupation. At the top of the stairs the immigrants were given what was termed 60 "the six second medical," a quick examination by doctors who watched for signs of illness or disease—heavy breathing, limping, and clumsiness. An inspector who found something wrong with an immigrant chalked a capital letter on the immigrant's clothing. An "L" meant lameness; an "H" meant heart trouble; an "E" indicated 65 an eye problem. An "X" meant the immigrant was healthy.

9   Those with curable infirmities were sent to the hospital building until they were considered well enough to go to the mainland. The incurable were cared for until a ship arrived to take them back to Europe. 70

10   Eighty percent of the individuals landing on the island passed through the examination and processing procedures in about four or five hours. Of the 20 percent detained for hospitalization or more extensive tests, most were admitted and released after only a few days. Less than 2 percent were sent back to their homelands at the 75 expense of the shipping company, and a good number of those tried their luck again.

11   During its sixty-two years of operation, more than 17 million
immigrants from all over the world were processed through the
Island of Tears. It is estimated that one out of every five Americans   80
alive today either came to America via Ellis Island or is the descendant of an immigrant who did. By 1954 Ellis Island had outlived its
usefulness as an immigration station and was abandoned. In 1955
the island was declared surplus and put up for sale.

12   Nearly eighteen years after Ellis Island opened its doors to   85
immigrants arriving on the East Coast, a small, little-known, and
even less cared about island in windy San Francisco Bay was
opened for processing immigrants on the West Coast. It was called
Angel Island. Angel Island was modeled after Ellis, and it was
selected as a processing center for many of the same reasons. As on   90
the East Coast, the previous immigrant depot was not adequate.
The constantly increasing number of immigrants necessitated
something bigger than the old two-story shed at the Pacific Mail
Steamship Company wharf. (Often 400 to 500 people were crammed
into "the wooden shack" at a time.) Also like Ellis, Angel Island was   95
located near a major U.S. city—San Francisco. Similarly, it was an
island which made it possible to isolate the immigrants. Many felt
that Angel Island would be like its neighbor, Alcatraz Prison—
escape-proof.

13   Outwardly, Ellis and Angel appear to have been quite similar. In   100
fact, Angel Island has often been referred to as "Ellis of the West."
However, the type of immigrants and the treatment they received,
particularly the Chinese, distinguish Angel Island quite drastically
from Ellis Island.

14   While Ellis was used in large part to process European immi-   105
grants, Angel Island, on the other hand, was used primarily for
Asians. Japanese picture brides were held there. Korean laborers
and Chinese immigrants or returning former residents coming to
this country to escape starvation and poverty in China—were processed at the island.   110

15   Like their counterparts on Ellis Island, Angel Island inspectors
would board each ship as it arrived in San Francisco. Those passengers with satisfactory papers were allowed to go ashore. The
remainder were ferried to the immigration station to undergo
inspection and careful medical examination and to await hearings   115
on applications for entry.

16   Medical exams were generally more extensive on Angel Island
than they were on Ellis. Soon after their arrival, immigrants were
taken to a hospital to be checked. They were often kept in the hospital for several days to undergo a variety of careful medical tests. The   120
"six-second medical" that was given to immigrants on Ellis was not
a part of the procedure on Angel Island. Those who passed the medical exams were returned to their dormitories to wait.

17   Unlike the immigrants that passed through Ellis Island, immigrants arriving at Angel Island were segregated according to   125
nationality and sex. As soon as the ferry docked, whites were separated from other races, and Chinese were kept apart from Japanese

and other Asians. Men and women, including husbands and wives, were separated and not allowed to see or communicate with each other again until they were admitted into the country. Children 130 under age twelve were assigned to the care of their mothers.

18   Immigrants were separated primarily to keep the Chinese away from the other races. This was done because the Chinese had to be held on the island longer than other races. They were held longer because of the strict exclusionary laws that were in effect in the 135 United States at the time. The laws stated basically that the Chinese immigrant was not a desirable alien, so strict quotas and regulations were imposed. As a result of these tight regulations, many Chinese immigrants were detained for extremely long periods of time.
                                                                        140
19   Like most Ellis immigrants, many of the immigrants who passed through Angel Island were detained for only a few days. The Chinese, however, were held much longer. For some the wait to get onto the mainland lasted for months or years. Compared to the average five-hour stay on Ellis Island, the average eighteen-month 145 stay on Angel Island must have seemed like an eternity to the Chinese. To pass the long hours, some of the immigrants scratched calligraphy into the walls—expressions of their despair and longing to be free: "Why do I have to sit in jail?" wrote one unknown poet. "It is only because my country is weak and my family poor," wrote 150 another. One man lived there, semi-forgotten, for twenty years. Immigration agents were changed so often that the man was lost in the shuffle. When the station was closed this immigrant was finally allowed to enter the United States.

20   While Ellis Island was in no way a popular place, it never came 155 under the fierce attacks and criticism that Angel Island did. From the day the facility was opened until it was closed thirty years later, the U.S. immigration service was under constant pressure to close Angel Island. Attacks came from all sectors—immigrants and immigration officials alike. Many considered it unsafe. "The living quar- 160 ters were fire hazards," said Immigration Commissioner Edward White. Many leaders from San Francisco's Chinatown claimed that the facilities were unsafe and unsanitary. Similar remarks were made by Assistant Secretary of Labor Edward Henning, who said, "The island facilities are filthy and unfit for habitation." Despite the 165 criticism, however, it was not until 1940, when the administration building was destroyed by fire, that the island was abandoned.

21   On November 5, 1940, the last group of Angel Island detainees was transferred to temporary quarters in San Francisco. During Angel Island's thirty years of operation, approximately one million 170 immigrants passed through its doors. Of those one million, over 175,000 Chinese immigrants spent, as one immigrant called it, "years of hell" on Angel Island.

22   Outwardly, Angel and Ellis appear to have been similar: both are islands located near major U.S. cities; they even have the same 175 number of letters in their names; and they were used for the same function. But the ways they carried out that function were

extremely different. It could be argued, at least from the Chinese
point of view, that while Ellis Island was a reception center, Angel
Island was a detention center.   180

23   One final aspect these two islands have in common is that they
have outlived their usefulness. Both Angel and Ellis Islands stand
abandoned today. All that remains on these two "islands of tears"
are skeletons of old buildings that have outlived their usefulness—
buildings that were once filled with immigrants seeking a new life.   185

---

*Many Chinese immigrants passed the long hours of detainment on Angel
Island by inscribing poetry into the wooden walls of their barracks. The
poetry recorded the immigrants' impressions of the long voyage to America,
their longing for families back home, and their anger and humiliation at the
treatment they received in America. (Photo by Mak Takahashi)*

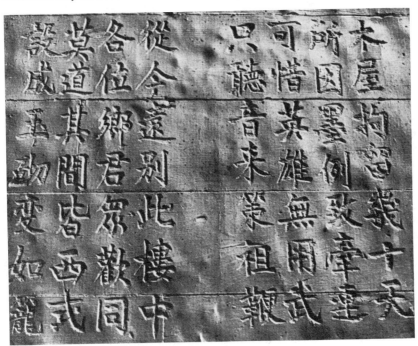

Detained in this wooden house for several tens of days,
It is all because of the Mexican exclusion law which implicates me.
It's a pity heroes have no way of exercising their prowess.
I can only await the word so that I can snap Zu's whip.

From now on, I am departing far from this building.
All of my fellow villagers are rejoicing with me.
Don't say that everything within is Western styled.
Even if it is built of jade, it has turned into a cage.

美有強權無公理，

囹圄吾人也罹辜。

不由分說真殘酷，

俯首回思莫奈何。

America has power, but not justice.
In prison, we were victimized as if we were guilty.
Given no opportunity to explain, it was really brutal.
I bow my head in reflection but there is nothing I can do.*

REVIEW | ANGEL AND ELLIS: ISLANDS OF TEARS

Comprehension

1. Why were Angel and Ellis called Islands of Tears?

_____

_____

_____

_____

_____

2. Which immigration station, Ellis or Angel, would an immigrant from the following countries most likely have been processed through?

a. Hong Kong _____   e. India _____

b. France _____   f. Poland _____

c. Italy _____   g. Korea _____

d. Thailand _____   h. Vietnam _____

---

*Poems and inscription reprinted with permission from Him Mark Lai, Genny Lim, and Jung Yung, *Island: Poetry and History of Chinese Immigrants on Angel Island, 1910–1940* (San Francisco: HOC DOI, 1980), pp. 58–59, 88–89, 135.

3. What factors caused Ellis and Angel Islands to outlive their usefulness?

_____

_____

_____

4. What part of the world did most immigrants entering through Ellis Island come from?

_____

5. A good title for this passage might be:
   a. Immigration in the United States Between 1892 and 1954
   b. Remembering Ellis Island
   c. Immigrants in the United States
   d. U.S. Immigration East and West

6. Give several reasons for your selection in question 5.

_____

_____

7. Which of the facilities, Angel or Ellis, was more carefully planned and organized? How do you know this?

_____

_____

_____

8. What race of people discussed in this reading received the worst treatment as immigrants? Why?

_____

_____

_____

9. Angel Island was never used as extensively as Ellis Island, yet there were more complaints about the facilities at Angel Island than there were about Ellis. Why do you think this is so?

_____

_____

_____

10. How long was the average stay on Angel Island for a Chinese immigrant?

_____

Textual Pattern: Compare and Contrast

1. In the space below list as many similarities and differences as you can between Ellis Island and Angel Island.

Similarities   *Differences*

2. Briefly outline the sequence of events an Ellis or Angel Island immigrant went through during his or her first few hours.

Ellis Island   *Angel Island*

Immigrants are inspected on board their ships.

Questions for Further Discussion/Composition

1. Why is "Island of Tears" an appropriate nickname for Angel and Ellis Islands?

2. If you had been an immigrant entering the United States in 1920, which immigration station would you have passed through? Briefly outline the treatment you would likely have received.

3. Since this article was written, the U.S. government has restored Ellis Island and made it a national park. Angel Island still remains deserted. Should the government restore Angel Island and make it a national park? Explain your answer.

PREVIEW | GOREE

Things to Think About

1. What were the major reasons immigrants came to the United States in the late 1800s and early 1900s?

_____

_____

_____

_____

2. Could slaves be considered immigrants? Please explain your answer.

   _____

   _____

   _____

3. Where did most immigrants entering the United States in the late 1800s and early 1900s come from?

   _____

4. Where did most slaves who entered the United States come from?

   _____

5. In what ways were slaves different from other immigrants entering the United States? You may want to review the reading "Why They Came" before answering this question.

   _____

   _____

   _____

Preview

1. To whom do "we" and "our" refer in the sentences below the title?

   _____

2. Scan the reading for answers to the following questions:

   What is Goree? _____

   Where is Goree? _____

3. Scan the reading for any dates. Write the dates down as you see them. What is the time frame for this reading?

   _____

   _____

   _____

4. Scan the reading for any indications of the textual pattern that is used in this reading. List any that you find.

   _____

   _____

   _____

READING FOUR

GOREE

As a Culture We Are Not a Small Minority. We Are Over 150 Million in Number, Stretching Throughout North, Central, and South America. For Many of Our Ancestors This All Began at the "Ellis Island" of Slavery, a Place Called Goree.

1   They may have begun their journeys in Ireland or Italy or Poland. They spoke different languages, practiced different religions. But what millions of Europeans coming to America had in common was an Immigration Center on a tiny island in New York harbor. Ellis Island was their first stop on the way to freedom and opportunity in the United States. And now their children, grandchildren, and even some of *them* are celebrating the centennial of Ellis Island and the Statue of Liberty, the two foremost symbols of America's "welcome mat" to the world. Nearly half the population of the United States can trace their roots to this site.

2   Tragically, there are millions of others whose ancestors did not come here in the name of freedom or opportunity. Blacks are the one single group of immigrants that came to America against their will. They are also the one single group that cannot, by and large, identify a place of origin more specific than an entire vast and diversified continent. There is one specific place, however, that black Americans can claim as a temporary ancestral home. Most of them are not even aware it exists.

3   Just outside the harbor of Senegal's capital city of Dakar lies Goree, an island tiny enough to explore on foot in a day. Half the slaves who left West Africa came to the Americas by way of this place. Over the course of three centuries, slave traders brought nearly 20 million slaves to this island, held them in slave houses, then boarded them onto ships that would carry them across the Atlantic. Another 20 million slaves left West Africa directly from Benin, Dahomey, Ghana and Angola, but Goree was the single most important center of the slave industry. It is every bit as significant to the American immigration story as Ellis Island.

4   Goree Island was "discovered" by the Portuguese in 1444. When the slave trade began a century later, they developed the island into a transit center because of its strategic location just off Africa's westernmost tip. Over the next 300 years, Goree passed through several hands. The Dutch owned Goree for the longest period, from 1602 to 1779. Then it passed back and forth between the British and the French until 1815, when the Vienna Treaty turned it over

5

10

15

20

25

30

35

Reprinted with permission from Shelley Moore, "Goree," *The Crisis*, June/July 1986, pp. 19–21, 56.

exclusively to France. There France continued to control the slave trade until it was abolished in 1848.

From various parts of Africa's Western bulge, slave traders brought their precious bounty to the island. Yorubas from Nigeria and Benin were especially marketable for their strong physiques. Mandinkas, Serers, Fulani and Wolofs were also sold in large numbers, although many traders considered the latter too delicately framed and too recalcitrant to make good slaves. Those who were accepted were taken into any one of 118 different slave houses on the island. One slave house has been restored as a museum—La Maison des Esclaves. It is a profound and vivid testament to slavery that no textbook can match.

Built by the Dutch in 1776, this two-story house of stone and wooden beams is washed in a faded pink. It is not a large house, yet as many as 400 slaves were kept here at a time. Off the central courtyard are doorways to small, dark cells. As many as thirty people were kept in a cell the size of today's average bedroom, chained to the walls. Smaller cells, the size of a walk-in closet, held 15 to 20 people. A few cells had small windows; others had none.

Men and women were held in separate rooms. One cell was reserved for little boys who were put on a special diet to fatten them up to a good selling price. Another relatively large cell held about 40 young women. They cooked for the slaves and also served as concubines to slave traders who lived in well-appointed rooms just upstairs from the crowded cells.

These young women were a relatively privileged group during the time the French controlled the house. While other slaves had only the common courtyard for a toilet, the young women had their own private hole in the ground within their cell. Those who became pregnant by the traders were set free to live on Goree, and their mulatto children given French citizenship. Some mulatto women, known as "Signares," ultimately became wealthy mistresses to French dignitaries. Some of them even owned slaves.

A tiny cave, better described as a hole in the wall, served as a dungeon-within-a-dungeon for re-apprehended runaways and other insubordinates. Sometimes as many as four people would be crammed inside at a time, with no room to stand or move.

The average length of a slave's stay at the house was 3–4 months. When ships arrived from Europe or the Americas, slaves were taken to a special room to be weighed, inspected and sold to captains. The men were rated according to physique; the women, by the size of their breasts; children, by the health of their teeth. They typically arrived at the slave house in families, and were usually separated before they left. Mother might board a ship for Charleston; father might be bound for Port-au-Prince; the children might be sent to Brazil. Tribal groups were split, too, since people who cannot understand each other's language are less likely to organize a successful shipboard insurrection. Each slave left Goree with a registration number in place of a name.

A central corridor runs through the house from the courtyard to a back door that opens out directly over the Atlantic Ocean. It is called the "door of no return." From this exit, slaves walked across a wooden bridge directly onto the ships. Their passage through the door marked their final contact with African soil. Some slaves chose to jump off the bridge rather than board the ships. In those days, the waters off Goree were infested with sharks. Those who jumped rarely survived. It is no wonder that of the 20 million slaves brought to Goree, an estimated 6 million never made it out alive. Dachau* could have been modeled after this place.

12   The slave trade ended in 1848, and Goree settled into a rela- tively uneventful existence, interrupted only by a yellow fever epidemic in 1878 and some fighting between the French and Germans during World War II. Slave houses evolved into homes and schools. The island remained in the hands of the French until 1960, when Senegal and much of the rest of West Africa gained independence. Leopold Sedar Senghor became Senegal's first president that year, moving into the former mansion of the French governors. High on a bluff overlooking the ocean, the mansion once afforded the governors an idyllic view of the slave ships coming and going at Goree. One of Senghor's goals was to establish a museum to commemorate Goree's role in the slave trade. He ultimately appointed a military man, Joseph N'Diaye, to set that goal in motion.

13   Joseph N'Diaye grew up on Goree Island. He never had any formal education about the island's historic role in slavery, but learned about it as a boy from the island's oral historians, or *griots*. To supplement his oral education, N'Diaye traveled to France, where far more information was available on the slave trade than he could ever have found in Africa.

14   "They took everything back to France when slavery ended," explains N'Diaye, "documents, artifacts, even the chains that shackled the slaves. Nothing was left behind." His research took him four years; much of that time was spent at La Maison de la Marine in Paris, which houses most of the materials on slavery. He also spent some time at a slave house in Nantes that served as a stopover for French slave ships on their way from Goree to the Americas.

15   N'Diaye returned to Goree and led the restoration of the slave house that finally became La Maison des Esclaves in 1969. Today, it is perhaps the most important tourist site in Senegal.

16   Goree is only a 20-minute ferry ride from downtown Dakar. In spite of its history, it is a pretty and inviting island of trees and flowers, people mingling at the marketplace, children playing at the beach. In contrast to downtown Dakar, with its modern post-war buildings, Goree retains an historic look with its mixture of Portuguese, Dutch and French architecture from centuries past. The streets are unpaved. There are no cars. Besides the slave houses, there are many other significant landmarks of West Africa's colonial history.

*Dachau is a city in Germany. It was in Dachau that one of the most infamous Nazi Concentration camps was built during World War II.

17   La Maison is a short walk up the road from the ferry. While many Senegalese tour guides are well-versed in the history of the [135] house, the luckiest visitors will find Joseph N'Diaye there to guide them personally, with the aid of an English-speaking interpreter. Still curator and director of La Maison at age 63, N'Diaye shows an enthusiasm for his work that is as youthful as ever. His knowledge of the slave trade throughout Africa and the Americas may be [140] unrivaled. Alex Haley was fortunate to have had him as an advisor for *Roots*. Though N'Diaye has no college degree, one is tempted to call him "Doctor."

18   N'Diaye tells the story of the slave house with a dignified passion that leaves most visitors speechless. By the end of the tour, [145] many visitors are found simply staring out the "door of no return," as the waves gently lap at the rocks below their feet. Some black American visitors leave the slave house feeling angry. Others weep.

19   Visitors accustomed to well-appointed museums with elaborate displays may find La Maison slightly disappointing. It is little more [150] than an empty building. Its existence is dependent upon private contributions, and those have been limited. Other than providing for occasional maintenance needs, the Senegalese government does not underwrite the house.

20   N'Diaye explains, "Goree isn't just about Senegal's history. [155] Goree belongs to Guinea and Benin and Nigeria. It belongs to the United States and the Caribbean and South America. But so far, those other places have given nothing." Some of the operating funds are raised from donations by visitors who chip a few francs into an old box at the end of the tour. There is no sales pitch, and probably [160] few of them realize that their contributions are critical.

21   Funds are also raised by N'Diaye's frequent lectures at conferences outside Senegal. In February 1986, he visited the United States for the very first time. Through the efforts of Dr. Chester Williams, a black theology professor at Boston University, N'Diaye [165] spoke before several university and church groups in Massachusetts, New York and New Jersey during his three-week stay. The story of Goree Island dumbfounded even black scholars.

22   The Senegalese government would prefer that N'Diaye stay closer to home. La Maison is an important tourist attraction, and [170] N'Diaye is its only expert. He has never had funds to train apprentices. It is therefore a profound relief to learn that N'Diaye has at least written down his knowledge. His book *L'Esclavage: Ses Origines et Ses Repercussions en Afrique* so far has been published only in French and only 1,000 copies are in print. Eventually he hopes to [175] publish it in English.

23   "If I had all the money in the world," N'Diaye dreams, "I would restore all 118 slave houses on the island. I would hire Senegalese artisans to make replicas of the chains. Maybe one day . . ."

REVIEW | GOREE

Comprehension

1. Why has Goree been called the "Ellis Island" of slavery?

   _____

   _____

   _____

2. Most slaves trace their origin to one place. Where? How does that make slaves different from other U.S. immigrants?

   _____

   _____

   _____

3. True or false? Most blacks in the United States today know about Goree. Explain your answer.

   _____

   _____

4. Exactly where is Goree?

   _____

   _____

5. Approximately how many slaves who left Africa were detained at Goree?

   _____

6. How many slave houses were used on Goree?

   _____

7. Briefly describe the living conditions inside the slave houses.

   _____

   _____

8. Who received the best treatment on Goree? Who received the worst treatment on Goree? Explain your answers.

   Best: _____

   _____

   Worst: _____

   _____

9. What is the "door of no return"?

_____

_____

_____

10. Explain why an estimated six million slaves never made it out of Goree alive.

_____

_____

_____

11. Why is Joseph N'Diaye called "Doctor"?

_____

_____

_____

12. Why did N'Diaye have to go to France to research Goree's history?

_____

_____

_____

13. What is Joseph N'Diaye's greatest dream for Goree?

_____

_____

_____

Skill Review: Detecting Sequence

The history of Goree presented in this reading covers nearly five hundred years. However, the historical events are narrated out of sequence and are frequently mixed in with descriptions of the island. In the table at the top of page 335, fill in as many significant events described in the reading as you can. List each event in its natural order. After you have listed each event, write a number in the column provided to indicate the order in which the author narrates that event. The first one has been done as an example.

Textual Pattern: Compare and Contrast

The three islands you have read about in this chapter—Goree, Ellis, and Angel—have certain similarities and differences. In the space pro-

THE HISTORY OF GOREE BY CENTURY

Century	Event	Narrated Order
1400 1444	*Goree was discovered by the Portuguese*	*1*
1500		
1600		
1700		
1800		
1900		

GOREE AND ELLIS ISLAND

Similarities	*Differences*

GOREE AND ANGEL ISLAND

Similarities	*Differences*

vided at the bottom of page 335, list as many similarities and differences as you can think of between Goree and Ellis Island and between Goree and Angel Island.

Questions for Further Discussion/Composition

1. What does N'Diaye mean when he says, "Goree belongs to Guinea, Benin, Nigeria, the United States, the Caribbean, and South America"?

2. Both Angel Island and Goree are reminders of unpleasant parts of U.S. history. Should we forget these unpleasant memories? Why?

PREVIEW | IS AMERICA CLOSING THE "GOLDEN DOOR"?

Things to Think About

1. Are there any restrictions on people who want to immigrate to your country? Explain.

   _____

   _____

   _____

2. Has your country ever had a problem of too many immigrants or refugees entering at once? Explain.

   _____

   _____

   _____

3. What kinds of problems would be caused by too many immigrants or refugees entering a country all at one time?

   _____

   _____

   _____

4. Is there any way a government can have *complete* control over the number of people who enter the country? Explain.

   _____

   _____

   _____

"What Happened To The One We Used To Have?"

From *The Herblock Book* (Beacon Press, 1952)

Preview

1. Scan the first sentence of each paragraph. Can you tell which textual pattern is being used?

   _____

2. What do the letters INS stand for?

   _____

3. What do *legals* and *illegals* mean?

   _____

   _____

   _____

4. What is the best meaning for the word *influx* in paragraph 6?

a. control

b. origin

c. entrance

d. growth

5. What is the best meaning for the word *forfeit* in the last paragraph?

a. destroy

b. forget

c. pass

d. lose

6. The author uses the term "golden door" in the title. Where has this term been used before in this chapter? What does it mean?

_____

_____

_____

7. What is the artist saying in the cartoon on page 337?

_____

8. Do the cartoon and the title of the next reading give any indication of what the content of the reading will be? Explain your answer.

_____

_____

_____

READING FIVE

IS AMERICA CLOSING THE "GOLDEN DOOR"?

1   America is and always has been a land of immigrants. With the exception of the native American Indian, there is no United States citizen who is not an immigrant or a descendant of an immigrant. Immigration into this continent started in the 1600s and continued nonstop and unrestricted until the late 1800s. Vast amounts of land   5 were available for the taking, and opportunities were limitless. To people in Europe and other parts of the world, where governments were often tyrannical, economies unpredictable, and food frequently scarce, this "new world" offered promise and hope. So they came; by the millions they came. Since the United States was a new   10 nation with a massive frontier and very few people to shape it, immigration was encouraged. By 1882, however, the expansive frontiers and open spaces were quickly disappearing. A country that had once had room for all was full, or so its citizens thought. Passing restrictive immigration (exclusionary) laws was their way of closing   15 the "golden door" on the constant stream of immigrants. With the passage of time, these laws became increasingly more strict, and by

1921 the first U.S. immigration quota system had been introduced. In essence, the quota system allowed only a pre-set number of immigrants to enter the country yearly. As time passed, stricter and 20 stricter regulations were imposed, until the annual quota reached an all-time low in 1960—of about 500,000.

2   Since the 1960s, the U.S. Immigration and Naturalization Service (INS) has been quite successful in controlling the number of "legal" immigrants entering each year. However, a rather predicta- 25 ble problem has resulted from the strict quota system: people's desires and needs to emigrate do not decrease just because a quota is imposed. Because the decision to emigrate is not an easy one to make, once it is made, people are often persistent about reaching their destination. If it cannot be reached legally, then they often 30 reach it illegally.

3   Illegal aliens have been a problem ever since the first immigration restriction was imposed, but the problem has never been as serious as it is now. No one really knows just how many illegal aliens are living in the United States. Estimates of the illegal popu- 35 lation range from a low of about two million to a high of ten million, and this population is growing. Estimates of the number of "illegals" entering each year vary from 100,000 to 500,000. The problem has grown to such proportions that there are nearly as many immigrants entering the United States today as there were at 40 the turn of the century, when there were few restrictions and immigration was at an all time high. According to one INS authority, in fact, "America has lost control of its borders."

4   The pressure this huge population of illegals is placing on the national economy is staggering. Demographically, a country is 45 never full, but economically it can only absorb so many people before someone is squeezed out of a job. The hardest hit in the U.S. workforce have been low-skilled American workers. Illegals often compete for jobs by offering to do the same work for far less pay and fewer benefits than American citizens. The economy is further dev- 50 astated by illegal immigrants' use of false identification papers. Illegals are using fraudulent I.D.'s at an alarming rate, to draw on services paid for by American taxpayers: food stamps, Medicare, unemployment compensation, Social Security, college loans and grants, etc. Such activities are costing American taxpayers millions 55 of dollars a year. In short, illegals are adding extreme pressure to an already over-burdened economy.

5   The economic problems caused by illegals are only the beginning of the problems. Ironically, the people who have suffered the most are the legal immigrants. As the economy continues to get 60 worse, and unemployment rates rise, it is usually the legal immigrant who cannot find employment. As a legal alien, a person must abide by strict regulations in job hunting or risk deportation. Consequently, the legal immigrant is out of work while illegals live better than ever before. Moreover, it is often the legal immigrant 65 who is most seriously ridiculed for the misconduct of illegals. America is quickly becoming an unpleasant place for immigrants to live.

According to one congressman, "If something isn't done soon, America may have to shut its doors altogether."

6   Solutions to such complex problems are not easy to find, and none are totally satisfactory. Some argue that the best place to attack the problem is at the borders. More intense border patrols would certainly limit, to some extent, the influx of illegals. More sophisticated night cameras and newer and greater numbers of vehicles would help, but only partially. The United States shares such massive borders with Canada and Mexico that it is virtually impossible to patrol them all.

7   Even if border patrols and equipment were upgraded, one source of illegal immigrants that could never be stopped is visa overstayers. In 1983, of the approximately 10 million people who entered on temporary visas, there were 2.1 million for whom the INS had no record of departure. It is unknown how many of these overstayers became illegal immigrants. The most realistic solution to this problem seems to be the greater use of the computer to keep track of all entering aliens. With the aid of computers the INS can more effectively seek out violators before they become too well-hidden in the mainstream of U.S. society. Currently, once a visa overstayer is in the country for more than six months beyond visa limits he or she is usually lost to the INS forever. Computers could also help authorities more effectively screen visa candidates before they enter the country. Such information as criminal record, previous immigration or visa violation, family records, or fraudulent documentation or declaration can instantly be checked by U.S. immigration officials. But computers too provide only a partial answer. They will be of little help along the borders, where the majority of illegals are getting through.

8   Historically, this country's solutions to immigration problems have been legislation: stricter quotas and restrictions. In the past, however, laws have obviously been ineffective. Stricter quotas only seem to worsen the problem. What is most needed is legislation that will affect the greatest number of illegals at one time. There are two types of laws that would accomplish this most effectively. First, laws would need to be aimed directly at the job market, since a majority of the illegals that come here do so for financial reasons. Such laws would have to make it more difficult for employers to knowingly hire illegals. In addition, heavy fines should be imposed on an employer who is caught violating the law. The second type of legislation needed is that which will channel more money into the Immigration and Naturalization Service. Such funds would enable the INS to update computers, hire needed personnel, and acquire much needed equipment. Legislation would not eliminate the illegal immigrant's motive for coming, but it would affect both border crossers and visa overstayers.

9   There is clearly no perfect solution to the problem of illegal immigrants in the United States, but one thing is certain: if the present problem continues, any solution will be too little, too late. As one congressman stated, "Unless we correct the situation we will

truly forfeit our heritage of taking care of legal immigration." If such were to happen, we would be closing our doors on the very people who built our nation.

120

REVIEW | Is America Closing the "Golden Door"?

Comprehension

1. Identify the following statements as either true or false.

    _____ Immigration to the United States started in the late 1800s and has continued ever since?

    _____ Immigration wasn't encouraged until 1882.

    _____ It was in 1960 that the United States first started to use immigration quotas.

    _____ The INS has failed to control the entry of illegal aliens.

    _____ Illegal aliens have been entering the United States at a rate of about 2–10 million each year since 1960.

    _____ Past legislation has been effective in controlling illegal aliens.

2. The first paragraph in this passage is quite long. What is the author's purpose in that paragraph?

    _____

    _____

3. What two groups suffer the most economic difficulty because of the large population of illegal aliens?

    _____

    _____

4. What are the two most common ways illegal immigrants enter the United States?

    _____

    _____

5. What effect does the large population of "illegals" have on immigrants who are in the United States legally?

    _____

    _____

    _____

6. Increasing patrols and using more sophisticated equipment at the borders are not very effective ways to decrease the number of "illegals" entering the country. Why?

_____

_____

_____

7. How is technology being used to fight the problem of illegal aliens?

_____

_____

_____

8. What kinds of legislation are being considered to solve the problem of illegal immigrants?

_____

_____

Textual Pattern

A. Cause/Effect. There are several paragraphs in this passage that emphasize the causes and effects of the illegal alien problem. In the space provided, draw cause/effect diagrams of those paragraphs.

Paragraph 2:

Paragraph 4:

Paragraph 5:

B. Problem Solution. In the table below write down the characteristics of the illegal alien problem and their solutions as they are
discussed in the reading "Is America Closing the 'Golden Door'?"

Problem	Solution

Questions for Further Discussion/Composition

1. If you were in a position to make suggestions on how to control the
   illegal alien population in the United States, what solutions would
   you offer for (1) visa violators, and (2) border crossers?

2. The author of this reading states that the United States has always
   had a problem of illegal aliens, but that the problem has never been
   as serious as it is now. Why is the problem worse now than before?
   What has caused the problem to get out of hand? What are some of
   the possible effects this huge problem will have?

3. In 1987 the United States government took two steps to solve the
   illegal alien problem. First, the government allowed illegal aliens
   who had been in the United States for more than ten years to apply
   for citizenship. Second, the government started to enforce very
   strict regulations similar to those described in this reading. Do you
   think these two solutions will solve the problem? Why or why not?

NOTES

NOTES

NOTES

NOTES

NOTES

NOTES

NOTES

NOTES

NOTES

NOTES

NOTES